PROMISED LAND

Death and Life
in El Salvador

Scott Wright

ORBIS BOOKS

Maryknoll, New York 10545

The Catholic Foreign Mission Society of America (Maryknoll) recruits and trains people for overseas missionary service. Through Orbis Books, Maryknoll aims to foster the international dialogue that is essential to mission. The books published, however, reflect the opinions of their authors and are not meant to represent the official position of the society.

Library of Congress Cataloging-in-Publication Data

Wright, Scott.
    Promised land : death and life in El Salvador / Scott Wright.
      p. cm.
   ISBN 0-88344-955-2 (pbk.)
   1. Catholic Church—El Salvador—History—20th century. 2. El Salvador—History—1979- 3. El Salvador—Church history—20th century. 4. Church work with refugees—Central America.
5. Christianity and justice—El Salvador. I. Title.
BX1446.2.W75   1993
282'.7284'09048—dc20
                                      93-42351
                                         CIP

PROMISED LAND

For Dora Menjiver,
killed August 30, 1984
at the Gualsinga River,

Sister Ann Manganaro, S.L.
who lived and worked in Guarjila,
and died June 6, 1993,

and the 75,000 Salvadorans
who were killed during the war.

"Nothing is as important
to the Church
as human life,
especially the lives of the poor
and the oppressed.

Jesus said
that whatever is done to the poor
is done to Him.

This bloodshed,
these deaths,
are beyond all politics.

They touch the very heart
of God."

Archbishop Oscar Romero
March 16, 1980

CONTENTS

THE HOUR OF THE POOR

BLOOD OF THE MARTYRS

PREFACE

I wish to dedicate this book to the martyrs of El Salvador, especially to the unknown martyrs whose names we may not know but whose spirits live on in the hearts of their people. The great suffering which they endured, and the great love to which they bore witness, will remain with us always.

I think especially of two women, Dora Menjiver, a young Salvadoran mother, who was killed with her five-month-old child Luis at the Gualsinga River massacre on August 30, 1984; and Ann Manganaro, a Sister of Loretto and a physician, who worked for five years in the village of Guarjila in Chalatenango before dying of cancer on June 6, 1993 at her home in St. Louis.

As this book was nearing completion Ann was struggling for life, surrounded by loving friends and family. At one point she told a friend Cathy, "Now I understand the wounds." "You mean *your* wounds?" Cathy asked. "No, the wounds." "You mean the wounds of the people in El Salvador?" "No, our wounds. The wounds of the entire world." Like the crucified people of El Salvador, Ann completed in her dying the suffering that was lacking in the passion of Christ (Colossians 1:24).

At her funeral Mass a friend, John Kavanaugh, S.J., recalled a time, ten years before, when Ann was working on the newborn intensive care unit of Cardinal Glennon Hospital in St. Louis, caring for a prematurely born child named Tamika, no bigger in size than Ann's hand. One day Ann even got the child to smile its one and only smile. After the child died John asked Ann, "What did that child *ever* have?" "She had the power to draw forth love from me," Ann replied.

This story from Ann's life expresses for me, in a most dramatic way, what I have tried to express in this book about El Salvador. Poverty, racism, and war threaten the poor with death. They are the sins and the evil against which we must fight. But there is hope, and specifically hope for life, in the poor and oppressed who organize and struggle for justice; and in the healers and teachers, the pastoral people and solidarity workers who accompany the poor in that struggle.

What did Dora and her five-month-old child Luis ever have before they were killed at the Gualsinga River? What did the children at El Mozote or at the Sumpul River ever have before they were so cruelly massacred? What did the four U.S. church women, the six Jesuits, and the two Salvadoran women who died at their side, ever have? What did Ann have?

They had — and have — in their great suffering and their great love, the power to draw forth greater love and greater solidarity from each of us. And where great suffering and great love converge, we are standing on holy ground.

This book is written in gratitude. First, to the Salvadoran people who have given their lives so generously, and shared themselves with those of us who had the privilege to accompany them in their struggle for life. And second, to my family and friends who sustained and encouraged me through the difficult years.

I am deeply grateful to my companion in life, Jean Stokan, who heard the stories and encouraged me throughout, not only by her affirmation but also by her example of passion for justice, gentle compassion, and faithfulness to the Salvadoran people. Without her friendship this book never would have been written.

I am especially grateful to my parents, Marian and Flavel Wright, for their love and encouragement; and to my brothers and sister for their constant support.

I also want to mention several communities which have sustained and challenged me through the years. The first is Tabor community, and in particular Peter Hinde, O.Carm., and Betty Campbell, R.S.M., whose letters back to us in 1980 from El Salvador were an important factor in my decision to work there. In addition to Peter and Betty, Ivonne Dilling, Tony Equale, and Mary Reisacher also worked with the Salvadoran refugees in Honduras. I would also like to thank Sally Hanlon, Ruth Fitzpatrick, Curt Wands, Konrad Ege, Martha Wenger, Jean Walsh, Joe Regotti, Leon Smith and Spike Zywicki. The spirit of Tabor, and the community of friends associated with Tabor through the years continue to be a constant source of support.

I want to thank the community of friends and co-workers with whom I shared the privilege of working in El Salvador the eight years I was there. I am especially grateful for the group of friends who met regularly to share the challenges that we experienced and the stories that we heard in the communities where we worked: Jim Barnett, O.P., Cathy Arata, S.S.N.D., Reverend Dan Dale, Nancy Jones, Eugene Palumbo, Reverend Bill Dexheimer, Elena Jaramillo, C.S.J., Lorraine Polacci, C.S.J., Franciscan Sisters Patty Farrell, Kay, Carole, and Nancy, Peggy O'Neill, D.C., Martha Thompson, Susan Classen, Peter Gyves, Reverend Phil Anderson, Larry Rosebaugh, O.M.I., Cathy Deriemer, Josie Beecher, Erica Dahl-Bredine, Peter O'Driscoll, Christine Rieser, Dean Brackley, S.J., Dennis Leder, S.J., and David Blanchard, O.Carm., and all the volunteers from the Mennonite Central Committee, the Jesuit Refugee Service, and Christians for Peace in El Salvador. The depth of the sharing around a common commitment to the Salvadoran people continues to be a source of lasting friendship.

I also want to thank the solidarity community in the United States, which sustained the struggle in the U.S. throughout the past decade. Their courage, dedication, creativity and self-sacrifice were exemplary in the struggle against U.S. intervention in Central America, and in building a people to people movement of solidarity. In particular I want to thank Minor Sinclair and Margaret Low, my co-workers at the Ecumenical Program on Central America and the Caribbean (EPICA).

I especially want to thank Eileen Purcell, José Escobar, Paul Scire, Teri Chin, Sheryl Bergman, Mike Hoffman, Gigi Gruenke, Kelly Josh, Barbara Schaible, Kathleen Kenny, Shana Grossman, Locke Shultz, Amy Crossed, Margarita Valencia, Ken Jacobs, Margie Clarke, and Lana Dahlberg at the SHARE Foundation; Barbara Wein, Betsy Shepherd, Christie Rodgers, and Jennifer Casolo at Voices on the Border; Tim Crouse at the Companion Communities Development Alternatives; and Angela Sanbrano, Leslie Schuld, Kate Thompson, Hugh Byrne, and Mike Zelinski at the Committee in Solidarity with the People of El Salvador.

I also want to thank Renny Golden, Cinny Poppin, and Michael McConnell at the Chicago Religious Task Force; Phil and Angie Berryman, Dick Erstadt, Sandra Pentland, and Darlene

xiv PREFACE

Graminski at the American Friends Service Committee; Lee Miller
and Margie Swedish at the Religious Task Force on Central America; Joe Nangle, O.F.M., Jim Wallis, and Joyce Hollyday at
Sojourners Magazine; Dan Long, Suzie Prenger, Jeff and Jackie
Schoonover-Higgins, Garth Cheff, and Betsy Ruth at Christians
for Peace in El Salvador; Margaret Sullivan, O.P., Amparo Palacios, Jo Owens, and Reverend Kim Erno at the Washington Office
of the National Debate for Peace in El Salvador; Shelley Mos-
kowitz at Neighbor to Neighbor; and Geoff Thale, Donna Mandel,
and Fran Teplitz at the National Agenda for Peace in El Salvador.

I also am grateful to Tom Quigley at the United States Catholic
Conference, Reverend Phil Wheaton at the Conversion for
Reclaiming Earth in the Americas, Gary MacEoin, Reverend
Richard Shaull, Mary O'Keefe, O.P., Heather Foote at the Uni-
tarian Universalist's Service Committee, Juan Mendez, Cindy
Arnson, Jemera Rone, and Gretta Siebentritt at America's Watch,
Moises Sandoval at *Maryknoll* Magazine, Marie Dennis at Mary-
knoll Justice and Peace Office, Jack Elder, Diane Elder, Stacey
Merkt, and John Blatz from the Sanctuary Movement, Don
Marengo, De Sanchez, Laura and Marcos Sanchez, Mike
McGuire, Patience Lee, Sonata Bohen, George Plage, Dennis
Dunleavy, Karen Sauer, Mary Slicher, Sister Pati Ann Rogucki,
Eileen Rudzinski, Gary Cozette, Rafael Tovar, Salvador Mejía,
William Hernández, Berta and Edwin Rodríguez, Roy Bourgeois,
M.M., Jim Harney, and the people of St. Aloysius parish in Wash-
ington, D.C., especially George Anderson, S.J., John Conlin,
S.J., Joe McCloskey, S.J., and John Dear, S.J.

Robert Ellsberg, the editor of Orbis Books, provided encouragement and friendship throughout, and the writings from the
Latin American Church and the Theology of Liberation which
Orbis has published over the past two decades have been a
source of inspiration.

Finally, I owe a debt of gratitude to the Salvadoran people,
especially to those friends with whom I had the privilege to share
life. In particular, I want to thank the Christian Base Communities
of El Salvador (CEBES), and the National Coordination of the
Popular Church (CONIP) for their courageous testimony and witness of life.

I am especially grateful to Jon Sobrino, S.J., and María

Eugenia of the Pastoral Center at the UCA, Monsignor Ricardo Urioste of the Archdiocese of San Salvador, Bishop Medardo Gómez of the Lutheran Church of El Salvador, and Reverend Edgar Palacios of the National Debate for Peace in El Salvador for their friendship, encouragement, and courageous witness for justice and peace.

INTRODUCTION

Truth Crushed to Earth Will Rise Again[1]

On March 15, 1993, the United Nations released the much-awaited "Truth Commission" report for El Salvador. It was entitled *From Madness to Hope: The Twelve-Year War in El Salvador*.[2] Reactions to the report have been varied, from outright denial of the conclusions by the Salvadoran military to calls for the full implementation of its recommendations by the FMLN (Farabundo Martí National Liberation Front) and civilian and church sectors of Salvadoran society.

The overwhelming evidence cited in the report makes it clear that the great majority of the crimes committed in El Salvador during the past twelve years, including the assassination of Archbishop Romero and the killing of the six Jesuit priests and the two women, were planned and executed by the Salvadoran military and its death squads. The FMLN is also cited in the report for violations of human rights, particularly the killing of town mayors in conflictive areas and of other right-wing opponents. Those giving testimony attributed 85 percent of the human rights violations to the Salvadoran military and death squads and 5 percent of the cases to the FMLN.[3]

Within days of the release of the Truth Commission report, President Alfredo Cristiani and the ruling ARENA party in the Legislative Assembly called for and passed a general amnesty. Archbishop Rivera Damas and the Jesuits in El Salvador, however, strongly opposed the amnesty, and insisted that truth *and* justice are absolutely necessary for genuine reconciliation to take place.[4]

The Truth Commission report also raised questions and stimulated debate about the role of the United States in the war and, in particular, its complicity in crimes committed by the Salvadoran military and their subsequent cover-up. The United States sent over $6 billion in aid to the Salvadoran government during the twelve years of the war, the majority of which was direct military aid and economic support to carry out the war and to keep the economy from collapsing.[5]

In addition, hundreds of U.S. military advisors participated in the day-to-day prosecution of the war, and entire elite military battalions, including the notorious Atlacatl Battalion responsible for the massacre of hundreds of people in the village of El Mozote in 1981, and for the killing of the six Jesuits and the two women eight years later, were trained by U.S. advisors.[6]

Initial reactions in Congress to the Truth Commission report included a call for an immediate investigation to see whether previous administration witnesses had lied to Congress about the extent to which human rights were being violated in El Salvador.[7] No Congressional investigation took place, but a special panel was set up by the State Department to assess how the Reagan and Bush administrations reported on human rights abuses in El Salvador.[8] Four months later, in July 1993, the panel issued its report.[9]

The panel identified the core question regarding human rights policy in El Salvador as "whether the improvement of the terrible human rights situation or prosecution of the war against the leftist forces should be the overriding goal of U.S. policy." But it refused to acknowledge any contradiction between the two goals: "Within the parameters of overall U.S. policy, the Department and Foreign Service personnel performed creditably—and on occasion with personal bravery—in advancing human rights in El Salvador."[10]

The panel did not even raise the question of the morality of U.S. intervention on the side of a military which systematically murdered tens of thousands of people during twelve years of civil war.

A Truth Commission for the United States?

It is instructive to look at what happened in El Salvador during the past decade in light of the crimes committed today against civilians in Bosnia. The bombing and massacre of the civilian population, the raping of women, and the forced displacement of entire villages which occurred in Bosnia in the 1990s, took place in El Salvador in the 1980s. One set of crimes was justified in the name of "ethnic cleansing," the other in the name of "fighting communism." The only difference is that the United States condemned the crimes committed in Bosnia, but continues to cover up its role in the crimes committed in El Salvador.[11]

For decades the United States used the argument of "fighting communism" to intervene in Third World nations like El Salvador. The roots of the conflict in El Salvador, however, had more to do with conditions of poverty and oppression, than with Marxist ideology. Since the collapse of state socialism in Eastern Europe and the break-up of the Soviet Union, the argument of "preventing a beachhead of communism" from being established on our shores has become totally discredited.

The real roots of U.S. domination of Third World peoples are found closer to home. Long before there was a Soviet Union, the United States found ways to justify the enslavement of African Americans and the genocide of Native Americans. It was a small step from oppressing people of color at home to oppressing them in Third World nations — in both cases, racism and oppression are linked.

Today the defense of free-market capitalism, national security, and the American way of life have replaced the war against communism as the essential elements of the "New World Order." The invasion of Panama in 1989, which caused thousands of civilian deaths, and the Persian Gulf war in 1991, which resulted in 100,000–200,000 civilian deaths, are the most blatant examples of the consequences of this new order.

Unless the truth about the U.S. role in El Salvador is acknowledged by the current administration, and justice exacted — at the very least a substantial commitment of financial aid for reconstruction, conditioned on the fulfillment of the Peace Accords — we can expect no fundamental changes in U.S. policy toward the region, indeed toward the entire Third World. The truth indeed will make us free;[12] that is why it must first be told. And it can only be told in its fullest sense from the perspective of the poor and the victims of lies and injustice.

The Greatest Scandal of Our Time

What is at stake is not only the truth about El Salvador, but the truth about the world itself and the poor in particular. After the death of the Jesuits and the two women, liberation theologian Jon Sobrino, S.J., spoke of "the massive cover-up" that hides from our eyes "the greatest scandal" of our time:

> Two-thirds of humanity are dying in poverty because wealth and power can exist for the few only when the many suffer and die in poverty. The martyrs of El Salvador were killed because they threatened the idols of wealth and power. My brother Jesuits defied these idols by telling the truth and unmasking the lies. To tell the truth is to defy the idols of death. [13]

Ignacio Ellacuría, one of the Jesuit martyrs, repeatedly called attention to the "crucified peoples" of the world, those who are condemned to death by crushing poverty, oppression, and war. They are "the Suffering Servants" of our time, disfigured by torture and death, whose appearance causes people to turn their heads away.

Throught his life, Father Ellacuría denounced the structural violence of injustice and the repressive violence of the state, and he gave critical support to the right of oppressed peoples to struggle for their liberation using violent means. Toward the end of his life, however, he came to the conclusion that the specific vocation of Christians in a revolutionary struggle is one of nonviolence:

> What we are called to do as Christians is to give the fullest and most complete testimony that we choose life over death, love over hate. The Christian attains this goal when he or she is willing to risk even life itself in defense of the poor and in the struggle against their oppressors. It seems neither daring nor cowardly to affirm that the Christian vocation calls us to use peaceful means to resolve the prob-

*lems of injustice and violence in the world rather than vio-
lent means, no matter how justified those means may be.*[14]

Eight months before his death, Father Ellacuría spoke at a
march organized by the National Debate for Peace in El Salvador,
in which he put forward the perspective of the poor:

*We need to work for peace from the perspective of the
orphans and the widows, and the tragedy of the assassinated and the disappeared. We must keep our eyes on the
God of Jesus Christ, the God of life, the God of the poor,
and not on the idols or gods of death that devour everything.*[15]

On November 16, 1989, Father Ellacuría and his fellow Jesuits
paid the price for their witness to the truth and their promotion
of justice. Their deaths, in no small measure, prepared the way
for the signing of the Peace Accords two years later.

On January 16, 1992, the Salvadoran government and the
FMLN signed the historic Peace Accords in Mexico, formally ending more than a decade of fighting. Two weeks later, on February
1, I joined two hundred thousand people as they converged on
the Plaza of the Martyrs in San Salvador, like so many rivers
flowing into one immense sea of people. There we sang the "Ode
to Joy" to mark the first day of the cease-fire.[16]

Two years later the cease-fire still holds. But the root causes
of the war—the extremes of wealth and poverty, the dominant
role of the military, and the absence of strong democratic institutions—still remain to be resolved.

El Mozote: The Lessons of History

There are important lessons of history to be learned from a
decade of war in El Salvador, so that the tragedy of seventy-five
thousand lives lost[17]—and $6 billion of U.S. aid to a cruel military
regime—are not repeated. And so that the struggle of the Salvadoran people for social and economic justice, real democracy,

and an end to military repression and impunity can illuminate
the struggles of other peoples.

The question Jon Sobrino asked immediately after the death
of his Jesuit brothers and the two women is as valid today as it
was then, and even more urgent in light of the Truth Commission
report:

> *When we look face to face at the Suffering Servant, at the
> crucified people of God today, we must ask ourselves:
> "How are we responsible for their suffering?"*[18]

One symbol of this suffering is El Mozote, a small village in
northern Morazán named in the Truth Commission report, where
hundreds of people were killed by the Salvadoran army in
December 1981. The name of El Mozote first appeared on the
pages of *The New York Times* and *The Washington Post* in January 1982.[19] At that time U.S. State Department officials denied
that any massacre had taken place.[20]

Eleven years later El Mozote was back in the news. It reap-
peared on the front page of the October 22, 1992 *New York
Times*, which pictured forensic teams digging up the skeletons of
thirty-six children killed by "American-trained soldiers." Five
months later, on the eve of the publication of the Truth Commission report, *60 Minutes* returned to the site of the El Mozote
massacre with Ray Bonner, the *New York Times* reporter who
first broke the story eleven years before, to once again disclose
the truth about El Mozote.

Hundreds of people were massacred in El Mozote on December 11–12, 1981, by the Atlacatl Battalion, the same army battalion that the Truth Commission held responsible for the
massacre of more than two hundred people in El Calabozo in
August 1982,[21] of one hundred eighteen people in Copapayo in
November 1983, of sixty-eight people in Los Llanitos in July
1984, of fifty people at the Gualsinga River in August 1984, and
of the six Jesuits and two women in November 1989. An elite
army battalion trained by the United States! More than five hundred victims were identified in Mozote and surrounding villages,
although the actual number of victims killed was much higher,
perhaps as many as one thousand.[22]

On Christmas Day, 1990, I went to visit El Mozote with a delegation of church people from the United States. There are few houses left standing in El Mozote. Everything has been destroyed, even the chapel. Only one person survived: Rufina Amaya. Rufina lost her husband and four of her children in El Mozote; she heard their cries as they were being assassinated. Miraculously, she escaped and lived to bear witness to what happened.[23]

We gathered that Christmas morning to hear Rufina's testimony again. As we stood in the ruins of the chapel and looked over the sea of little white flags people had planted in the ground two months before, I noticed a scrap of paper on the ground. I went over to pick it up and found the words of a song from the Salvadoran Mass, "The Lamb of God," written on the paper. Standing in the ruins of the chapel, we sang the song, then prayed in silence:

> *You are the crucified one,*
> *massacred by the powerful,*
> *and today your blood is spilled*
> *in the blood of our martyrs.*
> *We ask you, Lord, to hear us,*
> *to hear the cry of your people.*

This song tells the story, not only of the crucifixion of the Salvadoran people, but also of the witness of the martyrs and their love for their people. The poor of El Salvador cry to God to be liberated from their oppression; but they also cry to us to respond with faith, with solidarity, and with a commitment to end all the crosses that condemn the poor to an untimely death.

El Mozote is a symbol not only of the suffering of the Salvadoran people, but also of their hope. To the extent that the poor continue to struggle for justice, the truth about El Salvador will come to light, and the violence of the military and the death squads will become even more discredited. Only when the truth about the massacres is told, the military officials responsible for them are brought to justice, and Salvadoran society demilitarized will there be hope for genuine peace, justice, and reconciliation in El Salvador.

The Pastoral Legacy of Archbishop Romero

It is impossible to talk about El Salvador without mentioning the name of Archbishop Oscar Arnulfo Romero. Even though fourteen years have passed since he was gunned down by an assassin's bullet as he celebrated his last Eucharist March 24, 1980, his life continues to illuminate the journey of the Salvadoran people. "His death," liberation theologian Gustavo Gutiérrez remarked in one sweeping statement, "divides the history of the Latin American Church into a before and an after."[24]

Poverty for the poor of El Salvador has always meant death, and those who did not die slowly from hunger and disease were killed by the military repression. For generations, a wealthy minority continued to grow richer off the labor of the poor who harvested the coffee, sugar cane, and cotton produced for export, while a largely landless peasantry grew poorer. In 1932, when Farabundo Martí led a rebellion against the military dictatorship of General Maximiliano Hernández Martínez, 30,000 peasants were brutally massacred.

The rebellion was crushed, but its roots continued to deepen in the popular memory and the organizing efforts of the poor. By the end of the 1970s, after nearly fifty years of military rule, workers, peasants, and students were organized in a multitude of popular organizations to demand justice, bringing the nation to the brink of insurrection. The government responded with more repression, killing thousands. On January 10, 1981, the FMLN took up arms against the Salvadoran military in a war which would ultimately cost 75,000 lives.

This is the world in which Archbishop Romero lived and preached. His homilies and pastoral letters were significant events in the political turmoil of the nation. They had the power of truth in a country where the media is controlled by the government and given to falsifying reality in favor of the wealthy and powerful.

Each week Romero analyzed the social, economic, and political reality of the country, judging each political project according to the social teachings of the church and the gospel, and offering pastoral guidelines for action. "I am simply doing what Medellín recommends: conscienticizing my people on the need to organize

so that they may not be mere passive spectators but rather protagonists of their own destiny.''[25]

This capacity of the poor to organize in the midst of repression
bears witness to a gospel hope expressed in the words of their
martyred pastor. "Many times I have been asked here in El Salvador: 'What can we do? Is there no solution for the situation in
El Salvador?' And full of hope and faith, not just a divine faith
but a human faith, believing also in the people, I say: 'Yes, there
is a way out!' ''[26]

Archbishop Romero spoke very clearly about the role of the
church in the liberation struggle of the Salvadoran people:

> It is necessary to call injustice by its name, to serve truth,
> to denounce the exploitation of the people, to denounce
> discrimination and violence inflicted against the people,
> against their spirit, against their conscience and convictions,
> to promote the integral liberation of people, to urge struc-
> tural changes, and to accompany the people in their strug-
> gle for liberation.[27]

In this light, Romero denounced the political project of the
oligarchy as "defending the indefensible," he called the project
of the Christian Democrats "reforms with repression," and he
gave critical support to the project of the poor:

> I believe more than ever in the popular organizations, in
> the genuine necessity for the Salvadoran people to organ-
> ize; because I believe that the popular organizations are the
> social forces which are going to push forward and create a
> society with social justice and liberty.[28]

One month before he was assassinated, Archbishop Romero
was invited to give an address at the University of Louvain in
Belgium on the topic, "The Political Dimension of the Faith":

> Far from distancing us from our faith, these harsh realities
> have moved us to incarnate ourselves in the world of the
> poor. . . . The hope we preach to the poor is intended to
> return to them their dignity, and to animate them to be

protagonists of their own destiny. . . . In this situation of conflict the church has put herself on the side of the poor and taken up their defense . . . and this in turn has led to a new occurrence in the recent history of our church: persecution.[29]

Before his death, Archbishop Romero told a journalist: "I have frequently been threatened with death. I should tell you, as a Christian, I do not believe in death without resurrection. If they kill me, I will be resurrected in the Salvadoran people."[30] Twelve years later, on February 1, 1992, the first day of the cease-fire in El Salvador, the poor returned to the cathedral where Romero is buried to pay tribute to their beloved pastor. Hung over the front of the cathedral was a huge banner with his picture and the words: "*Monseñor Romero*, you have risen in the Salvadoran people!"

A Life-and-Death Struggle

There are many lessons that can be learned from the Salvadoran people. They teach us a deeper sense of what it means to live. I don't think it's possible to really live with integrity without struggling so that everyone has what he or she needs to live a dignified life: land, employment, food, shelter, health care, education. To be able to give your life for others, to have this capacity and this love to give up your life in a struggle so that all people have life, that is what the Salvadoran people teach us.

I recall so many experiences, so many moments of sharing life and hope with the Salvadoran people. There were moments accompanying the flight of the people through the mountains for days to escape the army; or moments sharing the anguish of a mother and her children in a primitive underground shelter when the villages were bombed. These were unforgettable moments of anguish and danger.

But there were also simple moments of great joy and hope. Moments sharing a tortilla with a campesino family, or spending the night in their little houses, so full of children and life. Moments of meditation in the night, surrounded by the beauty of nature and especially of the mountains. Moments spent accompanying the people, admiring their courage, their heroism, their sacrifice, and their love.

The Salvadoran people also teach us what it means to have faith. Like many Christians in the First World, I questioned how it was possible to believe in God when there is so much suffering. How could God allow so much suffering? In the refugee camps in Honduras I had seen children and babies die of malnutrition. I had seen the repression, found bodies by the roadside, and helped bury them.

I asked myself, how is it possible that these refugees have so much more faith than I? It's not that I didn't have faith, but it was certainly not as profound as theirs. What I discovered is that I had not sufficiently drawn near to their suffering, to their cross, to believe. In these past ten years I have found that only by drawing near to suffering, by trying to bear the same cross as those who suffer, can we discover the real meaning of faith. Only from the cross can we discover faith in a living God who wants us to have life and who announces resurrection.

I recall so many faces of women, children, old men, and their indomitable smiles in the midst of a cruel war, despite moments of danger and death. The Salvadoran people have a profound capacity to maintain hope and joy, to struggle for life and to celebrate, and to thank God for yet another day on this earth.

It seems foolish, or contradictory,[31] but it is only at the foot of the cross, only from a position of solidarity with the crucified peoples of the world in their struggle to eliminate all crosses — war, racism, poverty, oppression, nuclear and conventional arms proliferation, environmental destruction, sexism, homophobia — that we discover a deeper meaning of life, and of faith, hope, and love. And I believe it is only possible to do this if we build communities and cultures that resist injustice and struggle for life.

Truly, the Salvadoran people are heroic. So many people have given their lives in the struggle for liberation. Many have died in the armed struggle, but many more have died denouncing injustice, repression, and the war as they struggle for justice in the popular movement, in labor unions, in repatriated villages, and in Christian base communities. There is a very profound history of active nonviolent resistance, expressed in the organizing efforts of the poor in the popular movement which have opened political space, demanded justice, and pressed for a political and negotiated solution to the war.

Only when we see that it is possible to collectively change our own lives and our communities is it possible to change society and transform the world. This is the example that the Salvadoran people offer us as they struggle constantly to become a new people, a people of God capable of transforming this world through justice, solidarity, and the struggle for a dignified and lasting peace.

A Popular Theology of Liberation[32]

The poor who are active in the Christian base communities often do a critical reflection on their lives by asking what their faith was like ten or twenty years ago. At that time they had a very traditional, naïve faith without any commitment to the struggles of their people, without any participation in the church, or even any awareness of being church.

In the past decade, however, in places like the conflictive rural areas and the marginal neighborhoods of the capital, where there has been a history of evangelization and a promotion of base communities, the poor have discovered that they have a very profound experience of faith. By reflecting on their suffering *and* their commitment to justice in the light of the gospel, the poor have offered concrete signs of the Kingdom in their struggle to build a new life together.

People in the Christian base communities often speak of a God of life or a liberating God. These are not just words. They reflect real experiences of life and liberation, in which people have faced death and struggled to promote life and achieve liberation, drawing strength from their faith in a living God, a God who hears the cry of the oppressed and accompanies them in their struggle for liberation.

People in the base communities also reflect on the protagonistic role of the poor in the struggle for justice. The majority of these communities are situated in the marginal areas of the capital or in the conflictive areas of the countryside. Most of the people are poor; many are campesinos. It is precisely among the poor that you can see in practice what the liberation theologians and the social documents of the church teach: the poor become protagonists of their own destiny and the favored ones to announce the Kingdom.

It is in the world of the poor that we discover day by day how this *praxis* (action and reflection on action) of the poor becomes a reality. Only the poor—and those who identify with their cause—are capable of such sacrifice, of giving up everything, of committing themselves totally, even to the point of giving up their lives for others or of offering their children to the liberation struggle of their people.

These two things—faith in a God of life and the awareness of the protagonistic role of the poor in the struggle for justice—are sowing the seeds of a new model of church that many refer to as a church of the poor.[33] It is not only a church with a preferential option *for* the poor, or a church *with* the poor, but a church *of* the poor. It's the poor themselves who make this preferential option for the poor by their commitment to justice and to liberation, which provide the minimal conditions that make life possible.

This is the evangelization that is being promoted in the Christian base communities, in the conflictive rural areas as well as in the marginal areas of the capital. Solidarity, community, and commitment to justice are encouraged in the base communities; here the poor look at the gospel and each other with new eyes, and together begin to build the foundations of a new society.

In the reflections and liturgies of the Christian base communities signs of life, hope, and resurrection are announced. For example, where the community has been able to build new schools or clinics, or train their own teachers and health promoters, where the people work in cooperatives, where equality and participation of women in all aspects of community life is promoted, where there is solidarity—all these are signs of life and hope.

The Christian base communities also offer a prophetic witness in favor of peace and justice. In the past, when the military captured someone, people often encircled the soldiers and refused to leave until the person was released. Particularly in the areas most affected by the war, entire communities converged on the local army barracks to protest, day and night, until their community members were let go.

Throughout the years of the war, the Christian base communities always supported a political and negotiated solution to the conflict, and they continue to participate as active members of the National Debate for Peace in El Salvador—a coalition of more than eighty popular organizations and churches—which has mobilized the poor in dozens of demonstrations for justice and peace.[34] Here, too, in the struggle for justice, a genuine ecumenism has arisen.[35]

There is a profound sense of solidarity in the Christian base communities. Sometimes you find Salvadorans who think that solidarity is anyone or anything that comes from outside; for example, a delegation or a donation of food, clothes, or medicine. Or you find North Americans who think that solidarity means giving up what is left over, some spare time or extra money.

All this is good, but the poor who live in the base communities in El Salvador have discovered a more profound meaning of solidarity: to give all, even that which they themselves need. It was not rare to find a campesino family, for example, that would share with a stranger their last tortilla; or a family which had already lost three children in the war that would encourage their last son or daughter to take part in the liberation struggle of their people.

The struggle for liberation in El Salvador is a struggle against violence, particularly the dominant violence of poverty and military repression which condemns the poor to death. It is also a struggle for life, a struggle in which Christians have played a significant role within the popular movement, within the repopulated and repatriated communities of the rural areas, as well as within the marginal communities of the capital. The Christian base communities have provided a seed of the Kingdom of God, a vision of the new society and utopia to which the poor aspire and for which they struggle and give their lives.

Solidarity: Where Great Suffering and Great Love Converge

The next few years will be crucial for the peace process in El Salvador, and we must continue to be vigilant, to make sure that the Peace Accords are fulfilled. 1994 marks the first time since the Peace Accords were signed that elections will be held in El Salvador, and they will provide a testing ground for political pluralism. But democracy is more than elections, as the history of El Salvador has repeatedly shown.[36]

Real democracy requires strong democratic institutions that will guarantee the demilitarization of Salvadoran society, participation of the poor in the political process, and social and economic justice for the poor majority. For this to happen, the Peace Accords must be fulfilled, in letter and in spirit. But there must also be a commitment on the part of the international community, and particularly the United States, to make sure that sufficient economic aid reaches the poor and the organizations that represent them to make reconstruction possible.[37]

As people of the United States we are called to continue the work of solidarity, to denounce that which brings death, especially the economic domination and military intervention that have characterized U.S. policy in the region. But we are also called to support a project of life and the building of a new society whose seeds can already be seen in the repopulated and repatriated communities, in the organizing efforts of the popular movement, in the National Debate for Peace, and in the emergence of the FMLN and other opposition parties as actors in the political process. Each of these sectors contributes to the democratic revolution for which the poor struggle today in El Salvador.

As Christians we are called to bear witness to our faith and to promote justice: "Action on behalf of justice and participation in the transformation of the world . . . are a constitutive dimension of the preaching of the gospel."[38] We are further called to help build a church committed to the poor and to their struggle for justice. This is the challenge to which the gospel and the critical needs of the poor call us.

Perhaps the greatest lesson that the suffering of the Salvadoran people and their struggle for life teach us is that it is possible to transform this world of ours. We are not condemned to live in a world in which millions of children die of malnutrition each year and billions are spent on weapons of destruction; a world in which the dignity of so many men and women is not respected and human rights are forgotten; a world in which a few people have abundance and the majority who are poor have nothing.

It is possible to build a better world, a just and compassionate world in which genuine peace reigns, this *shalom* about which the prophets spoke and to which we are called by our faith in the gospel and by the critical needs of the poor throughout the world. The utopia that Christians call the Kingdom of God is possible, and signs of its coming can be discerned today in our own history and in the efforts of the poor to defend and to promote life.

The following pages tell the story of the twelve years I spent accompanying the Salvadoran people – eight of them in El Salvador – in their struggle to build a just society. It is one of countless stories that could and hopefully will be told. More than my story, it is the story of an oppressed people who struggle to build a new society, and their anguish and joy in living and dying to make that dream come true.

It is also the story of countless acts of generosity and innumerable campaigns and struggles of solidarity with the people of El Salvador undertaken by thousands of people in the United States and throughout the world. My hope is that telling this story may contribute to the ongoing struggle of the Salvadoran people for truth, justice, and reconciliation, and to our own efforts to call our government to rebuild what we destroyed in El Salvador. Only then can we move toward justice and real democracy, at home and abroad.

The history of the Salvadoran people is so dense, so filled with the drama of death and life, *"that the world itself could not hold all the books recording all that happened" (John 21:25).* Surely the Salvadoran people have, in the past decade, fulfilled what is still lacking in the passion of Christ. As a "crucified people" they are also the most credible witnesses to the resurrection.

Certainly there was great suffering and countless deaths – over 75,000 – during the twelve years of war in El Salvador. But there was also great love and signs of resurrection in the struggle of the poor for life. And where great suffering and great love converge, Jon Sobrino remarked in his homily in the UCA chapel a few days after the cease-fire, "we are standing on holy ground."

If the witness of the martyrs teaches us anything, it is that life is a gift to be shared with everyone. But it is a fragile gift, vulnerable to the threat of poverty, war, oppression, and death. And for the poor, life is not only a gift but a struggle — for survival certainly, but also for justice, liberation, and truth.

Archbishop Romero, one month before he died, described the most fundamental choice before us as a choice between life or death:

> *We see, with great clarity, that here neutrality is impossible. Either we serve the life of Salvadorans or we are accomplices in their death. And here what is most fundamental about our faith is given expression in history: either we believe in a God of life or we serve the idols of death.*[39]

Unless our faith leads us to a concrete solidarity with the poor and the oppressed, our faith is suspect. My hope is that this book will inspire solidarity, not only with the people of El Salvador, but with the people of Haiti and Guatemala as well; and with the struggles of Native Americans, African Americans, Latinos, Asian Americans, and all people of color in the United States for liberation; with the struggle of women for justice, dignity, and life; and with all peoples who struggle to beat swords into plowshares and abolish forever the scourges of war, racism, and poverty.

I would like to conclude this introduction with words from Dr. Marthin Luther King. More than ever, his words still speak to our times and bear witness to his firm conviction that "truth crushed to earth will rise again":

> *I am convinced that if we are to get on the right side of the world revolution, we as a nation must undergo a radical revolution of values. When profit and property rights are considered more important than people, the giant triplets of racism, materialism, and militarism are capable of being conquered . . . A nation that continues year after year to spend more money on military defense than on programs of social uplift is approaching spiritual death.*
>
> *These are revolutionary times. All over the globe people are revolting against old systems of exploitation and oppression, and out of the wombs of a frail world, new systems of justice and equality are being born . . . We must move past indecision to action . . . Now let us begin. Now let us*

re-dedicate ourselves to the long and bitter—but beautiful—struggle for a new world . . . The choice is ours.[40]

Let us choose life, then, so that the poor—and the earth which they will inherit—may live!

PROLOGUE

Unless a Seed Fall to Earth and Die

Palm Sunday 1981 . . . San Salvador

Today I woke up between the sound of gunshots and church bells. This morning the Christian base communities are gathering in the basilica of San Salvador to begin the celebration of Holy Week. It is one of the few places where people feel safe to gather. Many of the local parishes have been closed since the January 10 offensive of the FMLN three months ago and the outbreak of war. Since then the repression has intensified. It is not uncommon for twenty or thirty bodies to appear in the street with signs of torture, victims of the death squads. Simply to celebrate Holy Week is an act of courage.

The refrain from the Salvadoran Mass announced the hope of the people:

> *Lord of all the earth,*
> *Lord of all history,*
> *Who accompanies our people,*
> *Who lives in our struggles,*
> *Blessed are those who announce the gospel,*
> *The Good News of liberation.*

The people's reflection on the day's reading is profound: *"Humbling himself, he took on the human condition, even to the point of death on a cross"* (Philippians 2:8). "We must do the same," said María. "We've got to take up the cross and get involved with the people."

This is the people's exegesis, a rereading of the Bible from the perspective of the poor. Here the word *pueblo* (the people) expresses a living reality. The passion of the people is as profound as it is ordinary, drawn from everyday life.

In El Salvador it is a crime to practice the works of mercy. To feed and give shelter to the refugees, to bury the cadavers thrown in the street, to defend the political prisoners or search for the disappeared — these acts are punishable by the most horrible death.

Archbishop Romero said, "Sin is what brings death to the poor." We see the fruit of sin today in El Salvador: the untimely death of the poor and the unborn ripped from their mothers' wombs.

And we see the hope of conversion in the popular organizations and the Christian base communities, in the cry of the poor and in the struggle for liberation. These are the "signs of the time," signs that God has seen the humiliation of the people, has heard their cries and guides them now *"with an arm strong and mighty"* through the streets and hills to a Promised Land. The poor are struggling to build a new society based on justice and solidarity that make love effective.

But the Word of God has consequences. As we leave the celebration, the exits to the church are blocked by the National Police. Four young men are detained, their arms stretched against a wall of the church. They are searched as the police stand guard. Everyone leaves in haste. There is nothing we can do. As I look back, the sight of the arms stretched out against the wall leaves a vivid impression in my mind of the week's passion: the crucifixion of El Salvador.

Holy Thursday: Eucharist and Liberation

Today we gathered in the parish of Mejicanos, which has been closed since the January offensive. We return to celebrate Holy Thursday and to open the parish. Everyone is aware of the risk we are taking. Among the popular organizations and the Christian base communities, *entregada* is a key word: it means the offering of one's life to the people. The consequences of this act are only too well known today in El Salvador. In the words of Archbishop Romero, "the fate of the poor is to disappear, to be captured, to be tortured and thrown in the street as cadavers."

This is the price exacted from those who truly commit themselves to the people. So many people have willingly offered their lives. But this gift is life-giving! The hope on the faces of the people gathered here bears witness to the truth of the gospel: *"Unless the seed falls to earth and dies, it will bear no fruit. But if it die, how great the fruit!" (John 12:24).*

Today's reflections recall both the Passover in Egypt and the institution of the Lord's Supper. We began with these two historic events, recalling the daily exodus of the people in El Salvador.

"The Eucharist and the preparation for it bring about in each one of us a radicalization," said one woman, "a conversion from sin, which is necessary for us to unite together as a people toward our liberation." "This is the example Jesus gave us," said another. "To give up everything — body, blood, flesh, and bones."

"This is my body which will be given up (entregada) *for you. This is my blood which will be shed* (derramada) *for you. Do this in memory of me."* These two words — *entregada* and *derramada* — form the heart and soul of the Eucharist and the struggle for liberation. Every life given out of love for the people is offered, like Jesus' life, *"so that we might have life and have it abundantly" (John 10:10).* The prayers of the people form one great cry of anguish and hope. The Christian base communities offer new life to the people, a church born of the poor.

Tonight, as I returned home to our barrio to rest, shots rang out in the night. They bring to mind more profoundly the agony of Jesus in the Garden of Gethsemane, Jesus brought before the soldiers for interrogation and thrown into prison. How many times has this scene been repeated in El Salvador? Who at this moment relives in the flesh the torture and abandonment of our brother or our sister *Jesús?*

Good Friday: Way of the Cross, El Salvador

In this parish of San Francisco Mejicanos, Octavio Ortiz is buried. He was the first priest ordained by then Bishop Oscar

Romero, in 1974. Five years later Octavio was dead. He was killed early in the morning of January 20, 1979, when a tank broke through the gate of the retreat house of *El Despertar* in the parish of San Antonio Abad where he was staying, and National Guardsmen killed four boys and Octavio. Later Octavio's body was run over by the tank and his face disfigured.

Remembering Octavio's death, it's clear that the National Guard does not concern itself with religious sanctuary. In El Salvador *La Guardia* doesn't bother to knock. This is the daily tension under which the people live, and it is impressive to see the courage and hope they maintain despite a very natural fear.

Today we celebrated the stations of the cross, a dramatic rendering of a real-life *vía crucis* (Way of the Cross) lived each day by the people. The reading from the Suffering Servant of Isaiah is our meditation: "Who is this '*man of sorrows, acquainted with grief?*'" one of the catechists asks. "This '*disfigured one*' who does not appear to be human?"

> *Today in El Salvador, we are living through a true vía crucis, a cross which we encounter in the mountains, in the prisons, and at the military roadblocks, a cross which we meet in the tears and anguish of countless mothers whose loved ones have disappeared, a cross borne before the tribunals and in the agony of those tortured and assassinated by the military and their death squads.*

This *vía crucis* is nothing less than the daily path here in El Salvador that the poor must walk.

Suddenly a hush falls over the people. A rumor goes out: "*La Guardia!*" "The National Guard!" Looking back, we see nothing. The reflection continues, but the atmosphere has changed. Anxiety fills the air, and people are tense. What will happen? The result is a real-life *vía crucis.*

The adoration of the cross follows. A catechist leads the reflection: "This cross symbolizes not only the suffering of the people, but love of so many brothers and sisters who have given their lives for the liberation of our people." We all line up to kiss the feet of Christ on the cross as we anxiously await the arrival of the National Guard.

Finally we share the bread and wine of the Eucharist. Then we receive the final blessing. What will we confront on leaving? No *guardia* or soldiers appear. We disperse in silence; but the fear remains. At some determined hour tonight, or during the celebration tomorrow, they will come, together with the violence and threats that are part and parcel of the lives of the Salvadoran people.

Still there is peace and the commitment and testimony of love of these Christian base communities. *Vía crucis—El Salvador.*

Easter Vigil: Baptism and Liberation

Tonight I accompanied the Christian base communities to the parish of San Ramón, near the barrio of Zacamil. We were able to look out over the city of San Salvador and see the volcano to the north. On the table a single candle was lit.

We began with the account of the creation in the book of Genesis. With the approach of dusk, the celebration took on a new dimension: the victory and resurrection of Christ. We shared the bread and wine of the Eucharist, and sang from the Salvadoran Mass:

> *With this bread and wine*
> *The community lives,*
> *Sharing the goods of creation,*
> *A sign of liberation among the wolves.*

We continued the reflection with a reading from Exodus. People recalled the 430 years of oppression in El Salvador. "We, too, are passing through the Red Sea here in El Salvador, a sea of blood which drenches the people," one woman said.

Then we read from the letters of St. Paul to the apostles: *"The old within us is crucified with Christ . . . Whatever was enslaved to sin is destroyed"* (Romans 6:6). Structures of oppression that *"grind the face of the poor in the dust"* and sell their labor *"for a pair of sandals"* or a pound of coffee—"all this has been crucified with Christ," a man added. "The old has died and the new—a commitment to justice—is resurrected."

We went on to recall our baptismal commitments in the context of the social reality of El Salvador: "Do you renounce sin, oppression, and everything that brings death to the poor in El Salvador?" the celebrant asked. "We do."

"Do you believe in one holy and apostolic church? A church born of the people, where the poor believe in the poor and Christ lives in our solidarity? Do you believe in the communion of saints?" Pictures are held up and the names of fallen *compañeros* are called out. I looked at a picture as an old man held it up to the assembly. The woman next to me wept. "Yes, we believe."

"Do you believe in the forgiveness of sins? A time when field will no longer be joined to field, house to house, a time when the ancient yoke of oppression will finally be broken, *'and the lands which have been destroyed will be returned to their rightful owners'* (Isaiah 49:8)? Do you believe in the resurrection of the dead and life eternal?"

I thought of the words from the Salvadoran Mass and tried to imagine this day when the dead will come back and all will sit down together *"at the table of creation . . . where each one has a place and no one lacks for what he or she needs."* "Yes, we believe."

This is the hope of the poor. From the hills of Morazán to the waters of the Sumpul River in Chalatenango, all will come back to work the fields of their ancestors: *"They will build houses and live in them, plant fields and eat their fruit"* (Isaiah 65:21).

The poor will inherit the earth. This is the hope that fills the darkness of the present day with light, a hope that has overcome death and oppression—a hope that the poor of El Salvador live in the midst of the terror that surrounds them on all sides.

Just now another shot rang out; the rain makes it difficult to distinguish sounds. Tonight the electricity in the barrio has gone out. Only the light of the candle on the altar shines—the same light that gives warmth to the refugees in the mountains, and hope to the captives in the prisons and torture cells of the National Guard and the National Police.

Light of Christ! Easter has arrived. *"No greater love is there than to lay down your life for your friends"* (John 15:13). Christ is risen in El Salvador!

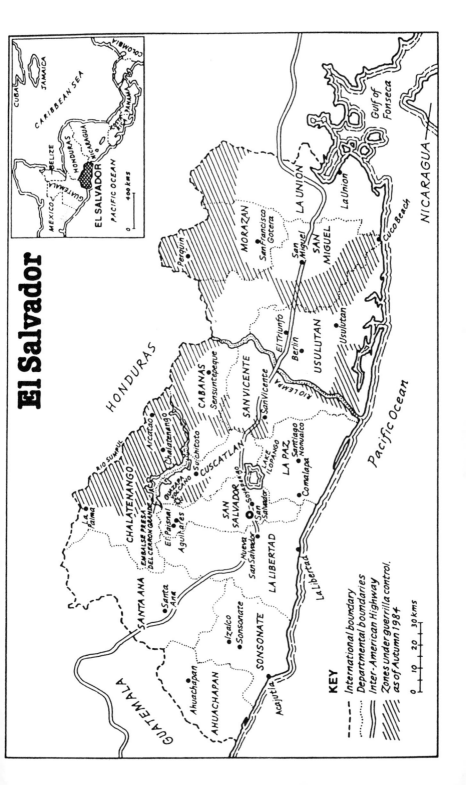

El Salvador

KEY

- --- International boundary
- .... Departmental boundaries
- ═══ Inter-American Highway
- //// Zones under guerrilla control, as of Autumn 1984

0 10 20 30 kms

GUATEMALA

HONDURAS

NICARAGUA

Pacific Ocean

Gulf of Fonseca

SANTA ANA
AHUACHAPAN
SONSONATE
LA LIBERTAD
SAN SALVADOR
CHALATENANGO
CABANAS
CUSCATLAN
LA PAZ
SAN VICENTE
USULUTAN
SAN MIGUEL
MORAZAN
LA UNION

Santa Ana
Ahuachapan
Izalco
Sonsonate
Acajutla
Nueva San Salvador
San Salvador
Comalapa
Santiago Nonualco
LAKE ILOPANGO
Aguilares
El Paisnal
Guazapa
SOYAPANGO
Suchitoto
EMBALSE PRESA DEL CERRON GRANDE
Chalatenango
Arcatao
LA Palma
RIO SUMPUL
ILOPANGO
San Vicente
Sensuntepeque
Berlin
El Triunfo
RIO LEMPA
Usulutan
San Miguel
San Francisco Gotera
Perquin
La Union
Cuco Beach

CARIBBEAN SEA
CUBA
JAMAICA
BELIZE
MEXICO
GUATEMALA
HONDURAS
NICARAGUA
EL SALVADOR
COSTA RICA
PANAMA
COLOMBIA
PACIFIC OCEAN

0   400 kms

EXODUS

1980–1983: The Institutionalization of Violence

The main characteristics of this period were that violence became systematic and terror and distrust reigned among the civilian population . . . There was a succession of indiscriminate attacks on the non-combatant civilian population and also collective summary executions, particularly against the rural population. There were appalling massacres . . . Organized terrorism, in the form of the so-called "death squads," became the most aberrant manifestation of the escalation of violence. Civilian and military groups engaged in a systematic murder campaign with total impunity, while state institutions turned a blind eye.
        —From Madness to Hope,
            Report of the Commission on the Truth for El Salvador, 27

1

THE BEGINNING
OF A JOURNEY
1981–1983

1980 was a watershed year for El Salvador. The cry of the poor in El Salvador for justice shook the consciences of people throughout the world. On March 24 Archbishop Oscar Romero was killed by an assassin's bullet while celebrating Mass.[1] On May 14, six hundred peasants were massacred at the Sumpul River. Huge military operations were carried out by the Salvadoran military throughout the year, killing peasants and destroying villages.[2] On November 27, six leaders of the popular movement were brutally assassinated by security forces in San Salvador.[3] Five days later, on December 2, four U.S. church women were raped and killed by the Salvadoran National Guard.[4] By the end of the year 12,000 people had been killed by the Salvadoran death squads and military.[5]

1980 was also a watershed year for the United States. The advocacy of human rights that had been a cornerstone of U.S. foreign policy under the Carter administration ended, and was subordinated to the ideological assault on communism that characterized the Reagan and Bush years. El Salvador became a test case of U.S. resolve to prevent a "beachhead of communism" from being established in the Western hemisphere, and polarized public debate on U.S. foreign policy. While Reagan officials proposed a hard-line military solution in El Salvador in order to avoid "another Nicaragua," opponents called for an end to U.S. intervention to prevent "another Vietnam."

Dozens of "religious task forces" and solidarity groups sprang up all over the United States to respond to the death squad killings and the massacres of peasants. I worked with the Religious Task Force on El Salvador, based in Washington, D.C., which

3

was set up by several Catholic Church organizations in the days prior to Archbishop Romero's assassination. The task force supported the Salvadoran people and the churches of El Salvador in their struggle for justice, and called for a total cutoff of U.S. military aid to the Salvadoran government.

By the end of 1980, thousands of peasants had fled their homes in the countryside. Thousands went to San Salvador and were given refuge in the churches. Thousands more fled to Honduras, where they were welcomed by the Honduran peasants along the border—and sometimes attacked by the Honduran army and turned back, as happened during the Sumpul River massacre. The number of Salvadoran refugees in Honduras at that time was estimated by the United Nations High Commission on Refugees (UNHCR) to be thirty-five thousand.

In March 1981 I went to Honduras. I arrived at the border on March 12, and visited dozens of hamlets where refugees were living. Many were living in crudely constructed shelters with thatched roofs, while others were sharing the homes of Honduran families. Three days later, I began to see signs of a military buildup, as Salvadoran planes could be heard bombing on the other side of the river and Honduran troops were sent to the border. Rumors began to circulate that the army was planning another Sumpul River massacre.

On March 18, during the early dawn hours, five thousand Salvadoran peasants crossed the Lempa River into Honduras. They were fleeing from the Salvadoran army that had attacked Santa Marta and several other villages near the town of Villa Victoria in Cabañas, but they had been unable to cross the border until now, because of the Honduran army. This morning, however, they found a breach in the border and crossed the river, reaching Honduras under fire from mortars and helicopters.[6]

That was my introduction to the war in El Salvador. In the weeks following the crossing, the UNHCR set up camps for the Salvadoran refugees in the town of La Virtud, about two miles from the border. For the next two years I worked as a member of the literacy team and the pastoral team of *Caritas*, a program of the Catholic diocese of Santa Rosa de Copán in Honduras. The experience of first-world people working together with Central American co-workers in a third-world context helped prepare me for the years to come.

We worked with small groups, helping to train teachers and catechists, while others worked to train health promoters. The process of learning was mutual. I shared skills and experiences from a first-world context, but I received much more in return. The method we used was one of empowerment, in which people value their own experiences, use the minimal resources at hand, and work cooperatively to solve their problems and to train others.

The refugees had a deep faith. They had a remarkable ability to identify their story with the biblical story. I recall one catechist's response to the readings that we shared that first Christmas in the refugee camp in La Virtud:

> Jesus was born a refugee. He, too, had to flee from one place to another. We should not be ashamed to be refugees; this is the same path that Jesus had to walk. God is very near to us. We are part of the people of God, we are on the way, and we are walking toward the promised land which is El Salvador.

In November 1981, the Salvadoran military attacked Santa Marta and several villages in Cabañas,[7] creating still another wave of refugees. Two weeks later, on November 16, two dozen Salvadoran soldiers and members of the paramilitary group ORDEN attacked the refugee settlements on the border, capturing and later killing seven refugees. These attacks continued until the refugees agreed to be relocated farther away from the border.

Between November 1981 and April 1982, thirty-four refugees had been assassinated, or detained and disappeared.[8] By May 1982, the UNHCR had relocated more than eight thousand refugees to camps in Mesa Grande, twenty miles north of La Virtud.[9] This effectively sealed the border and cleared the way for the Honduran and Salvadoran armies to cooperate in their war against the FMLN.

What follows is the story of those years and the beginning of a journey that would eventually lead the refugees back to El Salvador, to the promised land that they dreamed of building.

[1]

The Cry of the People

March 1981 . . . La Virtud, Honduras

The waters of the Lempa River divide the dry hills of Honduras from El Salvador, waters no wider than a stone's throw across to the other shore and just deep enough to reach over the head of a man or woman. On both sides of the river the hills rise sharply to a crest; cliffs and trees jut out into the water to offer protection from the sun.

Farther to the west flow the waters of the Sumpul River, where six hundred refugees fleeing from the repression in Chalatenango, El Salvador, were massacred on May 14, 1980, in the span of six hours by the Salvadoran army. Children were thrown up into the air as targets and shot. Some were bayoneted. Honduran troops turned back those refugees who managed to cross the river. Women carried babies and other children who died in their arms. Few survived; and those who did cannot forget. Esperanza told me this morning she dreamed again of the Sumpul River. A Salvadoran My Lai.

Who could believe it! Today, March 18, five thousand refugees crossed the Lempa River. In the darkness of the pre-dawn hours the refugees had begun to cross, cautiously. The hills were filled with men, women, and children—especially children. Cries filled the air. We heard the stories late this afternoon as a few of the refugee workers straggled into the town of La Virtud, exhausted by the day's ordeal.

Mortars fell on both sides of the river. Several men carried children on their shoulders and swam from one side of the river

7

to the other. Soon a helicopter appeared in the sky and made several sweeps over the river. The crackle of machine-gun fire filled the air. People rushed to safety behind the cliffs and trees, then returned to the river. Hundreds continued to cross. Everywhere cries filled the air.

Since September 1980, more than 11,000 Salvadoran refugees have crossed the river to the *aldeas* (hamlets) which are nestled in the hills surrounding La Virtud. The town itself has more than doubled in size to 3,000. Now, with the new arrivals, the number of Salvadoran refugees in the region of La Virtud exceeds 15,000 — nearly half the total number in Honduras. The impression which comes to mind is of a people on the march, trying to survive, hoping to reach a promised land.

Return to the Lempa River

One day after the crossing I returned with my co-workers to the Lempa River to look for survivors. Something happened here that we still cannot believe. The return is more difficult. By now the Honduran soldiers have mobilized. They check us every hundred yards along the way — opening our bags and asking for our passports. At the final checkpoint the soldiers inform us that they are prohibited from going any farther, and we travel at our own risk.

We approach the river with great anticipation. What will we encounter? And whom? The dead? The missing? Those who have managed to cross the river and survived?

Along the way we see unmistakable signs of the battle two days before. Rocks are piled up in circles like miniature caves behind which people hid from the helicopter fire. Huge holes gape in the ground where the mortars fell on Honduran territory. I reach down and pick up the lead fragments of a mortar.

Suddenly someone shouts out ahead: "We've found somebody! He's alive!" As we approach the river we find an old man; the gray in his hair and the features on his face reveal the trials he has borne. He can hardly speak because of fear and exhaustion. He lies still by the tree. Someone from his village recognizes him. "That's *Don* Felipe!"

A little farther toward the river we encounter more refugees:

three women and their children. What joy! As we come closer we find a small child, lying still on the rocks. Her mother turns the child over. The little girl cries out in pain. Half of her back is torn away, infested with flies and dirt. Her mother informs us a helicopter did it. *"Animales,"* she cries, referring to the helicopters and planes.

At last we reach the river and climb down the steep cliffs to the water. "Here's another!" There stretched out on the rocks is an old woman. Her mouth is open and turned toward the sky. Her hands, folded across her chest, are clutching a straw cross. Her clothes are soaked in blood. No one speaks. Only the water laps on the shore.

"Salvador!" Another man who is with us cries out to the other shore. "Salvador!" He is looking for his ten-year-old son who did not cross the river. We have to restrain him to prevent him from crossing over. "Salvador!" he cries again. "Salvador!"

The return home is somber. Exhaustion and the heat of the day subdue us. We carry the old man and the little girl in hammocks. The soldiers stop and search us and let us pass. At one checkpoint someone calls out for water for the little girl. The soldiers do not respond. Then one of them steps forward and offers her some water from his canteen. The little girl drinks thirstily. The soldier, no more than twenty years old, looks like the refugees. The woman next to me urges me to drink, too. Even though I am thirsty, I cannot bring myself to ask the soldier for a drink.

Finally we arrive in the village of Los Hernández. A makeshift clinic has been set up to treat the refugees. To one side I see a young man lying on the ground in agony, a gaping hole in his neck from a gunshot wound. A doctor treats the little girl. The old man rests in the shade.

Next to me a mother feeds her baby with a medicine dropper. On a cot another child receives nourishment intravenously. His belly is extended, his ribs pronounced, his eyes stare out into the distance. I reach out to touch his forehead. By morning both children are dead.

A Day with the Refugees

The village of Los Hernández is situated about two and one-half miles from the Lempa River. It is one of several *aldeas* that surround La Virtud, and the closest *aldea* to the point in the river where the refugees crossed. Before the crossing, hundreds of refugees lived here together with the Hondurans. Now there are five thousand more. Overnight the *aldea* has grown thirty times in size.

The daily life of the refugees is impressive. Day begins at 4:30 A.M. with the first signs of dawn. As far as we can see, people are stretched out on the hard rock ground with nothing more than the clothes on their backs. Here and there fires dot the ocean of people. Everywhere the cries of young babies can be heard.

Already the men are hard at work gathering firewood; women are grinding corn and washing clothes in the river; children are fetching water in clay jugs, which the girls balance gracefully on their heads and the boys on their shoulders.

"We work hard," one man says, his worn face and hands testifying to his words. "We want to plant a *milpa* (a cornfield)." The crowd of men who have gathered around all agree. The creativity, the industry, the pride and joy of work are evident in the activity around us. *"Somos trabajadores,"* the same man says. "We're working people."

"Primero Dios!" Everywhere I hear this expression, almost as a greeting. "God willing!" This is how people deal with their anxiety about the future. Their gratitude is profound. "How else can we explain it?" Lino, one of the catechists, asks. "It was like the exodus story in the Bible. God divided the Salvadoran and Honduran armies like the waters of the Red Sea, so we could cross the Lempa River to safety in Honduras."

Three days they fled the bombings, day and night, without food. By the time they reached the river, the Salvadoran army was close behind them. The next morning, when the Honduran soldiers moved farther downstream, a handful of guerrillas provided cover for the refugees to cross. In one day five thousand refugees, the majority of them women and children, crossed the river. Two were killed by helicopter fire, eleven drowned, and hundreds are still missing on the other side of the river. But five thousand crossed over to safety! "God is great and all powerful!" Lino concluded.

But the reality is still grim. Most of the refugees have been in flight from the Salvadoran army at least since August 1980, and some longer. Nearly nine months on the run, fleeing from the invasions and the bombings. "The soldiers burned our homes in June." "They killed my niece, seven months pregnant with her first child, and threw the fetus to the dogs." "The soldiers have no compassion." "These are things of the devil."

Nine months in flight: men, pregnant women with babies in their arms, young children, the old, and the lame. Days without food or water, and nights under the rain with no shelter. Each night a different spot, and always the fear of being killed. "How long have you been in flight?" I ask. "Two years," says one. "Three years," says another. There is no end to this testimony of suffering, this Calvary, it seems.

By now it is evening. People return to their few square feet of ground to sleep. The ground is bare and rocky. Here one sleeps a bit more securely. But the fear remains: fifteen people have been captured and seven others killed by the Honduran army in a week's time here. Four of the bodies were found with their thumbs tied behind their backs — a trademark of the Salvadoran death squads.

People from the Salvadoran paramilitary organization ORDEN have been seen here collaborating with the Honduran soldiers, pointing out refugees along the way who are targeted to disappear. Few are willing to speak out. The United Nations High Commission on Refugees (UNHCR) even went so far as to congratulate the Honduran military for their cooperation with the refugees. In the distance, we still hear the bombs explode.

But there *is* peace here. The peace the people nourish in their hearts that one day, *"Primero Dios,"* they will reach the promised land and return to El Salvador. Theirs is the hope of the psalmist:

> *They went away, went away weeping,*
>   *carrying the seed;*
> *they come back, come back singing,*
>   *carrying their sheaves. (Psalm 126:6)*

Songs of Liberation

Tonight marks my fifth day with the refugees. Already there is a little more security and food, thanks to the efforts of the Honduran churches and the United Nations. The night again is clear. The stars are brilliant, and the moon rises over the mountains. Here and there fires dot the landscape. People are asleep.

Suddenly, voices break the silence. Then music:

> *March twenty-fourth,*
> *People will never forget,*
> *Another bloodbath*
> *For one who spoke the truth.*

It is the eve of the first anniversary of Archbishop Romero's martyrdom, an event that will be commemorated throughout the continent. Even the FMLN (Farabundo Martí National Liberation Front) has declared a day of cease-fire in commemoration of his death. Throughout El Salvador church bells will ring at 6 P.M.

The songs from the Salvadoran Mass continue:

> *Come, let's go to the banquet,*
> *To the table of creation.*

The words recall the life of Rutilio Grande, a Jesuit priest killed by the Salvadoran military in 1977. Here at the table of creation, all are equal, all will eat together and share the goods of creation.

People have begun to join in the singing. Now and then there is applause. Surrounding the camp in the darkness are the Honduran soldiers. But here, for the moment, there is peace:

> *When the poor believe in the poor,*
> *We can sing of freedom!*
> *When the poor believe in the poor,*
> *We will live together as brothers and sisters.*

The whole camp comes alive; the words and music renew the bodies and spirits of everyone:

> *You are the God of the poor,*
> *A human and humble God,*
> *A God who sweats in the street,*
> *A God with a worn face.*

This is the God of the poor, leading them through the hills of Santa Marta in El Salvador, shielding them from the bombs and the repression, guiding them through the Lempa River to refuge in Los Hernández, Honduras. The God of Abraham who called him to leave his country and set out for a new land; the God of Moses, who led the people of Israel through the Red Sea with a strong and mighty arm. The God of the refugees.

The hope of the Salvadoran refugees is as bright as the pillar of fire that led the people of Israel through the wilderness, and as certain as the vision of Moses on the mountaintop to reach the promised land.

Building Houses To Live In

Today the first hundred men left Los Hernández, walking an hour to reach La Virtud. It is the first time since crossing the Lempa River that the soldiers have given them permission to leave. Today they will begin to build the refugee camp in La Virtud, where the United Nations says there will be more security, farther from the border.

Below the hill where we sit, overlooking the future site of the camp, lies a huge cornfield, fallow and bordered on one side by a small stream. The men climb down the hillside to begin the work of clearing the stubble away from the earth. I join them, hauling lumber and constructing simple tent-like shelters. The work is long and hard beneath the hot sun, but there is a spirit of joy and cooperation in being able to work again.

I stop to rest beneath a tree. An old man, his face worn and tired, looks up at me and smiles through his toothless mouth: "When they mistreat and persecute you." He stops to scratch his head, trying to remember a few words. Then he smiles, *"Blessed are you when they mistreat and persecute you, for one day you will be rewarded."* I smile in return.

Today in the refugee camp the first child was born. Healthy and full of life, the people say. Looking over the field and the work, there is a sign here of a new day. A day when the poor will inherit the earth, when those who work the land will enjoy the fruits of their labor. A day when those who join house to house and field to field, excluding the poor, will be banished from the earth.

The people already have a new name for the camp here. They will call it "La Victoria," which means "victory" — the name of the town they left behind in El Salvador. This is a sign of *"the new heaven and new earth"* promised by the prophet Isaiah, the beginning of a new life when children will no longer die of malnutrition before their time, and babies will no longer be ripped with machetes from their mothers' wombs.

It is a new day that approaches, a day of judgment for the rich and powerful who manufacture and use arms of war to massacre innocent peasants and their children; and a day of liberation for the masses of poor, the peasants and workers in El Salvador — and all of Central America — when they will inherit the land of their ancestors, as God promised: *"Woe to you rich! Blessed are you poor!"* A new day dawns over El Salvador.

[2]

Breaking the Veil of Darkness

December 1981 . . . La Virtud, Honduras

Nine months have passed since the Lempa River crossing. There are three refugee camps now, called *campamentos*, which are spread out along the edge of the town of La Virtud, beside a little stream called the Gualguís. More than 3,500 Salvadoran refugees live there now, in primitive tent shelters with hot canvas roofs. Another five thousand refugees live in the different *aldeas* surrounding the town.

Today is the beginning of Advent. Lino, one of the catechists in the camps, told me today that he left his home in the village of Santa Marta exactly one year ago during an invasion by the Salvadoran army. "I have learned one thing," he said. "If we don't pass through this martyrdom, this suffering, we will never understand the gospel." Lino's hope, like the hope of all of the refugees, is born in the crucible of violence, blood, and death. His hope is the hope of a people in exile: to return one day to his native land, El Salvador.

Tonight another group of refugees arrived in the rain, mostly women and children. Family by family they make their way down the mountainside in the dark to the camp below. Like each new wave of refugees, their stories are tragic. They have been in flight for sixteen days, fleeing still another invasion of their village of Santa Marta by the Salvadoran military. Exposed to the rains, with nothing to eat, their faces are weary, their feet bare and bleeding.

15

Only a flaming torch, a fire-lit stalk of corn, lights their way into the camp, illuminating their faces and the hope, expressed so well by the Advent readings:

> *The Lord will not be silent about Jerusalem . . .*
> *until her integrity shines out like the dawn*
> *and her salvation flames like a torch.*
> *(Isaiah 62:1)*

Tonight in our *campamento*, a light shines in the darkness.

A People Who Walks in Darkness

The next day the catechists got together and read from the prophet Isaiah: "*Console my people, console them*" *(Isaiah 40:1)*. The situation of the refugees is strikingly similar to the exile in the time of Isaiah. The refugees yearn to hear a message of hope, just like the people of Israel, and prepare the way for their return to El Salvador:

> *Prepare the way of the Lord in the wilderness,*
> *make straight in the desert a highway for our*
> *God. (Isaiah 40:3)*

Like the message of John the Baptist in the wilderness, this hope is prophetic, inviting the people to prepare the way for the coming of the Lord in this time of exile:

> *Let every valley be filled in,*
> *and every mountain and hill be laid low.*
> *(Isaiah 40:4)*

The prophetic word can make a way out of no way, creating new options that open paths of salvation in history. The Lord saves people in history, with unexpected historical possibilities.

Not only do the words of the prophet illuminate the dramatic situation of the refugees on the border; their suffering provides fertile soil for the message to take root and blossom with hope.

When new refugees reach the camps after fleeing for days in the mountains from the Salvadoran army, their feet swollen and bare, there is a great outpouring of grief, but also of compassion and amazement. *"Milagro!"* the people say. "It's a miracle! A sign of God's favor."

The suffering of the people is profound. Their struggle is much like the dramatic struggle to be born that is recounted in the story of Advent: the flight from the repression, the struggle to find shelter, and the slaughter of innocent children. But the faith of the people and their ability to resist are even more profound. They have a deep faith that God will accompany them in times of distress and give them strength to resist. "We will prevail," Lino said, "because we know how to suffer."

These two things—the flight of the people, the terror, persecution, repression, and resulting exile; and their struggle and hope for liberation—profoundly mark the experience of the refugees. The more devastating the experience of exile and suffering, the more profound the hope of liberation, a definitive liberation that touches on all aspects of life: social and economic transformation, political participation, and a deepening of one's faith and commitment to the people.

It is as though a veil has been lifted. A people who have literally walked in the darkness of ignorance, domination, humiliation, and repression are now awakening to a new hope that breaks through this veil like a bright flash of light.

The Death of a Child

The pervasive presence of children is a striking reality in the refugee camps. They are everywhere, in the processions, around the manger scenes. These camps are truly a world of children. At times it seems that the adults are here simply to provide for their children and to prepare the way for the next generation.

Perhaps this impression is because survival is at stake. Children die so frequently here in the camps. The doctors say they die from a combination of factors: malnutrition and susceptibility to infectious diseases, especially diarrhea and pneumonia. During the first month in La Virtud, at least two children died every day.

Still, hardly a day passes that a child does not die.

It is a common sight in the early morning to see the carpenters hard at work building a coffin. Each day measurements must be taken to determine the size of the coffin, depending on the age of the child to be buried.

I have seen children who have died, and I have been to the cemetery to bury them. I have been with children near death. I can still remember, just after the Lempa River crossing, sitting with a tiny child who was severely malnourished. Unable to feed him intravenously, his mother fed him during the night from an eyedropper. By morning he was dead. But I had never seen a child actually die—until today.

I could hear a group of women in a nearby tent quietly singing in chorus. It sounded much like early morning prayers in the refugee camps, with one woman leading and the others repeating. I asked Consuelo, "What is that singing?" "It's the child," she said. "The child is dying." She invited me to come with her, and we made our way to the tent and entered. Nine or ten women were gathered in a circle around the young mother and her dying child. A single candle burned. Between the verses of the song, the anguished cries of the mother filled the air.

I will never forget the child's expression. There in the center, in his mother's arms, was the child. His eyes were open and expectant, as if overcome by the whole spectacle before him. His mouth, too, was wide open, but he did not cry. The mother, overcome by grief, was no longer able to hold the child in her arms and she passed him to another woman standing nearby. Then she covered her face with her hands and rocked back and forth, crying aloud. One of the women marked the sign of the cross on the child's forehead while the child looked at us fervently, as if expecting an answer.

"I am the bread of life," was the reading in the Gospel that day. *"He who comes to me will never be hungry; he who believes in me will never thirst"* (John 6:35). The question the child does not quite ask, and the answer we are unable to give, are both bound up in the mystery of the body of Christ, crucified and broken for us in the body of this child. I walked away in silence, and soon the singing stopped. A moment later Consuelo told me, "The child is dead."

This evening we heard more tragic news. This morning four National Guardsmen from El Salvador crossed the border into Honduras. They came to the house of Lucio, a catechist, took him outside, and bound his thumbs behind his back so they could take him back to El Salvador. When he tried to escape, they shot him — once in the back, once in the head.

We read the story of the resurrection of Lazarus at Lucio's vigil. His pregnant wife and five children gathered around the coffin as a single candle burned in the darkness. *"I am the resurrection; whoever believes in me, though he die, shall live"* (John 11:25). At these times the immensity of evil weighs heavily upon us. Who can understand? Here you are killed first with *"la lengua,"* people say, pointing to their tongue, as those who remain faithful to the gospel are singled out and falsely accused of being "subversives."

Three days after Lucio was killed, the forced relocation of the refugees in the *aldeas* began. Some five hundred of them were loaded onto the trucks with their few possessions and driven six hours north of the border to a new camp in Mesa Grande. Nearly ten thousand refugees will be relocated over the next six months. People do not want to go, but they have little choice other than to comply. As the trucks loaded with people pass along the road, it is difficult to see any light in the darkness.

Jesus Was Born Poor and Persecuted

The following week we met again with the catechists to prepare for Christmas. Such gatherings are significant moments in the journey of the people, times when the Word of God galvanizes their spirits with hope and transforms their passive lives in exile into an active struggle for the liberation of their people. It is the power of hope and love to create new options.

We read the birth narratives in the Gospel together and chose three questions to help the catechists in their reflections with the people. The questions were: "Why was Jesus born poor?" "Why was Jesus persecuted?" "Why do we feel joy at the birth of Jesus?"

Cristóbal said, "Jesus was born poor because of a system of

oppression. Just like today, our children are born on the bare ground or in the mountains because of this oppression." Santana continued. "Christ was born poor because of his love for the poor, and because of this love he struggled against poverty." "But why was Jesus persecuted?" someone asked. "Because he came to proclaim another Kingdom, another King," Albertina replied.

"And why do we feel joy?" Lino asked. This was a more difficult question to answer, particularly because so many people in the camp are filled with sadness at this time of year when they remember loved ones who have died. "Because we follow the same path as Christ," Aparicio ventured. "Because Jesus was born poor just like us," Santana concluded, "and accompanies us in our sufferings. That's why we feel joy."

Later that week we celebrated the Christmas vigil with the beginning of the *posadas*. As is the custom when evening draws near, small bands of children, dressed as shepherds, pass from tent to tent singing an ancient round taken from the drama of José and María as they look for shelter at the inn.

The drama is profound in its simplicity. Even the devil appears at times, for comic relief, chasing the children through the camps. It is a reminder of the actual drama that the refugees live, a story that began as the search for refuge, and continues in the flight from persecution; a drama of the powers of light and darkness. The tragic experience of the refugees gives new meaning to this drama that has been handed down and kept alive for centuries.

"We, too, are passing through the same situation as José and María," Lino said. "This Christmas we will celebrate as they did, looking for a place where our children can be born." Luis recalled the news of the star that appeared in the East. "We, too, hope for this star to shine, a star which illuminates a new dawn, a day of justice, of liberty, of joy."

Cristóbal mentioned that some people "do not want our children to be born." They show a disregard for children "as in the day of José and María." Santana recalled the laments of Rachel in the wilderness, refusing to be comforted, and Herod who tried to assassinate the child Jesus and "so many other children who are the future of our people."

The slaughter of innocents continues today in El Salvador.

Already 25,000 people have been killed in the past two years. But it is the death of children that is especially sad. Their deaths are so common in the camps—and so profound—because they remind us of the life-and-death struggle of the poor for survival in all of Central America and throughout the Third World.

A Light Shines in the Darkness

The next day we celebrated Christmas in the camps. A profound peace filled the air, as we reflected on the meaning of Christ's birth today in our midst: *"A light shines in the dark, a light that darkness could not overpower" (John 1:5).* This mystery became even more real to me as I looked around at the refugees in the camp. "Jesus was born a refugee, too," Lino observed, "just like everyone here." Suddenly everything was transformed.

"This news should not make us feel ashamed or sad," Luis said. "We should be proud that we are refugees, that we pass through difficult times. Jesus as well passed this way. It is a sign that the Lord draws near to his people in such moments."

Behind a cross on the altar, in a little tent that served as a chapel, the mountains of El Salvador rose in the distance. As I looked upon the hills on Christmas morning, I remembered how much sadness they have brought in the past, hills filled with soldiers and mortar fire. But now there is joy in these hills, the anticipation of a message of peace: *"How beautiful on the mountains are the feet of one who brings good news, who heralds peace" (Isaiah 52:7).* Today the hills surrounding the camps are radiant in the morning sunshine. People are joyous, as they share freshly baked loaves of bread and tamales with each other.

"The Word was made flesh, and dwelt among us" (John 1:14). This promise lives on in the lives of the poor today in Central America, the poor who are, in Archbishop Romero's words, "the body of Christ in history." The Word is born in history, and "pitches its tent" among the thousands of refugees throughout Central America. Jesus was born and *is* born each day in these camps, as a refugee.

Nowhere have I seen the presence of this liberating Word

expressed so profoundly as in the Christmas celebration here. We are certain that this Word is addressed to the poor of the earth tonight as it was to the poor two thousand years ago in a stable surrounded by shepherds from Bethlehem.

We experience this Word of hope as the living unity among us, and the hope of liberation for El Salvador. We feel all of this profoundly when we take hold of the rough and expressive hands of the Salvadoran campesinos and campesinas, worn by labor with the machete and grinding stone. We feel this hope as we raise our hands together to give expression to our faith.

The light shines in the darkness, like the cornstalk torch leading the new refugees to shelter in the camp; like the evening star that shines over the camps recalling the people's journey to freedom; like the candle burning over the body of Lucio, an offering of love and sacrifice. A light shines in the darkness over the camps tonight. Christ is born as a refugee!

IN THE WILDERNESS

1983–1985: Violations within the Context of the Armed Conflict

During this phase, the military development of the war caused the armed forces to view the civilian population in areas of conflict as "legitimate targets for attack." Indiscriminate aerial bombings, massive artillery attacks, and infantry advances were carried out, all of which resulted in massacres and the destruction of communities in an effort to deprive the guerrillas of all means of survival. Because of the systematic use of this tactic by the armed forces, in violation of human rights, this phase was characterized by vast numbers of displaced persons and refugees.

> —From Madness to Hope,
> *Report of the Commission on the Truth for El Salvador, 32*

IN THE WILDERNESS
OF CHALATENANGO
1983–1985

During the two years I worked in the refugee camps in Honduras, I heard hundreds of stories from the refugees of their dramatic plight and their suffering. Every two or three months I went to the border to receive hundreds of new refugees who continued to flee from El Salvador and seek safety in Honduras. Many of them were barefoot and possessed nothing more than the clothes on their backs. Many of them had not eaten for weeks, and some of them had lost children along the way. They told us the same stories of terror, of bombings and invasions of their villages by the Salvadoran army.

These were the years in which the major massacres occurred, first at the Sumpul River in Chalatenango in 1980, then at the village of El Mozote in Morazán in 1981, then at the village of El Calabozo in San Vicente in 1982.[1] By 1983 more than thirty thousand civilians had been killed by the military and death squads in El Salvador, and hundreds of thousands of people had been displaced from their homes by the violence.[2]

In March 1983 a new wave of refugees reached the refugee camps in Mesa Grande, this time fleeing from as far away as the Guazapa volcano.[3] They told stories of indiscriminate bombings and more than one hundred civilian casualties near the village of Tenango, where A-37 fighter-bombers dropped bombs on people as they fled from the army.[4] On March 14 Marianela García Villas, president of the non-governmental Human Rights Commission (CDHES), was killed by the army in Guazapa as she was investigating the army's use of white phosphorous and napalm against the civilian population.[5]

Each story the refugees told planted a seed in my heart and

challenged me to draw closer to the suffering of the people. It was difficult for me to imagine the suffering that they had experienced. I longed to see for myself the villages they had left behind and to share more of the life of these people who had become my friends.

In June 1983 I responded to an invitation to accompany the civilian population in the conflictive areas of Chalatenango. I worked first with a literacy team and then with the National Coordination of the Popular Church (CONIP), which coordinated the pastoral work in the area. At that time five thousand people were living in villages without any protection or legal documentation, in permanent flight from the Salvadoran army.

The counterinsurgency war that the military waged against the FMLN was based on a strategy of depopulating the area of civilians through invasions and bombings, in clear violation of the Protocols of the Geneva Conventions that protect the lives of civilians in internal conflicts such as occurred in El Salvador.

By 1984 the FMLN had emerged as a military and political power to be reckoned with in El Salvador, controlling nearly a third of the countryside, including northern Chalatenango, Cabañas, San Miguel, Morazán and La Unión, and parts of Cuscatlán, San Vicente, and Usulután. People in those areas were trying to create a new life in their communities based on justice, on equal respect for all, and on solidarity. They established community councils to direct the work of agricultural production, health care, and education, and local elections were held to choose community representatives for each area of work.[6]

During my eighteen-month sojourn in Chalatenango, from June 1983 to January 1985, I heard firsthand accounts from the survivors of several massacres. On November 4, 1983, at least one hundred eighteen people were killed in the village of Copapayo[7] in Cuscatlán; on July 22, 1984, sixty-eight people were killed in the village of Los Llanitos[8] in Cabañas; and on August 30, 1984, fifty people were killed at the Gualsinga River[9] in Chalatenango. All three massacres were committed by the Atlacatl Battalion, an elite army battalion trained by the United States. Despite clear evidence to the contrary, Assistant Secretary of State Elliott Abrams declared that the last two massacres "never happened."[10]

As a result of the "scorched earth" policy carried out by the Salvadoran military against the civilian population in conflictive areas like Chalatenango, tens of thousands of people were displaced from their homes. More than 1,500 people fled to the refugee camps in Honduras in the latter half of 1984. Chalatenango looked like a desert wasteland. Several towns had been destroyed by the army and abandoned by the people, including San Antonio los Ranchos, Las Vueltas, San José las Flores, Nueva Trinidad, and Arcatao. Everywhere I met people who had been displaced from their homes. Their faces, gaunt and weathered by the war, reflected the devastation of the land around them.

I remember a liturgy we celebrated with one of these displaced communities in the ruins of a house. One of the catechists chose a reading from the prophet Isaiah. *"How long?"* Isaiah asks. How long before there will be justice in the land? And God answers Isaiah:

Until the towns have been laid waste and left without inhabitants; until the houses are deserted and the fields ruined and ravaged." (Isaiah 6:11)

Still, the destruction will not be complete; a remnant will remain:

And though a tenth of the people remain, they will be stripped like a terebinth of which, once felled, only the stock remains. This stock is a holy seed." (Isaiah 6:13)

Despite the destruction and cruelty of the war, a remnant did remain in Chalatenango that prepared the way for the Salvadoran people to return to their homes. Their presence made possible the repopulations of the displaced people in 1986 and the repatriations of the refugees in 1987 when they returned from Honduras to their homes in Chalatenango, Cuscatlán, and Cabañas. Even in the midst of so much darkness and desolation, there was hope.

For the next eighteen months Chalatenango would be my home. I give thanks to God — and to the Salvadoran people — for that experience. I believe it's in the most painful moments, when we feel we don't have the strength to go on, that we discover a profounder meaning of faith. In such moments God becomes present, not only in a mysterious way, but incarnated in the poor, in their sense of community, in their solidarity, and in their willingness to give their lives for their people.

[3]

The Signs of the Time
in Chalatenango

March 1984 . . . Patamera, Chalatenango

It is March now, more than nine months since I first set foot in Chalatenango. Here in Patamera, a beautiful little village near the town of Arcatao tucked deep into the hills along the Honduran border, it is a warm spring day. Already signs of the rainy season appear with the return of the swallows and the singing of the cicadas in the evening. The people say that the *asacuanes* (swallows) and the *chicharras* (cicadas) are signs of the approach of Easter. About two hundred campesinos live here with their families.

For moments we forget that we are in the midst of a war, and we are able to enjoy the beauty of the countryside around us. But always, in the distance, the sound of bombs exploding and the flight of reconnaissance planes overhead remind us that the war is not that far away.

Just three months ago, on December 28, the day of the Holy Innocents, two U.S.-supplied A-37 fighter-bombers dropped eight bombs over this village in a lightning raid that terrified everyone. One five hundred pound bomb landed within a few feet of a primitive shelter dug into the ground where a dozen women and children had taken refuge. Miraculously it did not explode. Days later, I went to see the bomb after it had been dug up. It was as tall as I am. Since then, we are on constant alert, and at any moment we expect the planes to return.

Seeds of the Revolution

Today I spent the morning with Esperanza. I had not seen her
since Honduras, when she crossed the border and lived for a
number of months in the *aldeas* there as a refugee before returning to El Salvador. Her home had been completely destroyed in
the bombing raid last December. She had just enough time, along
with her children, to jump into a trench a few feet from the house
before the bomb exploded. That saved their lives.

I asked Esperanza to tell me her story:

*We lived in a small village called El Sitio, not far from
Patamera. We were poor, and I never attended school. My
mother was an early widow, and only through great sacrifice was she able to raise nine children. Each year my
mother rented a manzana of land (about one and one-half
acres) and paid the local landowner 100 colones (about
$40) so we could plant our spring crops of corn and beans.
After buying fertilizer and insecticides, we were left with
nothing after the harvest.*

*In 1975 the Farm Workers Union (UTC) began to organ-
ize in the village where we lived. Everybody understood
the need to organize ourselves in order to demand lower
rents from the landowners. So we joined the UTC. Church
people came to our community to encourage us in our
struggle. We studied the Bible, and they helped us see that
the way the world was ordered was not according to God's
plan but as the landowners wanted.*

*Throughout Chalatenango, the government responded
to the demands of the campesino organizations by spread-
ing terror and death in the countryside. People were taken
off buses and killed, and their bodies thrown into the rivers.
They even accused us of being guerrillas just for going to
church. We didn't even know what a guerrilla was, and we
insisted on our right to continue our Bible reflections.*

*The government and the military tried to eliminate eve-
ryone who was organized in the Farm Workers Union. I
remember in 1979 the army killed seven women in the*

neighboring village of El Rincón. The soldiers raped them.
They ripped open the wombs of the women who were
pregnant and threw the fetuses to the dogs. Then they threw
the women on a woodpile, poured kerosene over them,
and lit the fire.

We have lived through such hard times and so many
massacres, like the army invasion of May 1982. We had
just put the children to bed when one of the community
leaders came to warn us that the army was going to invade
our villages. He told us to wake the children and pack our
blankets, that we were going to leave on a guinda—that's
what we called it when we had to flee all of a sudden. That
was especially hard for us because we had to leave everything behind. All we took with us were the clothes on our
backs.

Now as I look back on that time, it reminds me of the
story of Exodus in the Bible, and how the people complained to Moses when they began to suffer: "Why did you
take us out into this wilderness to die?" they cried. Some
people lost all confidence and exclaimed: "There's nothing
to eat here. We're going to starve!" More than six thousand
of us fled through the mountains then, with nothing to eat.

I always remember Archbishop Romero's visit to Arcatao,
and how he told us not to get discouraged when we were
persecuted. All these obstacles, he told us, were tests for
our faith to see how strong we were. I thought about this a
lot when we had to flee to the mountains. Hopefully, those
of us who are still alive today can strengthen each other,
and continue to struggle.

Esperanza's story moved me. I had heard so many stories like
hers in the refugee camps, but each story was so compelling that
it riveted my attention to the suffering of the people and their
capacity to endure and to resist.

The sympathy that Esperanza and campesinos like her have
for the revolution in El Salvador has roots that are deeply planted.
Their love for the land and the irrevocable loss of their loved ones
give meaning to their hardship and struggle. It is *their* children

who are fighting with the guerrillas to defend the land their ancestors worked for generations, before it was taken from them.

Seeds of a New People

When I first arrived in Patamera in June 1983, the FMLN had
already established control over large portions of the countryside
in Chalatenango. During the previous year they had occupied
dozens of towns, including Arcatao, an hour's walk from Patamera. Government soldiers and National Guardsmen were forced
to abandon their posts, and the mayor fled to the nearest military
barracks in the departmental capital, Chalatenango. Soon after,
people fled Arcatao when they were told they would be considered subversives if they stayed.

In 1983, in the absence of any official government authority,
a popular government was set up in twenty-four villages throughout the eastern third of Chalatenango where more than 3,500
displaced campesinos and their families lived. María Serrano, a
catechist from Arcatao who was well liked by the campesinos,
was elected the first president of the popular government. "My
house was so close to the National Guard post in town," she told
people, "that I could hear the screams of people being beaten
and tortured at night."

Not surprisingly, none of the people in these twenty-four villages participated in the March 1984 national presidential elections. They were occupied with trying to survive a counterinsurgency war being waged against them by the Salvadoran
army. "Even if we could have voted, who would we vote for?"
many remarked. "One candidate is a *guerrerista* (a war-monger)
and the other is an *escuadronero* (a death squad assassin)."

The two candidates were Napoleón Duarte, during whose time
as head of the civilian-military junta in 1981–1982 more than
thirty thousand people were killed in El Salvador, and Roberto
D'Aubuissón, head of the death squads and reputed intellectual
author of the assassination of Archbishop Romero.

Against this background, the efforts of the local community
councils in the twenty-four villages to galvanize the support of the
campesino population behind the political project of the FMLN

were remarkable. I went to one of the weekly assemblies held in the village of Patamera. The problems that the people in the communities struggled to resolve were problems they had faced for generations, only now they had a voice of their own and community organizations to resolve their needs.

Many of the questions focused on new forms of production. One campesino commented: "We have always worked the land, but we only produced for our own families. Now we need to work together so we can help the people in our community who cannot provide for themselves, like the elderly, the widows, and the orphans."

Another spoke about buying and selling: "We used to sell the corn and beans we produced for profit, but now we try to think of the needs of the entire community and agree on a fixed price for everybody."

Some of the discussion focused on the schools and clinics the popular government had established. "When I was growing up we worked in the fields," one man said, "because we never had schools. But now that we are building our own, we should encourage our children to learn to read and write." One of the women added: "It's true, we have a health clinic now, but we must try to help our children before they get sick. That's why we must keep our homes clean."

Much of the structure and the vision of the popular government was given by the FMLN, and a political representative was often present at the assemblies. But the questions the people raised were genuine, and the decisions reached were generally responsive to the needs of the community. For a people who had never experienced real democracy before, it was a first attempt under the extremely adverse conditions of the war.

Here production is oriented toward the entire community. In the past, most of these campesinos paid dearly to rent the land; now it is free, and both seed and fertilizer are provided when they are available. Most of the people divide their time between family and community plots, working three days on one and three days on the other. The corn and beans they produce on the communal lands serve as a reserve for the community in times of emergency, such as when the Salvadoran army invades and they are forced to flee or when new families who are displaced arrive. The prices of basic items like corn, beans, salt, and lard are regulated to prevent speculation.

Social services as well are oriented to serve the needs of the community. In a country where 75 percent of the children under the age of five are malnourished, every community is served by a clinic and a health promoter. Emphasis is placed on preventative care, and some natural medicines are produced locally and used to treat diseases. And in a rural area like Chalatenango where illiteracy is as high as 90 percent, schools and literacy teachers provide these villagers with a basic education.

It was primarily in these two areas, health care and education, that international solidarity workers in Chalatenango offered our services, training health promoters and literacy teachers and helping set up clinics and schools in each of the twenty-four villages. The learning experience, however, was mutual. We were provided with a unique opportunity to see the world from the perspective of the poor in the Third World (and in El Salvador, a world that was at war) and to help plant the seeds of democracy and community empowerment. What we discovered, in turn, was the remarkable tenacity, creativity, and faith of these campesinos who taught us about their struggle for liberation and the meaning of the gospel for their lives.

[4]

The Way of the Cross

April 1984 . . . Los Amates, Chalatenango

Spring has come to Chalatenango. Already people are beginning to plant corn and beans in the rocky soil. This morning I accompanied Chepe, the local catechist from Patamera, to the neighboring village of Los Amates to celebrate the beginning of Holy Week. Chepe is fifty-seven years old. He used to be the sacristan in the church in Arcatao before the people abandoned the town. Now his lined face reveals the trials he has weathered all these years, but his spirit is resilient and I have to struggle to keep up with his swift pace.

Throughout Chalatenango you find remnants of Christian communities that were able to survive the repression of the 1970s. Since January 1981 they have continued to live and work in areas under FMLN control. Most of the pastoral workers are lay catechists, local campesinos who celebrate the liturgy of the Word as they have done for a decade or more in dozens of rural communities here. Working under the adverse conditions of the war, they offer a heroic witness to their faith in a liberating God, and in a God of life. They are the seeds of a new model of church committed to the poor and their struggle for justice.

When we reached Los Amates, which lies along the banks of the Sumpul River, we stopped to rest at a small church where hundreds of people had already gathered. Women and children were busy cutting bright green leaves from the mango trees to decorate the church. For a moment, as I looked at the faces of the people around me, I forgot the suffering of the war and was lost in the excitement of the people gathered for the celebration.

As we rested, Chepe recalled the May 1982 army invasion of
Los Amates. It was the first military invasion undertaken by the
Ramón Belloso Battalion just weeks after finishing their training
at Fort Benning, Georgia.

> *Two years ago thousands of these same villagers fled from
> a surprise attack by the Salvadoran army. Hundreds of peo-
> ple were slaughtered in the days that followed. We used to
> speak of the passion of Christ as though it were something
> which happened in the past. Now we live this passion every
> day in the suffering of our people. But we are people of
> faith, and one day this suffering will bear fruit in the liber-
> ation of our people.*

Toward evening we reached Jicarito, just as the first sound of
the bell called people to the Holy Thursday celebration. We gathered in an open space in front of the church. Twelve children —
six boys and six girls — sat around a table like the twelve disciples
to reenact Jesus' washing of the disciples' feet. Tomás, one of
the catechists, sat at the head of the table and shared a tortilla
and a bowl of water with the twelve children. Then he washed
their feet.

Israel, who used to be the sacristan of the church in the town
of San Antonio los Ranchos, began to read from the Bible:

> *You shall eat hastily, for it is a Passover in honor of the
> Lord. During the night I will pass over Egypt and bring
> death to the first-born of Egypt. But the houses marked
> with the sign of blood I will pass over. (Exodus 12:11–12)*

The story describes a situation of persecution very much like
that which people are experiencing today in El Salvador. At any
moment they, too, may be forced to flee.

"What is this sign of blood," Israel asked, "if not the sacrifice
of our people? We must not dwell on the invasions and the bombings but trust in the promise that is ours. God has chosen to
accompany us in our struggle for liberation. Let us look forward

to the day when we can celebrate with our loved ones in the streets of San Salvador."

The Gospel text recalled the story of Jesus and the washing of the disciples' feet: "This is a symbol of how the church should serve our people," Israel continued, "a people who are poor, persecuted, and massacred in El Salvador. The task of the church is to denounce sin, to denounce injustice, and to take up the defense of the widow and the orphan."

As the liturgy came to a close, I looked around me at the faces of those gathered as we stood in a circle under the open sky: faces of children, of mothers, of the old. On each face I could see the evidence of a people worn by years of war, poverty, and persecution, but determined to hold on to the hope of one day being free and seeing the promised land. "I'm fifty-seven years old," Chepe told me later that night, "but I still hope to see the day of our liberation."

Every Day Is Good Friday

The next day we returned to the church to prepare the fourteen stations of Christ's passion. Again, because of the pending threat of an air strike, the procession was put off until late afternoon. Fourteen crosses were planted along the path.

As people began to gather in the late afternoon, the procession got underway. Israel announced each station, while Tomás offered a reflection. *"First station: Jesus is condemned to death."* "In our day," Tomás began, "the people of El Salvador are condemned to death by the Pentagon, D'Aubuissón, and Duarte, and the war they wage against our people."

As we walked along the way, a child laid a wreath of white flowers on the cross at each station. *"Second station: Jesus takes up the cross."* "For generations," Tomás called out, "the people of El Salvador have submitted to the crosses of exploitation and oppression. Thousands of our people have been cruelly assassinated." Our procession recalled not only the crucifixion of Jesus two thousand years ago, but the crucifixion of an entire people today in El Salvador.

When we reached the eighth station Israel called out: *"The women weep for Jesus." "Don't weep for me,"* Jesus tells them, *"weep for yourselves and for your children."* "How many mothers in El Salvador can we recall today," Tomás asked, "who weep for their sons and daughters who have been assassinated or disappeared?"

We walked a little farther. *"Tenth station: Jesus is stripped of his garments."* Once again Tomás called out: "We, too, have been stripped of the fruit of our labor, our land, our work, our dignity, our children, and our martyrs like Archbishop Romero."

In the distance the sun had set. Francisca, a beautiful white-haired grandmother, stood beside me. Dozens of children surrounded the cross where we stopped. "The authorities say we are anonymous masses hiding in these hills," Tomás observed. "But look around you and see for yourselves. We are a people with names and faces!"

By the time we reached the twelfth station, it was nearly dark: *"Jesus dies on the cross."* "We are a people nailed to the cross," Tomás reminded us. "Every day in El Salvador our children are assassinated by the army or killed by the bombing raids. More than fifty thousand people have been killed."

We walked a little farther. *"Thirteenth station: Jesus is lowered from the cross."* "What mother here does not know the agony of recovering the cadaver of one of her children?"

By now we have reached the church and enter. *"Fourteenth station: Jesus is buried in the tomb."* Once inside, Israel invited us not to dwell on the dead but to remember their example: "Whoever dies out of love for justice never dies but lives on forever in the hearts of our people. The dead we must not mourn, but imitate in the struggle!"

It is a Salvadoran Way of the Cross. Here the stations of the cross illuminate the crucifixion and resurrection of the Salvadoran people. "In El Salvador," Israel concluded, "every day is Good Friday."

Abel, a catechist from Los Amates, finished with this reflection: "The way of the revolution is the way of sacrifice, the Way of Calvary. The Gospel tells us, *'Unless a grain of wheat die, it will bear no fruit (John 12:24).'* We must live with the hope of resurrection, too, and the hope that the struggle of our people for liberation will one day bear fruit."

Do Not Look for Me among the Dead

Early the next morning we crossed the Sumpul River and made our way to the next stop on our journey, the village of Tequeque near the town of Arcatao. By late morning, people had begun to gather for the celebration.

"Today, Holy Saturday, we traditionally bless the water and the grains to be sown this year by the community," Israel explained to the people. One by one they presented their offerings to be blessed: seed corn, beans and containers filled with water. As Israel pronounced the blessing, he read from the first chapter of Genesis. "The creation was given to all of us," he said, "to work and to bring forth fruit, not just to those few who amass land and leave the rest of us empty-handed."

The reading from the Gospel followed: *"Why look for the living among the dead? . . . Jesus is risen!" (Luke 24:5–6).* Several mothers nursed their babies. Moments before, these same women had recalled the army invasion of May 1982 when they were separated from their children. "We must not dwell on times past," Israel concluded, "but look ahead to the hope of liberation which awaits us."

As we walked home in the darkness, a fire burned in the mountains in the distance where the earth had been scorched to prepare for the spring planting. Along the way several houses were lit by fires to prepare the evening meal. When we reached Chepe's house, Elida, his niece, had already prepared the evening meal for us. On the table a single candle burned. We sat down together to eat and to share the light of Easter.

The following morning I saw Israel and Chepe off to celebrate the liturgy of resurrection in the villages near the Honduran border. This day, two thousand years ago, the disciples gathered behind closed doors for fear of the authorities. There Jesus appeared to them and said: *"Peace be with you!"*

It was a time of persecution, perhaps not much different from what these communities in Chalatenango are experiencing. On the eve of a growing threat of U.S. intervention in Central America, in the midst of recurrent army invasions and bombings, the

Salvadoran people proclaim once again their hope in the resurrection.

Why look for the living among the death and destruction of the war? Jesus is risen in the struggle of the people of Central America for liberation!

[5]

The Cry of a Crucified People

May 1984 . . . Sicahuite, Chalatenango

It is May now, and spring planting continues in Chalatenango. Since Holy Week I have been working with the catechists in their pastoral work of accompaniment. This month the pastoral team met in Sicahuite, a village near the town of Las Vueltas. As in Patamera, the local church supported the efforts of the campesinos to organize in this area during the 1970s. I asked Manuel, one of the catechists, if he would share with me the history of the area.

> *This valley, and principally the village of El Jícaro, was one of the first areas to organize with the UTC, the Farm Workers Union, in 1974. In the beginning we had to meet in small groups during the night and in remote locations, because it wasn't safe to meet openly. We struggled for a reduction in the price to rent a manzana of land for our milpas, for the right to organize as farm workers, and for a just wage in the coffee harvests. But every time we demanded our rights, we clashed with the security forces.*

Manuel, who is originally from El Jícaro, also recalled the invasion of Las Aradas, the name of the hill overlooking the Sumpul River where one of the worst massacres of the war took place on May 14, 1980. Thousands of people fled north from different

41

villages toward the Honduran border in order to escape the army. More than six hundred people from El Jícaro, Yurique, and Las Aradas were killed by the Sumpul River in a single afternoon.

As Manuel talked, I looked out over the beautiful mountains that rise above these tiny villages. I tried to imagine all the suffering these hills had witnessed and the secrets that remained buried in their silent beauty.

The following day, as we were leaving Sicahuite, I stopped in the plaza next to the church that had been destroyed by a bombing raid last January 6. As I looked directly in front of me, where before the wall of the church had stood, the view opened out onto the hills. Above me the sun shone through the rafters of the partially destroyed roof. The floor was covered by the rubble of the broken roof tiles and the remains of the adobe walls.

At that moment it seemed to me the authentic place of the church should be here, in the midst of this destruction, accompanying the poor in their struggle to defend life. Here, in the ruins of this church, the very stones cry out to vindicate the lives of fifty thousand dead in El Salvador.

Blood of the Martyrs

A few weeks later I accompanied Manuel to the monthly pastoral meeting in the village of Haciendita, near the town of San José las Flores. We were going to make a retreat with a dozen catechists who had come from as far away as the Guazapa volcano across Lake Suchitlán. Many of the catechists shared with us their harrowing experiences. The previous week seven Salvadoran army battalions had invaded numerous villages near the Guazapa volcano, forcing thousands of people to flee.

Father Rutilio Sánchez, affectionately known as Tilo, had also come from Guazapa with the catechists. He was tired, but greeted us with a smile. I had heard about Father Rutilio from the refugees in Honduras, where we first read his letter to Bishop Rivera Damas announcing his decision to take up the pastoral work of accompaniment in areas controlled by the FMLN:

The pastoral needs in the area where I am going are great
. . . The suffering of the people living in these valleys and

*mountains calls us to commit ourselves to the struggle for
liberation . . . I only want to take up the cross and follow
Jesus in the ravines, the hills and the trenches where the
Kingdom of God is being fulfilled, in which there will be
enough bread for everyone, and our people will not die
young.*

Father Rutilio, together with two other priests, David Rodríguez
and Trinidad de Jesús Nieto, courageously accompanied the civilian population in Chalatenango, Guazapa, and San Vicente, all
areas of intense conflict. I talked at length with Silvia, one of the
catechists from the Guazapa area. Silvia told me she was nineteen
years old. I was struck by a long scar across her face that made
it difficult for her to smile.

Silvia described to me in great detail the events surrounding
the massacre last November 4, 1983, in her village, Copapayo,
near the town of Suchitoto. Nearly half of the community of three
hundred were assassinated in a single day by the U.S.-trained
Atlacatl Battalion. Silvia's sister, her brother and his wife, and
their small child were killed in the massacre:

*We left Copapayo on Monday before the massacre and
crossed Lake Suchitlán to Chalatenango. The next two days
hundreds of people crossed over in small boats and took
refuge in the abandoned town of San Antonio los Ranchos.
On Thursday, one of the guerrillas in the area told us they
had intercepted a Salvadoran army radio communication
announcing the end of the invasion. But it was a trick. The
army deceived us. When the people returned to Copapayo
on Friday, the entire village had been surrounded by the
Atlacatl Battalion.*

As Silvia spoke, I struggled to remember every detail. I had
heard news of the massacre last November, but this was the first
time I had come face to face with any of the survivors. Silvia's
story was all the more poignant to me, knowing that her family
was killed by Salvadoran troops trained by the United States:

*Dozens were assassinated by the lake as they tried to escape
in a boat. The soldiers threw grenades at them, and*

*machine-gunned them without mercy. Those who re-
mained on the shore were taken to a neighboring village,
La Escopeta, and then to a third village, San Nicolás, where
they were kept under guard in a house. All of the young
girls were taken away from the house and raped, first by
the soldiers, then with bamboo sticks, and killed. The young
men were also separated from the group, tortured, and
assassinated. The remaining women and children were
machine-gunned to death the following day in that house.*

*"Arrepiéntense!" Colonel Monterrosa screamed. "Re-
pent, subversives! Today you're going to die!" The people
were gunned down in cold blood by .50 caliber machine
guns placed in the windows and the door of the house.
"Finish them off with a grenade," one soldier called out.
"Cave in the walls," another shouted. Finally the roof collapsed, leaving a pile of corpses buried beneath the broken
roof tiles. Seventy-two children, including an eight-day-old
baby, were slaughtered that day. Only three children survived beneath the pile of bodies. That's how we know what
happened.*

Four days later, A-37 fighter-bombers dropped eight bombs
on the town of San Antonio los Ranchos where Silvia had taken
refuge with her mother and sister. The last bomb exploded beside
a stream where Silvia and her sister had gone to wash clothes.
Silvia was struck by a piece of shrapnel, leaving a long gash across
the side of her face.

As Silvia told her story, a reconnaissance plane known as the
Push-and-Pull made several passes overhead. A hush fell over
the village of Haciendita where we were meeting. Nobody
moved, and fires were carefully tended so as not to give off
smoke. These reconnaissance planes are the eyes of the A-37
fighter-bombers, marking potential targets with the rockets that
they fire.

I felt trapped beneath the roof of the house where we were
talking. My first impulse was to leave. We were so vulnerable
there. But such a move could be disastrous if the pilot detected
any signs of movement below. There was nothing to do but wait

in silence until the plane passed, hoping that nothing would happen.

The stories of suffering are endless. I have heard so many stories like Silvia's from survivors of other massacres since I first came to the border of El Salvador three years ago! Each year the army invasions are more terrifying than the previous ones. At times like these I feel compassion, and a challenge to draw nearer to the people in their suffering. But there is little that any of us can do to make a difference. As long as the United States continues to fund the war, the suffering of the people will continue.

That evening I sat with Chepe in the pastoral center in Haciendita. Dora, a young woman who lived next door, came to sit with us as she nursed her two-month-old baby Luis. She had fled with her family from her home in Santa Bárbara, a village near the town of Cinquera, and come to Chalatenango a few months before. Two of Dora's sisters, their children, and her mother also joined us. Her mother, like many of the old people here, often complains of aches and pains in her neck and back. The last time the Push-and-Pull plane made several passes over the village her pain got worse.

As we sat talking, I looked up on the wall of the adobe house where a poster of Archbishop Romero hung. In the picture he is walking with dozens of people through a slum in San Salvador; the children are leading the way. On the bottom of the poster these words are inscribed: *"The Good Shepherd does not want security as long as his flock has no security."*

Like the ruins of the church in Sicahuite, this poster symbolized for me the challenge to the church to accompany the poor in the midst of the war and all of its destruction. Our fidelity as Christians requires us to stand in solidarity with the poor and to struggle for justice; and the consequence of that fidelity, the war teaches us, is costly. The fate of the poor will become our own.

Tonight, with the other catechists, we reflected on a passage of Scripture I had not read for years, but one that illuminated the situation of the people here:

Take note of the countless witnesses who form a cloud around you. Meditate on Jesus who suffered countless abuses, but did not tire or become discouraged. Now you are face to face with evil, but you have not yet had to resist to the point of blood." (Hebrews 12:1– 4)

Like countless Salvadorans who have died during the past four years of the war, or disappeared ignominiously in the streets of the capital, we witness the passion of Christ in the passion of the Salvadoran people who suffer *"outside the walls of the sanctuary" (Hebrews 13:12)*. Their cry reaches up to the heavens and penetrates the hearts of all those who draw near.

[6]

Hunger in the Land

July 1984 . . . Jicarito, Chalatenango

It's now one year since I first arrived in Chalatenango. I'm beginning to feel at home here, despite the war. The past two nights I stayed with Manuel in his home in Haciendita. His "home," like everybody else's here in the village, is the shell of an adobe house with few of the roof tiles still intact. Many homes have only a corner of the house covered by a roof. Still, it is enough to provide shelter from the rain. In the evening our neighbor, Dora, prepared supper for us. She and her family have become good friends of ours. We finished off a delicious meal of hot tortillas and beans.

Later that night, as I lay awake, I was surprised by a shrill whistling in the air. Suddenly the stillness of the night was broken by a resounding explosion in a hill above the village. Mortars began to fall all around us. My first impulse was to call out to the family next door, but there was no time. So I made my way, as best I could, through the darkness to a trench dug into the earth, a few feet behind the house. I lay down for what seemed to be an eternity until the attack was over. Then I went to visit Dora and her family to see if they were all right. We stayed up the rest of the night talking, staying alert for the next attack.

The next morning I set out to visit the village of Jicarito and other rural communities south of Haciendita. It is July now, and the fields are ripe with corn. Along the way I stopped to visit Beltrán and his family. Beltrán is a catechist and also serves as president of the local community council. The catechists are often

47

the only people in their communities who can read and write, and for that reason they have been chosen as leaders. In five of the seven local community councils in this part of Chalatenango catechists serve as presidents.

As I visited with Beltrán and his family, several women came to buy grain for their families. The price fixed by the community councils is fifteen cents a pound. This is done to prevent speculation and also to make grain available to people in the communities at a low cost. During these last few weeks before the August harvest food is scarce, and only *maicillo* (sorghum) is available to eat.

"More than three hundred people have come to settle here in the past three months," Beltrán told me, "fleeing the repression in their villages near the Guazapa volcano." The number of displaced people from Guazapa and Cinquera who have fled to Chalatenango in the past year now exceeds one thousand. The hospitality they have received here is a testimony of how the poor take care of the poor.

I reached Jicarito that evening and went to stay with Tomás. I had not been to Jicarito in three months. Tomás, fifty-seven, is the catechist. Like all the people in this valley, he lives in a tiny *ranchito* made of mud and stick walls and a tin roof. The entire community fled when the army attacked their village, Los Guillenes, two years ago. When they went back to the village, they found that their homes had been burned to the ground, so they came to settle in this valley. This was the second spring they have planted, and the hillsides are ripe with corn.

Tomás has seven children. Bernalda, his wife, told me she had given birth to fourteen children, but seven had died in infancy. Bernalda shared her story with me:

I used to work in the fields with my father and brothers during the time of planting and harvesting. I planted corn and beans this year as well. My father was killed two years ago by members of the paramilitary group ORDEN who lived in the village of Concepción. They dragged him outside his house in full view of my mother and killed him. That's why I say I can't live with the people who killed him. Shortly after his death we moved to this valley.

The following day Neto stopped by Tomás' home. Neto is a young catechist from the village of San Antonio in Guazapa. He is twenty-five years old. I first met him two months ago at the pastoral meeting in Haciendita. Neto coordinates the pastoral work of several villages near the Guazapa volcano. Last week he came to visit his family. They had fled their home in Guazapa months before and had come to live in Jicarito.

I accompanied Neto to a liturgy of the Word. "We must never lose sight of the value of these celebrations," he said. "That's how many of us first became aware of the causes of the poverty in which we live, by meeting in small groups and reflecting on our lives in light of the gospel."

During the celebration Neto appealed for support for the people displaced from their homes. Already this morning I have seen dozens of displaced people going from house to house to look for food. Beltrán, who is the president of the local community council, proposed that a collection of corn be made to distribute to the displaced families. Chavela, his wife, said that 16 *medios* (about 320 pounds) of *maicillo* had already been donated to the displaced by the families here in the valley.

The Power of the People

The next day I went with Tomás and his family to inscribe their names in the civil register of the local community council. Beltrán sat at a table receiving a dozen women and their children. They each were given a slip of paper with a seal that said: *poder popular* (people power). It was signed by María Serrano, the president of the popular government in Chalatenango.

You can begin to see the fruit of this "people power" in the social services of these rural communities. Tomás' daughter, Dinora, is a community health worker. Although she is only fifteen years old, she has considerable responsibility in the community. She treats people at the community health center three hours each morning and three hours each afternoon, six days a week. Dinora is in her fourth week of a six-week training course. She meets three days a week with five other health workers and a health professional to continue her training.

In the afternoon I stopped to visit Marina at the primary school. Marina, who is thirty-two, has taught school for the past two years in Jicarito. She teaches two classes each day, first and second grade. She is also a catechist. Today seven children, ages five to ten, are present. "These months of spring planting and harvest always bring a drop in the enrollment," Marina explained, "since the children are helping their parents in the fields." Her dedication and enthusiasm for teaching are exemplary.

As we observed the class, Marina told the children:

Before the revolution, we did not have the opportunity to learn to read and write. We were illiterate. Now that we have the opportunity to learn, we must never forget to share our knowledge with each other. You are the future of our people. One day you may leave your mark in life by teaching somebody to read and write.

Today marked the fifth anniversary of the Sandinista revolution in Nicaragua. Posters are tacked on some of the *ranchitos* in the community and along the paths that lead from one village to the next. A popular assembly was held in the afternoon to commemorate the anniversary. Leaders from two popular organizations, the Federation of Farm Workers (FTC) and the Association of Salvadoran Women (AMES), also participated in the celebration. Attempts are now underway to rebuild these organizations in order to give voice to the demands of the poor.

During the assembly people recalled their participation in the struggles of campesinos to achieve just wages, improved working conditions in the coffee and sugar cane fields, a reduction of rent for the land that produces their annual crops of beans and corn, and the right to organize in farm worker unions. These efforts were met with repression and violence, as the history of the 1970s vividly demonstrated.

The organizers of the assembly also noted the present economic crisis in El Salvador. "The prices of basic necessities have doubled since the war began," one man observed. "The cost of the war is immense," another added. "Millions of dollars are spent each day by the government to buy arms, train soldiers, and bomb the countryside, which only brings more suffering to our people." "We are tired of the war," a woman responded, "but we must go forward. What else can we do?"

Among the Displaced

The following day I went with Marina and her sister to the next village to visit the families that had been displaced from Guazapa before fleeing to Chalatenango. Some of these families are relatively settled now and able to plant a small cornfield and bean crop to provide for their needs. But most of them are newer arrivals, and they lack sufficient food to feed their families.

At the first *ranchito* where we stopped, we met families from San Antonio and Guadalupe, two villages near the town of Suchitoto. Several children gathered around us as we talked. "Each day we go from village to village looking for grain," one woman told us, "while the men go out to scavenge for roots or seeds." "I haven't had a tortilla to eat for days," another man told us.

One mother held in her arms a small child who was severely malnourished, his ribs protruding and his eyes sunken, perhaps no older than six months. I asked her how old the child was. "Two years," she told me. I was shocked. Many of the children of these displaced families are in a similar condition.

In the next few houses we visited families from La Criba, Azacualpa, and La Escopeta, all villages near the town of Cinquera in the department of Cabañas. "The day before yesterday the army invaded our villages on the other side of Lake Suchitlán. We could see smoke from the burning houses and fields in the direction of Azacualpa. We even heard the sound of helicopters in the distance across the lake."

"We had been expecting the invasion for days," several people told us. "It's supposed to be the beginning of Plan CONARA. First they mount a huge invasion with thousands of troops. Then they take up strategic positions in the surrounding hills. For weeks soldiers patrol every inch of ground in between, burning homes and fields, and killing any living thing in sight."

Plan CONARA, which stands for the National Commission for the Restoration of Areas, is the government pacification plan for El Salvador, modeled after a similar program used by the United

States in Vietnam fifteen years before. It is a "scorched earth" policy, designed to destroy the social base of the FMLN by driving the civilians living in FMLN-controlled areas into areas controlled by the army and setting up "civic action" programs to pacify the population.

Hardly a week went by before the next invasion. "Sometimes two or three invasions occurred in a single month," one woman told us. "Sometimes they bombed every day. The planes flew so low they nearly touched the tree tops!" Two months ago two thousand civilians were surrounded for days by the army as they hid in the ravines. "You should have seen how the children cried!" an older man added. *"Solo Dios con nosotros,"* he concluded. "Only God can save us."

"With the current invasion," Neto told us, "these families can expect to lose the crops of corn and beans they planted in their villages last spring, not to mention their homes." The possibility that they can return to their homes near Cinquera is more remote each day.

One of the men told us of the frustration he felt going from house to house to beg for grain. "We've never had to beg for food before. We've always worked the land," he said. "In most homes people are generous; they share what few tortillas they have." Perhaps the most generous, I thought, are these displaced families who welcome visitors like ourselves and are so gracious with their time. This communal spirit, no doubt, is born of their suffering and their struggle to survive.

[7]

When the Poor Believe in the Poor

August 1984 (1) . . . Jicarito, Chalatenango

These past few weeks in the village of Jicarito have been special ones for me. The war has torn apart so many families and so many communities, it's a real blessing to be able to live with Tomás and his family. I'm beginning to know my way around here and to go on my own to visit neighboring villages. Today, as I was out walking, I stopped by an abandoned church where Marta and her five small children were living. She invited me in to rest. Two women from Guazapa were sitting on the step leading into the church, talking to Marta.

As I listened, Marta began to tell her story, the same story I had heard from Tomás' wife Bernalda who grew up in the same village as Marta. "Our village had been terrorized for years by the paramilitary group ORDEN. They even killed a woman who held a child in her arms, beating her to death with machetes as they formed a circle around her house. 'Ay, ay, ay, ay!' she cried out, 'Don't kill me!' You can't imagine how terrible it was to hear those screams." Marta told us other equally horrendous stories, of a man beaten to death with a machete and of a woman whose fingers were cut off one by one.

As we sat together, Marta's three daughters listened while they plucked ripe beans from the vines brought in from the fields. Now and then the two women from Guazapa nodded as if to say they understood only too well the story Marta told. Then one of them began to tell her story. "Month after month our village was attacked by the army, bombed by A-37s, and rocketed by helicopters. Each time we escaped into the hills and ravines for days, suffering beneath the rain." I asked her how long this had been going on. "We left our homes more than five years ago. In all these years we haven't slept in a bed or returned to our house."

It's a common sight to see these women from Guazapa pass from house to house in search of grain, sharing their plight with the women here in Chalatenango. These years of war, which have divided so many families, ironically have brought people from neighboring villages and departments together for the first time under the same roof. "I've learned," one of the women from Guazapa told us, "that my family is all of the Salvadoran people."

As the two women left the church which Marta had made her home, I remembered the liturgy of the Word celebrated in Jicarito yesterday. Tomás shared with those present the plight of these displaced people, recalling how they pass each day from house to house, seeking a bit of grain or food. "The Gospel tells us," Tomás concluded, "that whenever we give hospitality to the least of these, we receive the Lord as well."

Already a popular assembly had been called to discuss the problems of the displaced and to see how the community could respond. "Tomorrow a local health worker will visit the displaced people," Tomás added. "Many of them are already suffering from malaria, dysentery, and malnutrition, particularly the children and the elderly."

Planting Fields To Harvest

Later that morning I passed by several houses where displaced families were living. In every family I saw signs of malnutrition and illness, especially in the children. Almost every day I met women and children along the path looking for wild fruits or seeds. Many families use one pound of the *maicillo* they receive to make the day's tortillas, and the other pound they use to plant.

Beltrán, the president of the local community council, had told us earlier that seeds would be given to the displaced families to plant a crop of beans in August, and additional grain would be given to the families to guarantee a supply of food until the harvest of *maicillo* in January. "With seed in the ground," one man smiled, "we have hope to go on."

I also heard more details from these families of a massacre that had occurred in the village of Los Llanitos, near the town of Cinquera in the department of Cabañas. On July 19, sixty-eight people were assassinated by the army. Some forty-two *manzanas* of corn (about seventy acres) were destroyed, and thirty houses were burned to the ground. "This was the government's reply," one man told me, "to the FMLN attack last month on the army barracks near the hydroelectric plant at Cerrón Grande."

"Twenty-five cadavers were found stuffed into a hole in the ground which served as a latrine," one woman told us. "Bodies were found burned to a crisp, and others sliced to bits by machetes." These details are still unconfirmed, but what appears to be certain is that dozens of civilians were killed by the army. The latest news is that the government has mounted still another invasion to cover up the massacre. "On August 15 the army plans to put Plan CONARA into effect in Guazapa," another man told us, "to destroy homes, crops, and any living thing in sight."

Despite the hardships these displaced families face, their creativity and industry are truly amazing. They produce miracles with a minimum of resources. In one house two small children were weaving strands of palm leaves together to make straw hats. In another house a woman was making pots from the clay she found in the hills. Some people were making soap from the *aceituna* seeds taken from the trees that grow in the valley, while others were making straw mats called *petates* from a reed that grows wild here.

In the afternoon I went with Tomás and his children to harvest beans from the field. The hillsides are covered now with the August crop of corn and beans. Along the path you see clumps of beans strung across dry corn stalks to dry, the colorful red vines spotting the countryside. In the distance the Sumpul River winds its way through the valley and the mountains of Chalatenango. There is a natural beauty in these hills and in the fresh earth that is healing. I sometimes forget that we are living in the midst of a cruel war. At any moment we may be obliged to run for cover from an air strike or to flee for days from an army invasion.

Along the way we passed a group of forty men and children working in the fields. They, too, were gathering in the ripe beans that the men had planted as part of a community cooperative. This harvest will serve as a reserve for the needs of the village, as well as provide food for the displaced families. The joy and enthusiasm that people feel as they work the land together are contagious, and their communal spirit inspires hope again. I thought of the words of the psalmist:

> The earth is the Lord's and the fullness thereof,
>   the world and all that dwell in it . . .
> The Lord has founded it upon the ocean,
>   and set it firmly upon the waters.
> Who will go up to the mountain of the Lord
>   and enter into the sanctuary?
> Those whose hands are innocent
>   and whose hearts are pure. (24:1– 4)

The Miracle of the Loaves

The next day three women and their children stopped by Tomás' home looking for a pound of corn. Tomás had to tell them he had no grain to offer. In the meantime one of the women went to a neighboring *ranchito* while the second woman began to help Tomás' daughter prepare tortillas. The third woman remained seated and began to tell us her story.

"I came to Chalatenango nine months ago and already I've buried two children here," she began. "How did they die?" Tomás asked her. "They starved to death," she said. "Three months ago I returned to my home in Guazapa to help my brother plant to see if we could make ends meet. But the last army invasion burned our crop to the ground."

In the course of the conversation Tomás began to tell his own story:

I first joined the Farm Workers Union (UTC) in 1975. At the time I was living with my family in the town of Aguilares where Father Rutilio Grande worked, promoting Christian base communities and lay catechists. Most of the farm workers in Aguilares had organized with the Federation of Christian Farm Workers in El Salvador (FECCAS); I worked with the UTC in the sugar cane fields and at the sugar refineries in San Chico and La Cabaña.

After I moved back to Los Guillenes from Aguilares, I continued to work with the UTC here in the valley. In 1979 I was involved in a land takeover. We took over seven manzanas of vacant land (about twelve acres) near the Lempa River and planted corn. When the local landowner finally tried to evict us, we refused to leave. That's when the National Police were called in. The landowner paid them off with 2,000 colones ($800). Two police and an inspector were killed in the clash.

I was taken prisoner with six others. They bound me to a wooden post and tortured me for forty-two hours. Several times they held a machete to my throat, but I never lost my faith. I've faced death many times since then, but now I feel a new freedom to proclaim the gospel. In 1981 I moved with my family to a neighboring village. That very night members of ORDEN came to our house and destroyed everything. The following year my second home was burned to the ground during an army invasion. That's why we moved to Jicarito.

During the conversation Tomás' daughter Santanita and her adopted child Lucía stopped by. Lucía, eight, lost her father and four-year-old brother months before when a bomb exploded near their home in Guazapa as they ran for cover. Lucía alone survived. Her mother later left her three surviving children, including Lucía, to live with another man. Lucía's older brother lives with Tomás' mother-in-law in a neighboring village.

"You know," Tomás continued, "my mother died when I was very young. We were seven children at the time. We supported my father when he decided to remarry. My father was a good man," Tomás concluded, "who loved children. We wept when he died."

By this time the first woman had returned from the next house.

She was unable to find any corn. Tomás asked his daughter to offer each of the three women two tortillas for their journey. They shook hands and went on their way. *"Dios se lo pague,"* they called out. "May God repay you." Only then did I realize that Tomás had shared his own lunch with them. It was one of countless examples of the hospitality I have witnessed here, where the poor take care of the poor.

Early the next morning two small children from the displaced families in the valley stopped by Tomás' *ranchito*. They sat for a moment as Tomás' wife Bernalda prepared the morning tortillas. The older child, a boy of eight, told us, "My father tried to return to our home in Guazapa to sell his crop, but the recent invasion there made that impossible." Bernalda gave them each fresh ears of corn and the younger child, a girl of six, placed them in her shoulder bag. They each shared a tortilla before departing.

Today's Gospel reading during the liturgy of the Word provided us with ample reflection on these past weeks spent among the displaced. It was taken from the multiplication of the loaves and the feeding of the five thousand: *"The disciples asked: 'How are we going to feed this entire crowd before us?' and Jesus told them: 'Feed them yourselves' "* (Matthew 14:16).

It's a story that illuminates the situation here very well. For weeks now these displaced families have sought to buy grain, going from house to house and village to village. Hardly a day passes without seeing women or children along the path as they go in search of food.

The miracle, however, is that the poor share with the poor. In each household that opens its door to these displaced families, a pound of grain or a single tortilla bears witness to the solidarity among the poor that enables these dispossessed families to survive until they are able to harvest their newly planted crops of corn, beans, and *maicillo*. It is one more example of what the song from the Salvadoran Mass proclaims:

> When the poor believe in the poor,
> Then we can sing of freedom;
> When the poor believe in the poor,
> Then we will build a beloved community.

[8]

In the Valley of the Shadow of Death

August 1984 (2) . . . Haciendita, Chalatenango

Early this morning we heard bombs exploding in the distance. "Where is that?" I asked Manuel. "In the direction of San Antonio los Ranchos," he replied. *"Lejos,"* he added, to reassure me. "Far away." These past few days the pastoral team has been meeting in Haciendita with catechists from the Christian base communities of both Chalatenango and Guazapa. The last time all of us were together was three months ago.

Emilio, a catechist from Cinquera, brought news of the recent army massacre of sixty-eight people from the village of Los Llanitos. I listened to his testimony and the testimonies given by other survivors. The first declaration was given by Mirna, an eight-year-old girl, who was wounded in the leg and the forehead by shrapnel from a grenade. Her mother and her fourteen-year-old sister were killed at her side, along with six others, when they were ambushed by soldiers of the U.S.-trained Atlacatl Battalion:

When the army invaded Los Llanitos, we hid for three days and three nights in the ravines and hills. One day the soldiers found a group of mothers and their children hiding near us in a cave beside the river. When we heard the burst of machine-gun fire and the screams of the children, we fled.

The next day we were overcome by the smell of burning

59

*flesh. Later people told us that the army had set fire to the
cadavers of the women and children killed the day before.
Only the charred bones remained, including those of a sev-
eral-month-old baby. We continued to flee, fearful that the
soldiers would find us, too.*

*That's when we were ambushed, near the village of Las
Tortugas. They killed my mother. I felt her hand slip away
as she fell by my side. My sister ran ahead and was shot
down as well. They split her head open with a bullet.*

Emilio's testimony confirmed this account of the massacre. We
spent the entire day together before I realized that his twenty-
year-old daughter, Ana Gloria, had been killed as well. She died
in the same ambush as Mirna's mother and sister. "This is the
'Christian democracy' we have here in El Salvador," Emilio concluded. "While President Duarte campaigns for human rights in
Europe and the United States, the civilian population is massacred in El Salvador."

I sat with Emilio while we plucked beans from the vines. "The
war is cruel," he emphasized. "I always think of the passion of
Christ and the three times that he fell with the cross along the
Way of Calvary." We continued plucking the beans in silence.
"Our cross is Cinquera," Emilio added, referring to the town near
the site of the massacre. "I remember Jesus' prayer in the Garden
of Gethsemane: *'If it be possible, take this cup from me.'* There
are times when we don't want to suffer anymore."

The Bombing of Jicarito

This morning the news came as a shock: "Jicarito was
bombed!" The bombing we had heard in the distance yesterday
took place in Jicarito, the village where I had lived the past month
with Tomás and his family. Eight people were killed and five
injured, nearly all of them women and children. The wounded
had been taken to an FMLN field hospital for treatment.

I reached the field hospital near Haciendita at 8 A.M. and met
with Francisco, an FMLN doctor. Then I went to see the children
who had been wounded. They lay stretched out on bamboo cots

called *tapescos* in a wooded area used by the FMLN as a field hospital to treat both civilians and combatants. Tomás' eleven-year-old son Santiago was there and sat up to greet me. His face was bandaged where shrapnel had sliced his cheek, and his ankle was also wrapped in tape. I asked Santiago what had happened.

> *I had gone to the fields to take lunch to my father and was on my way back with a load of firewood when I stopped at Petronila's house to rest. She never refused a tortilla to anybody. She was still grinding corn and praying aloud when the first bomb exploded. The shock wave lifted me off the ground. I crawled on my hands and knees to a nearby ravine, and then the second bomb exploded.*

Next to Santiago lay another child, Zoilita, who was nine years old. She was half-conscious and cried out in pain. Francisco, the doctor, told me he did not know if she would live. She was wrapped in bandages soaked in blood. I recognized her father, Chando, sitting next to her. He had just come from burying the child's mother and told me in detail what had happened:

> *When Zoilita heard the first bomb explode she ran with her mother to a nearby shelter dug into the ground. Marta and her two small children were already there. The A-37s dropped eight bombs over the community. It all happened so fast. One bomb landed above the shelter and buried Zoilita and her mother alive. My wife was eight and a half months pregnant at the time. She was still alive when we dug her out of the debris, covered with mud and blood. She died shortly after.*
>
> *Marta and her six-year-old daughter Irma also were killed. Only a three-year-old boy, Fredis, and Zoilita survived. We found Fredis in his mother's arms, still unconscious from the shock of the explosion, but his mother was already dead. Please, God, help my child to live! She's all I have left.*

Later that morning I went with Beltrán to see the damage caused by the air strike. The destruction was massive. We passed

Petronila's house, close to where the first bomb exploded. "She was struck in her throat by a piece of shrapnel and died four hours later," Beltrán told me. "She was eighty-four years old." Two other people, a father and his son, were also injured here as they stopped to ask for grain.

As I walked with Beltrán through the village, we passed a second house where a man was repairing the damaged roof of his home. "Two women and their children had come to ask for grain when the bomb hit my *ranchito*. One woman was killed instantly. The other woman survived, but her son died in her arms, killed by the shock of the explosion." Still farther up the valley we reached the underground shelter where the two women and the three children were buried alive. The inside of the shelter was soaked with blood and filled with mud and shreds of clothing.

A War against the Children

I have been thinking these days how we used to commemorate each year the victims of the atomic bombs dropped by the United States on Hiroshima and Nagasaki August 6 and 9, 1945. The massacre which occurred last month in Los Llanitos and the bombing of Jicarito have made the link between Hiroshima and Central America more present to me. One link is simply *the survivor*. As I listened to the testimonies of Mirna and her father, who survived the massacre of Los Llanitos, and of Emilio, whose daughter Ana Gloria was killed there, an indelible voice was imprinted in my memory—the voice of the survivor.

I thought of another link between Hiroshima and Central America: *the children*. When I think about children, I remember eight-year-old Mirna describing how her mother's hand slipped from her own hand as her mother was killed by the soldiers; and nine-year-old Zoilita lying in pain in the hospital, her back ripped open, her vertebrae protruding, after a bomb exploded over Jicarito. I think of Zoilita's mother, eight and a half months pregnant, who was buried alive at her side in the same shelter.

The survivors, the children, and *the dead*. These are the links that bind the bombings of Hiroshima and Nagasaki to the war in Central America: two events that took place forty years apart and on opposite sides of the globe. The voices of the survivors remain with us forever. Our memory of them is our conscience.

The cry of the poor of Central America is the cry of these survivors, the cry of these children, the cry of the dead. A cry that awakens the cry of our own hearts and calls us to take sides with the defenseless, to make the cause of the poor our own, and to work for justice and peace so that others—the Mirnas and the Zoilitas and countless children like them—may live.

I thought of one even more disturbing link between Hiroshima and Central America, in addition to the survivors, the children, and the dead. These atrocities were committed with U.S. weapons in our names, invoking God's blessing.

According to testimony from the victims, this policy of indiscriminate bombing has continued unabated for ten weeks since June 1, when Napoleón Duarte took office as president of El Salvador. More than six hundred bombs have been dropped over ninety villages throughout the country, resulting in the loss of innumerable civilian lives.

In the past five years alone the human cost of the war has been tremendous: fifty thousand people dead, most of them civilians and most of them victims of government repression. In addition, hundreds of thousands of people have been displaced from their homes and forced to flee to the mountains or into exile.

A few days after the bombing of Jicarito, I went with Chepe to celebrate a liturgy of the Word with the displaced families. Mirna and her father were there, as well as dozens of newly displaced people who were fleeing from the current army invasion in Guazapa. They had come to join their families here in Chalatenango. Chepe chose a reading from the psalmist:

> *Though I walk through the valley of the shadow*
> *of death,*
> *I will fear no evil,*
> *for You are with me.*
> *Your rod and your staff*
> *comfort me. (23:4)*

Many of the displaced families recalled the past months they had spent in flight and the countless army invasions they had suffered in Guazapa and Cinquera. "We walked for days and nights in the shadow of death," one woman said, recalling the words of the psalm, "hiding in dark ravines from the soldiers. But we must go on, despite the sacrifices required."

Suddenly, two A-37 fighter-bombers made passes overhead. I followed the women and children as they scrambled to an underground shelter dug into the hillside. Once inside the shelter, I was struck by the faces of a dozen children who surrounded me, including Mirna's. As the A-37s continued to circle overhead, threatening to bomb us, it seemed to me that the war in Central America was not only a war against the poor; it had become a war against the children.

[9]

A Spectacle for the World

August 1984 (3) . . . Gualsinga River, Chalatenango

Toward the end of August the pastoral team met again in the village of Jicarito. We celebrated a liturgy of the Word to commemorate the victims of the bombing who were killed here three weeks before. I looked around me at the people gathered and saw many familiar faces. Chando was there, but Zoilita was still in the field hospital recovering from her wounds, as was Tomás' son Santiago. Other people, however, were noticeably absent, like Petronila, the eighty-four-year-old grandmother who had been killed in the air strike.

These celebrations bear witness to the determination of the people in this rural community to continue the struggle for the liberation of their people. Many people responded to the occasion as a time to recommit themselves, to join together, and not to lose hope. It was the first time since the bombing that the community had met together openly. They were fearful of another air strike over their village. Still, people were determined to rebuild the ruins of the destroyed homes and comfort the families that were victimized by the bombing.

The following day I set out early with Chepe for the village of Haciendita. We planned to visit there before crossing the Sumpul River and returning to Chepe's home in Tequeque. As we crossed the Guancora River in the dawn hours, we heard heavy gunfire and mortars near the road that leads from Chalatenango to the town of San José las Flores, about half an hour away. Helicopters passed in the distance. "We better not go to Haciendita," Chepe advised. "There's another path which will take us to the Sumpul River." So we decided not to cross the road to Guarjila and continued on to Los Amates, the next village, an hour south of San José las Flores.

As we reached Los Amates, we were met by several families who had come for the afternoon celebration to baptize their children. "Don't you know the army has invaded?" Chepe asked. "We've walked for hours just to get here," one man replied. "Won't you come?" We decided to cross the Sumpul River to the village of Santa Anita and celebrate there instead, awaiting further notice to depart. Several young mothers and their babies were present, along with the babies' godparents.

During the celebration a reconnaissance plane circled above us, firing rockets in the distance. Every now and then people looked up nervously to the sky to follow the flight of the plane. "We must commit ourselves to defend the lives of these children," one parent said. "But it's the entire community who will have to take responsibility for these children if their parents are killed," another added. Several people spoke of their commitment to struggle for a just society for these children to grow up in.

As we finished the celebration, we were alerted by the community council of the advance of the army and advised to retreat farther into the hills to safety. We walked silently beneath the rain to the village of San Juan, near the town of Nueva Trinidad, and departed from the beaten path down a dark ravine where a shallow stream flowed, walking in the water to avoid leaving any trace of our footprints behind. There we settled in for the night.

I was overcome by the sight before me. We lay down on the rocks beside the stream and tried as best we could to cover ourselves with sheets of plastic. The water from the rain rushed all around us and soaked our clothes. Only the warm rocks provided some measure of comfort. Several mothers tried to hush their children's cries. There was nothing we could do but try to sleep and wait until morning.

The Gualsinga River Massacre

For days we hid in the hills until we received word one morning to return home again. A man from the next village came to tell us that the army had retreated. Most families returned to their homes to prepare their first hot meal in days. I went with Chepe to his niece's house in Tequeque, near the town of Arcatao. That's when we first heard news of the massacre that had taken place days before at the Gualsinga River.

The day the army invaded, hundreds of families left their homes in the villages of Haciendita and Tamarindo, near the town of San José las Flores, and fled to the Sumpul River. At dawn the next morning they crossed the river. Soldiers fired on them from a distance, but the people escaped. The following day helicopters came and transported soldiers from the U.S.-trained Atlacatl Battalion into the area. They quickly surrounded the families near the banks of the Gualsinga River. Dozens of people were shot down, and dozens more were captured.

I went with two others the next morning to look for survivors of the massacre. As we reached Guisucre, a village near the junction of the Sumpul and Gualsinga rivers, we met several families in a state of shock. People simply stared into the distance, with blank expressions on their faces. A few people had lit fires and were grinding corn to prepare tortillas. In one house several wounded people waited for medical attention.

I spoke to a number of families I knew from Tamarindo and Haciendita. They had hidden for three days in the underbrush, terrified that the soldiers would return. As we talked, two men carried a wounded woman in a hammock slung over their shoulders and laid her down on the path. I recognized her immediately.

"Beatriz!" I called out, and ran over to where she lay on the ground. I was shaken. Beatriz had been shot in the back and was in a state of shock but still conscious. I asked her about her sister Dora and the rest of her family. She only shook her head and wept, unable to speak.

As I talked to the survivors, dozens of families passed by, exhausted by their ordeal of terror and exposure to the elements. People from Guisucre offered them food and shelter in their homes. Several families joined together to husk corn and prepare tortillas for supper. Several pigs were slaughtered as well. This would be their first meal in five days.

I never saw Dora again. At midnight, as most of us lay asleep, news came that the army had returned to Haciendita and taken up positions near the Sumpul River, just an hour from where we were hiding. As I looked across the river, I could see fires burning in Haciendita, the village Dora had left behind. "It has to be the army," a man beside me said. Once again we fled into the darkness, this time with the three hundred survivors of the Gualsinga massacre, and walked for hours beneath the rain. By dawn we reached several empty houses near the abandoned town of Nueva Trinidad where we settled in for the day to await further news.

About 1 P.M. we were forced to retreat again as a reconnaissance plane circled overhead and fired rockets over the village of Guisucre, just two hours away. Each time the plane made its pass and left, twenty or more people filed out of the house where we were resting and fled to a nearby ravine for safety. By evening, we were ready to continue our journey to the town of Arcatao where we settled in for the night, bedding down on the hard floors of several abandoned houses.

At the break of dawn we retreated into the hills overlooking Arcatao, a half day ahead of the Atlacatl Battalion. "The army has already occupied Guisucre," one man announced, "and now they are advancing on Arcatao."

Flight to the Mountains

We had been walking for two nights, immersed in the immense solitude of a September night in the hills of Chalatenango. Now and then we would stop along the path and listen, waiting for the footsteps of those behind us to catch up. Now and then the cry of a child would pierce the night air. Mothers would hush their children, wrapped in rags, and hold them more firmly to their breasts to nurse although many had no milk.

The silence of the old people, weary with years, was poignant. Up ahead I could just make out the figure of a young boy mounted on his father's shoulders. Everywhere there were children. We were three hundred or more pilgrims on this road, fleeing from the Atlacatl Battalion.

I carried a little lame boy named Manuelito in my arms. His mother and little sister walked beside me. One night someone asked me if I would carry the boy. I hoped that someone else would offer. I was exhausted, but how could I refuse? The night was dark, with no moon. It rained. I followed the sound of the footsteps ahead of me on the damp path and reached out to touch the person ahead of me to guide my way.

A thousand thoughts raced through my mind: "Where were we going?" "What would happen to us?" "What was I doing here?" Suddenly, Manuelito whispered something to me in my ear, *"Ya no aguanto."* I didn't quite hear. "I can't take it anymore," he whispered again. I wanted to cry out, but who would hear? Here in the immense solitude of our march the cry of a small child expressed the drama that we all felt in our hearts. A cry of abandonment.

The mountains enveloped us in their silence. I thought of a passage from the Bible I had often read in more tranquil times, a passage that came to life in the present circumstances: *"The whole creation groans as in the pain of a woman in childbirth, right up to the present moment. And not only creation, but we ourselves"* (Romans 8:22–23). I held Manuelito in my arms as we continued our journey up the mountains. I had no words with which to comfort Manuelito, only *"the Spirit who intercedes for us with groans that words cannot express"* (8:26).

Most of the people here are survivors of the Gualsinga River massacre. Most of them hid for days in the underbrush, terrified the army would find them. Many families count children or loved ones dead or missing. Most lost what few possessions they carried on their backs, and most were barefoot, especially the children. They have gone for days without a single tortilla and have slept on the hard ground in the cold and rain. What little food people did bring with them, a handful of corn or sugar, was consumed in a day.

The drama, of course, is seen especially in the advance or retreat of the Salvadoran army. Silence and discipline are essential but nearly impossible, since most of the group are young children who are tired and hungry. To move by day is risky because of the reconnaissance planes overhead. The cry of a single child could easily give our hiding place away to the army that continues to pursue us. What movement we do make is at night, often in pitch dark, over muddy and difficult paths.

By the end of the fifth day we received news that the Atlacatl Battalion had retreated. What joy people felt to come out into the open and walk freely again! Still, we were cautious, and occasional flights overhead by reconnaissance planes forced us into the underbrush along the side of the road to escape from being detected. By evening we were in Guisucre again, husking corn and preparing our first meal in five days.

The plight of the displaced in El Salvador has truly become a "spectacle for the world," a drama that surely rivals the people of Israel in the wilderness or the early Christian communities in the catacombs:

> *We have become a spectacle for the world . . . To this very hour we go hungry and thirsty, dressed in rags, mistreated, as we flee from place to place. We have become the wretched of the earth, the refuse of the world. (1 Corinthians 4:9–13)*

Mothers with babies, old people leaning on sticks, little children holding on to their parents' shoulders . . . each one is a living testimony of what it means to be hungry and thirsty, mistreated, and dressed in rags as they flee from place to place to escape the army. Each story, it seems, is the same; and yet each is absolutely unique.

[10]

The Peace of the Cemeteries

September 1984 . . . Haciendita, Chalatenango

It has been three weeks now since the Gualsinga River massacre. Today I returned to the villages of Haciendita and Tamarindo. What a shock to see these two communities, once the center of so much activity, now abandoned! As I walked along the path between the two villages, I met two women carrying a few meager possessions. They were moving to Conocaste, a neighboring village. "Did you hear that the people who had been captured by the army at the Gualsinga River have been turned over to the International Red Cross?" they asked me.

The following day the pastoral team held its monthly meeting in Haciendita. It was almost one month ago today that we last met in Jicarito, where we commemorated the deaths of the eight people killed in the bombing August 8. On Sunday, Tomás and Chepe held a memorial service for the victims of the Gualsinga River massacre. At least sixteen people of the fifty people killed were from Haciendita, and dozens more are still missing or have been captured. Not a single family has been left untouched.

Tomás read from the prophet Isaiah: *"How long, O Lord?"* Isaiah asks, and God replies:

> *Until the towns have been laid waste*
> *and left without inhabitants;*
> *until the houses are deserted*
> *and the fields ruined and ravaged.*
> *(Isaiah 6:11)*

71

The words described the desolation around us. Then a word of hope illuminated the darkness:

> And though a tenth of the people remain,
>   they will be stripped
> like a terebinth
>   of which, once felled,
>   only the stock remains.
> This stock is a holy seed. (Isaiah 6:13)

Chepe followed, reading from the Gospel: "*I will build my house upon a rock. The wind and rains will come, but in the end the house will remain standing*" (Matthew 7:24). "This is the faith we must have," Chepe concluded, "a faith built on a firm foundation. We have been tried these past weeks by violent winds, but our faith remains firm."

Tomás added, "We have been tried by days of hunger and thirst during this last invasion. Some of us have been tempted to flee to the safety of the refugee camps; one person even accepted the government amnesty. But we must stand firm. Jesus remained faithful to his people, and his faith enabled him to resist to the end."

The Cry of a Child

It is now one month to the day since the Gualsinga River massacre took place. We are in our third day of flight from still another army invasion, the second in Chalatenango in as many months. Two days ago a dozen mortars fell over Haciendita and Tamarindo. Four of them exploded fifty feet from the pastoral center where I had stayed the night before. Four hours later eight more mortars, fired from the army barracks in the town of Chalatenango, exploded over the same two villages. Four of the mortars fell in the exact location they had fallen hours earlier, seriously injuring two people: a ten-year-old boy and a twenty-five-year-old man named Pedro whose mother was killed at the Gualsinga River.

"It seems that the timing of this invasion was not accidental," one man told me. "On the day it began the families of the fifty people captured at the Gualsinga River last August 30 were meeting in Haciendita. They were planning to go the next day to meet with the International Red Cross in the town of La Laguna to negotiate the release of their loved ones. Because of this invasion, however, they were unable to complete their mission."

When I passed through Haciendita two nights ago, I found people preparing to flee to the hills for safety. Fires dotted the ruins of the houses as families packed their few possessions and prepared tortillas for the journey. How sad to see these same families, so decimated by the death of parents, spouses, or children, once again in flight. Especially the elderly, bent over and wearied by the weight of their years, and the children, who have never known what it is to live in peace, evoke compassion.

I looked for Manuel in the confusion, hoping I would find someone with whom to share the journey. Usually there is a plan of evacuation for each village and sufficient time to flee. This invasion, however, had taken people by surprise, and instead of crossing the Sumpul River to safety during the night the plan was to hide in underground shelters that had been dug in the area, where they hoped to escape detection.

The thought of hiding for days in an underground shelter, surrounded by soldiers, frightened me. I would much rather flee, as we had in past invasions, playing a game of cat-and-mouse to evade the army. But this time the decision had been made, and I resigned myself to an uncertain fate.

As I lined up with others along the path, preparing to leave the village under cover of darkness for our underground shelter, I caught sight of Esperanza. My eyes lit up upon seeing a familiar face. "I'm going to try to go back to Patamera to reach my family," she told me. "Evaristo's coming too. Do you want to join us?" I jumped at the chance. As long as we could keep moving I felt hope, and my fears dissipated.

We walked for eight hours through the night, Evaristo leading the way, crossing the Sumpul River in the early dawn hours. At 8 A.M. the next morning the first mortars began to fall over the villages we had left behind, and they did not stop until 5 P.M. All morning the reconnaissance planes and the A-37 fighter-bombers rained down rockets and bombs, strafing the banks of the Sumpul

River less than an hour's walk from where we had taken cover. We spent the entire day hidden in the underbrush waiting for the protection and shelter of the night. The next morning we reached the village of Guisucre.

Already people were preparing to retreat farther into the hills. As we waited for everyone to get ready, Sonia, a nineteen-year-old mother with a three-week-old baby, came up to me and asked, "Can you help me with the child?" I could see the anxiety on the faces of the people around me. During these days and nights of flight, mothers carry their babies and nurse them until their milk runs dry. Even then, they press their children against their breasts to hush their cries.

If the army is nearby, the drama begins: Will the child cry? Will the soldiers hear? What will happen? In some cases, children have suffocated and died as their anguished mothers stuffed rags into their mouths to quiet them, fearful that the army would hear and the entire community would risk death.

I recall vividly one moment in particular. Everyone's attention was fixed on one child. The mother struggled to hush the child's cries and nurse him in the ravine where we hid, even though she had no milk. We looked anxiously at the mother, praying for the child to stop crying. In the distance beside a tree we could see the soldiers, standing still for a moment as if to listen. And there in our midst was the child, struggling for life.

Before I could respond to Sonia's question, she placed her baby in my arms and ran off to fetch a blanket she had left behind. I felt the child's warm body, bundled up in a cloth, pulsate with life in my arms as it cried out. In an instant my fears seemed to dissipate as I held the child. No longer was it simply a matter of personal survival. I had someone to care for now, someone to protect. That was a lesson in solidarity for me; I felt humbled by this gesture, and ashamed that I had thought only of my own survival.

War Returns to Chalatenango

That same morning we retreated into the hills for safety. Toward evening, the soldiers departed. We emerged from our hiding place in the ravine and returned to Guisucre, where we spent the night in an abandoned house. During the early morning hours I awoke and walked outside. For a moment, I felt a sense of tranquility and beauty in these hills that I did not feel during the day.

But the reality of the war soon invaded the night's tranquility. From these hills above the Sumpul River I looked out across the river to the villages on the other side now occupied by soldiers. In the distance I could just make out the village of Haciendita, where smoke had risen the day before from the burning houses. As dawn approached we got up and continued our flight. It began to rain.

The army invasion ended three days later when the Atlacatl Battalion returned to the army barracks in the town of Chalatenango. The results of this second invasion were devastating. Many people were captured, especially the elderly and the children who did not know where to turn for protection. This was particularly true of the displaced families from Guazapa living in Haciendita. They did not know the surrounding terrain like the people of Chalatenango, and few of them had prepared underground shelters where they could hide.

"The army was only a half hour away," Evaristo told me later, "when we crossed the Sumpul River with Esperanza to the other side. The next morning soldiers occupied Haciendita and Tamarindo, destroying houses and combing the surrounding area for people. The village of Sicahuite, near the town of Las Vueltas, was also hit by mortars and bombs, and thirty-six people were captured."

"The soldiers left word with the storekeepers in the village of Zapotal that they would be back within fifteen days," Evaristo added. Once again, war has returned to Chalatenango.

[11]

A Reason for Our Hope

November 1984 . . . Haciendita, Chalatenango

A month has passed since the last army invasion of Chalatenango. Last night I returned to the village of Haciendita for the first time in weeks. Along the path leading to the village I met a group of women and children on their way to the refugee camps in Mesa Grande, Honduras.

"Did you know," one of the women asked me, "that thirty-four women and children were captured by the soldiers near Haciendita? They were discovered hiding in a ravine the morning after the invasion began. A child cried out and the whole group was detected by the soldiers. All thirty-four were flown by helicopter to the village of Zapotal, near Las Vueltas, and later transferred to the military barracks in Chalatenango."

As I passed through Haciendita this morning, silence hung over the community like a shroud. The houses were all in disarray and empty. I noticed that the poster of Archbishop Romero no longer hung on the wall of the pastoral center. Behind the house, about fifty feet in the distance, I could see the destruction caused by the mortars that had fallen over the village a month before. The only sign of life were three small children playing beside a broken water spigot.

These last two invasions have virtually destroyed the community of Haciendita. Half of the people in the community have either been killed or captured by the army. At least sixteen of the people killed at the Gualsinga River massacre were from this village, and thirty others were captured there. Another thirty-four

76

women and children from Haciendita were captured in this last invasion, making a total of eighty persons from this village who are either dead or missing.

We celebrated a liturgy in the evening with the people of Haciendita. It was for me one more affirmation of the power of the Word to call people together in moments of affliction and to strengthen them. It is a power that manifests itself in the ability of the people to come together in community, to reflect on their situation in light of the gospel, and to continue to struggle.

The reading chosen for this evening was filled with hope: *"For they will build houses and live in them, plant fields and eat their fruit"* (Isaiah 65:21). Israel, one of the catechists, led the reflection:

> *We have all witnessed the destruction of houses, fields, and entire communities during these past two invasions. We have seen men, women, and children killed by the army. Isaiah tells us that things can change. The Lord can make a way out of no way, cast off the weight of a sinful past, and open to us the future in new and surprising ways. But we have to do our part, too.*

Later, I thought about what had been said tonight. Despite all of our failings, our faint-heartedness, and our lack of solidarity in moments of danger, there is still hope one day to rebuild what the war has destroyed and to begin life anew. This is the hope for which so many have given their lives in anticipation of the day when justice and peace will come to El Salvador.

A People of Faith

The past four days have been uneventful. Rumors of another invasion persist, but nothing has occurred. Already it is November 2, All Souls' Day. I went with Tomás to his home in Jicarito. Three months ago this village was decimated by an air strike that took the lives of eight people and injured five, the majority of them women and children. Today Tomás and Marina, the catechists in this community, and seventy-five others gathered to cel-

ebrate a liturgy of the Word in the village cemetery overlooking
the valley below. In the distance we could see the Sumpul River
winding its way through the hills of Chalatenango.

Marina stood beside a wooden cross, covered with flowers,
and read from the prophet Isaiah, the same reading we had read
days before in Haciendita: *"My servants will eat, but you will go
hungry; my servants will drink, but you will thirst; they will
rejoice, but you will be humiliated" (Isaiah 65:13).* It is the story
of the last judgment, the separation of the just and the unjust,
which precedes Isaiah's great message of hope to a people in
exile: *"I will create a new heaven and a new earth . . . My people
will build houses and live in them, plant fields and eat their fruit"
(Isaiah 65:17–21).*

Marina's words spoke to the anguish and the sorrow that people felt in their hearts:

> *Today we gather to commemorate the victims of the August
> bombing of Jicarito. After two army invasions in Chalaten-
> ango and the anticipation of still another, many people are
> demoralized. We are a people who have been humiliated
> by many years of war. We know what it is to go hungry
> and to thirst. But the day will come when we will rejoice
> and eat of the harvest we have sown. The day will come
> when we will build houses and live in them. The day will
> come when those who humiliate us now will be humbled
> by the Lord.*

Several people lay flowers on the graves of the eight persons
who were killed in the August bombing. Some lit candles beside
the crosses that marked the graves of their loved ones. In one
single plot three people were buried: Marta, her six-year-old
daughter Irma, and Irene, who was eight and a half months pregnant with her second child at the time of her death.

Tomás continued the reflection, reading from the Gospel story
of the resurrection:

> *Let us remember all those who have died during the past
> year. They did not waver in their struggle to be faithful to
> the end. We are passing through difficult moments now,*

and we will pass through more difficult times in the days ahead. Many people, in their desperation, are tempted to flee to the refugee camps. But we must not lose heart. We all long to see the day when El Salvador will be free. The disciples believed because they saw with their own eyes. Blessed are those who believe in the day we cannot yet see!

Sometimes It's Difficult To Believe

The invasion came as promised, the third in Chalatenango in as many months. I was in the village of Haciendita when the first mortars fell over the community, signaling the advance of the army. This time we were better prepared and headed in the direction of the Sumpul River for safety.

Each invasion and each flight are different. This time María Serrano, the president of the popular government here in Chalatenango, directed our group to safety. Her presence instilled confidence and discipline in the people. Several hundred men, women, and children walked hours through the dark night.

The tall grass brushed against our faces and arms, and shielded our darkened figures as we passed through the fields. Only the sound of our footsteps, the dry grass against our bodies, and an occasional metal cup falling to the ground broke the silence. We crossed the Sumpul River in the early dawn hours and spent the next few days hiding in the hills until the army retreated.

Yesterday, when I returned to Haciendita after more than a week's absence, I was shocked. The destruction of the community, especially after this last army invasion, was total! Houses had been burned to the ground with only the adobe walls left standing. Clay pots and jars had been shattered and kitchen utensils were strewn over the ground. Every sign of life had been crushed out; even the papaya trees that grew near the pastoral center had been cut down. Not a single clay roof tile was intact; they were scattered in pieces over the dirt floors.

As I walked through the ruins, I stopped to visit a family and to share the noon meal. Felipe and his wife lived in this house, together with their eight children. The oldest daughter was grinding corn for the day's tortillas on a stone. As we talked, I mentioned Dora to Felipe. "We knew the whole family," Felipe began. "Do you know how she was killed?" I asked. "Yes, they were ambushed by the army at the Gualsinga River. Dora, her baby Luis, and her mother Dorila were all killed. Another baby was killed, too."

"Whose child was that?" I asked. I recalled the accounts I had heard before of Dora's death, but never the mention of two small infants. "Marta's," he replied, and he pointed to his daughter who was grinding corn. Only then did I realize that I had seen her before in the field hospital, visiting the surviving members of Dora's family. Marta told this story:

> When the soldiers began to shoot, we ran along a path near the Gualsinga River to a hill called Las Córdobas. Jaime, who is my husband and Dora's brother, carried our five-month-old daughter Norma in his arms. We walked for about half an hour, and when we approached some trees, Dora whispered to Jaime: "Look, soldiers." Before we could respond, they began to shoot.

"Dora was your sister-in-law?" I asked.

"Yes. We were from the same village, Santa Bárbara, in the department of Cabañas."

"And what happened next?"

> We ran to save our lives. Jaime was shot in the side and in the leg. He told me later he put the child on the ground and ran. He thought that if the soldiers killed him, at least they wouldn't kill the child. The soldiers combed through the underbrush looking for the rest of us to kill us. I could hear my child crying. Then I heard the soldiers approach, another burst of gunfire, and then silence.

"They killed your child?" I asked in disbelief.

"Yes."

We finished our meal in silence. I thanked them and continued to walk through the ruins of the village. Toward evening I met Manuel and accompanied him as he went to make arrangements for supper. Here and there we spoke with families as they toasted day-old tortillas over an open fire beneath the ruins of the houses. A sense of gloom penetrated the air in the face of so much death and destruction. Two elderly women greeted us. "We don't have any more tortillas, but you're welcome to our fire." It was a gesture of friendship and warmth in the midst of so much darkness.

These last days of November and the brisk winds that accompany them signal the end of the rainy season and the beginning of the dry season. As Advent approaches, I am struck by the gospel challenge to proclaim a message of hope in a time that seems so filled with despair, a message of liberty to a people that is held captive by the threat of yet another army invasion.

"Always be prepared to give a reason for your hope," Peter tells the early Christian communities (1 Peter 3:14). Advent is both a time of waiting and a time of hope: *espera* and *esperanza*. A time when we are called *"to prepare a way in the desert"* for the One who comes in history to make all things new again. Sometimes it's difficult to believe anymore.

〚 12 〛

A Light Shines
in the Darkness

December 1984 . . . Arcatao, Chalatenango

It's nearly December now. Life is beginning to return to normal. Today I set out with Chepe for the village of Santa Anita, near the town of San José las Flores. We crossed the Sumpul River and arrived in the village in time to attend the popular assembly there. María Serrano, the president of the popular government in Chalatenango, was there to talk to the community about the dialogue between the FMLN and the Salvadoran government. The first dialogue had taken place October 15 in the town of La Palma, Chalatenango. Three hundred women and children, including María, her two daughters, and Esperanza, had walked three days and three nights just to be there.

María told people that a second dialogue was about to take place in the town of Ayagualo near San Salvador. "What's going to happen at the next dialogue?" someone asked and María responded:

> *The FMLN has made several proposals to humanize the conflict. These include an end to the bombing and the army invasions; identity documents for the civilian population in areas controlled by the FMLN; and a return of the refugees from Honduras to their homes in El Salvador. We're going to insist on our right to live on this land and to work it, and the army's not going to be able to do anything about it!*

It was hard to imagine that the refugees in Honduras would one day return to El Salvador. It was even harder to imagine that people in Chalatenango would no longer have to flee through these hills to escape the army.

I recalled a conversation I had had a week before with Eva, a widow and mother of eight small children. Eva is Tomás' sister-in-law. She was leaving for the refugee camps in Mesa Grande, one of the 1,500 people in Chalatenango who have fled to Honduras these past three months.

"What do you think I should do?" she asked me. "Once I leave Chalatenango it might be years before I can return. My mother refuses to leave. But how can I go on like this with eight small children? We barely survived the last invasion, hiding from the soldiers in the underbrush."

A few days later I met Eva's mother, a beautiful white-haired woman named Angelina. She was anxious because her only daughter was going to leave her behind. I mentioned to her that I would be seeing Eva again. "You tell my daughter she should have more faith," Angelina replied with conviction. "We've suffered so much already and look, we're still alive. *Dios es grande!* God will see us through."

A Cry of the Poor against Poverty

Today we began our celebration of Christmas in the village of Jicarito. Three hundred people came from the surrounding villages to gather for the evening liturgy. The reading for the day from the prophet Zephaniah brought a message of hope to the people gathered:

> *Cry out with joy, O daughter of Zion;*
> *rejoice, O people of Israel!*
> *Sing joyfully with all your heart,*
> *daughter of Jerusalem!*
> *Yahweh has lifted the sentence of your condem-*
> *nation*
> *and has driven your enemies away.*
> *Yahweh, the King of Israel, is with you;*

> *do not fear any misfortune.*
>   *(Zephaniah 3:14–15)*

"What does this message have to say to the people of El Salvador?" Father Rutilio asked. "That we need not be afraid," a woman called out. "God is with us. God is with the poor."

The Gospel also recalled a message of hope, the birth of a Savior. It was the story of the visitation of Mary to Elizabeth, the mother of John the Baptist.

"Why was Jesus born poor?" Father Rutilio asked.

"Because he identifies with the poor. He's one of us," a man replied.

"But what does Jesus teach us about poverty?" Rutilio continued. "Did he teach us to be poor?"

A discussion ensued.

"Jesus was born poor to cry out against poverty," Father Rutilio concluded. "Christ was born poor and cries out against the poverty in which millions of children throughout the world are born today."

The celebration ended with the baptism of a dozen children, the Eucharist, and the final blessing. As we departed in the darkness, the stars illumined the path over which we passed. I felt a renewed sense of hope and unity tonight. Surely "God is with the poor."

The following morning we continued our journey to the town of San Isidro, which was abandoned years ago. Now it is the home of many displaced families from Guazapa. The church there had been destroyed, so we gathered under the shade of some trees beside the ruins of several houses. The trees served as a cover for us, so that the planes could not detect our presence and strafe or bomb the community. Several women brought flowers to decorate an old table that served as an altar. Dozens of children gathered nearby.

Today's reading recalled the birth of Samuel, consecrated to a life of service to the Lord by his mother Anna when she was barren.

"What example does this mother offer us?" Father Rutilio asked the people.

"Our children are a blessing from God," one woman replied.

"They are the future of our people," another woman responded, nursing her child. "We must also be willing to offer our children to the struggle of our people."

The Gospel reading followed, from the Magnificat of Mary:

> The powerful will be cast down from their
>   thrones,
>   and the humble uplifted.
> The hungry will be filled with good things,
>   and the rich sent away empty.
>
>   (Luke 1:52–53)

"Where was Christ born?" Rutilio asked.

"In Bethlehem," someone answered.

"In a stable," another called out, "where the animals are fed."

"And who today is born as Christ was born?" Rutilio asked.

I looked around me at the dozens of children present, many still nursing in their mothers' arms.

"How are children born today in El Salvador?" Rutilio asked.

Several mothers recalled the birth of their children on a dirt floor or in a ravine during flights from the army.

"In these past three months fifteen children were born to mothers hiding in these hills," Rutilio continued, "in conditions equal to or worse than the stable where Christ was born." Then he added:

> All of us had to choose, years ago, whether we would go
> with our people to the mountains or remain with the army
> in the towns. Since then we have been forced to live a
> clandestine life, persecuted by the authorities. We have suf-
> fered, but we still have joy. The struggle gives meaning to
> our lives. We still love life, but we have learned to sacrifice
> our lives so that our people may live.

As evening drew near we celebrated the Eucharist, and several children were baptized. Then people departed for their homes just as they had left them a few hours before. Yet I sensed that something had changed. A feeling of unity, solidarity, and hope had grown up among us. I remembered the words spoken by

Archbishop Romero years before: "No one," he said, "has a right to despair. All of us have the responsibility to search for new paths to bring hope into the world."

It's not easy to keep hope alive, especially when there is so much death and destruction around. But these celebrations are a confirmation of Archbishop Romero's words: "With people like these, it's not hard to be a Good Shepherd."

One More Chapter of Our Bible

The following day we set out for the town of Arcatao. We crossed the Sumpul River in the afternoon and reached the town by nightfall. Arcatao was once the center of commercial activity for rural communities near the Honduran border. At one time fifteen thousand people lived in the surrounding area. In January 1983 the FMLN attacked and destroyed the National Guard post in the town. When the military threatened reprisals against the people if they stayed, thousands left. Now the streets and houses are empty; only a few families still live in the town.

We gathered in the evening in the church to celebrate the Christmas Eve Mass. Hundreds of families came from the neighboring villages. "If the walls of this church or the stones of these streets could speak," Father Rutilio began, "they would cry out against the terrible repression which occurred in this town. Hundreds of people were captured, tortured, and assassinated by the National Guard. Who recalls these terrible things?"

"I remember when the National Guard threatened Archbishop Romero when he came to visit us in August 1979," a woman recalled.

"The National Guard captured several young people right here in this church," a man called out, "and dragged them away to be tortured."

"These are terrible things," Rutilio concluded, "but what virtues can we recall? This town has also been the center of great virtues."

"The courage of countless campesinos who organized, despite the repression," one man called out.

"The hospitality we have shown to neighboring communities,"

another recalled, "including people from Honduras."

A man from a neighboring village added, "I'm grateful for the welcoming reception which we have received today. You have not rejected us, even though we fled to the side of the army years ago."

This last reflection, in particular, touched all of us and gave us hope, a sign of reconciliation between neighbors that the war has divided.

Chepe began to read from the prophet Isaiah by the light of a kerosene lantern. Isaiah's words spoke of God's faithfulness to the poor and the hope of the exiles—and the people gathered tonight—to return to their homes:

> *For love of Zion I will not be silenced,*
> *For Jerusalem I will not remain tranquil*
> *Until justice shines forth*
> *and salvation is brilliant like a torch.*
> *(Isaiah 62:1)*

The Gospel reading followed: *"Glory to God in the highest and peace on earth to men and women of good will"* (Luke 2:14).

"Christ is born poor in a manger because there was no room in the inn," Father Rutilio began. "This occurred during the *pax romana*, the 'peace' of the Roman Empire. But what kind of 'peace' was it that governed the poor in Israel at that time? The peace which God promises us? Or the peace of the cemeteries? What does this peace mean to us? Who will bring peace to El Salvador today?"

I looked out over the faces of the people gathered, faces worn by years of suffering, illuminated now by the dim light of the lantern.

"The day in which all of us, organized and unorganized, peasants and workers, children and old people, men and women, all agree to end this terrible war in El Salvador and bring justice to our people, we will have peace," Rutilio concluded.

At midnight Chepe rang the church bell as he had done for years when he was the sacristan of the church. The sound filled the silence of the empty streets of the town tonight and reached up to the hills that surround Arcatao. I imagined a day when all the church bells in El Salvador would ring forth the good news promised to us on this Christmas Eve: *"How beautiful on the mountains are the feet of one who brings glad tidings, announcing peace!" (Isaiah 52:7)*.

"This year our people have written another chapter of their Bible," Father Rutilio continued, "the story of a people who struggle to be free. What kind of world will we prepare for our children?"

One by one the people shared their hopes for the future, above all for a just and lasting peace.

"*Primero Dios*, we will have peace next year," an old woman called out.

The Mass concluded with the celebration of the Eucharist and the final blessing. Fireworks lit up the night sky. Freshly baked bread and coffee were served to the entire community. Tonight there is joy in Arcatao, a moment of peace in the midst of so much suffering and sadness. The words of the prophet Isaiah written so long ago to another people in bondage illuminated the darkness of this present exile of the Salvadoran people and offered comfort and hope:

> *No longer will you be called "Abandoned,"*
> *nor your land "Desolate,"*
> *But the Lord will take delight in you*
> *and your land will have a spouse.*
> *(Isaiah 62:4)*

PROMISED LAND

1985–1987: Violations within the Context of the Armed Conflict

In 1985 there was a marked stepping up of violence in military confrontations and operations in the areas where the guerrillas were active . . . There were intensive aerial bombings and mass displacement of the peasant population in rural areas . . . The FMLN began to make widespread tactical use of mines in areas under its influence. Vast numbers of people were displaced from their places of origin when they fled the counter-insurgency operations. Those affected established the National Coordination of Repopulation, which sought to regain the rights of the civilian population to live in the areas from which they had come . . . The violence continued.

—From Madness to Hope,
Report of the Commission on the Truth for El Salvador, 36

A NEW HEAVEN AND
A NEW EARTH
1985–1987

I returned to the United States in March 1985 and began to help translate into English a biweekly newsletter from the Jesuit University in San Salvador called *Carta a las Iglesias* as part of a project of Christians for Peace in El Salvador (CRISPAZ). The letter was filled with testimonies of suffering and hope, and accomplished in a unique way the challenge that Archbishop Romero had presented to the church: "to be the voice of the voiceless." Known as "Letter to the Churches" in English, the newsletter brought these testimonies to hundreds of people in the United States. Many of these testimonies were eventually published in a book, *El Salvador: A Spring Whose Waters Never Run Dry.*

Meanwhile, the suffering of the people of El Salvador deepened. With the election of Napoleón Duarte as president in 1984, the illusion of "democracy" in El Salvador provided the United States with an excuse to increase aid to the military, and with it the bombings of civilians and the attacks against their communities in the countryside intensified. Thousands of people were killed, and tens of thousands more were displaced from their homes.

In January 1986 the Salvadoran military began "Operation Phoenix" and literally bombed the Guazapa volcano back to the stone age, killing 245 people and displacing thousands more.[1] Window glass in San Salvador, fifteen miles away, shook under the impact of the heaviest bombing to date in the war. Reams of testimonies about human rights violations, bombings, and invasions were published by *Tutela Legal*,[2] the Legal Aid Office of the Archdiocese of San Salvador, and by the nongovernmental

Human Rights Commission (CDHES). The United States Embassy, for its part, tried unsuccessfully to discredit both of these human rights institutions.[3]

One of the more moving stories from Guazapa was that of Laura López, a catechist and mother of five children.[4] She was killed April 24, 1985, by the Salvadoran army during a massive invasion of the Guazapa volcano. Her thirteen-year-old daughter lived to tell how her mother had given up the protection of an underground shelter to make room for another family, only to be shot down as she fled from the invading army. In one of her last letters, she wrote:

> *Since the electoral campaign began, we have been subjected to terrible repression on the part of the government troops and the Air Force. Day and night the bombardments and invasions come our way. From January 17 until March 8, a total of 81 bombs and 69 rockets have been dropped on villages near the town of Cinquera. Five invasions left six dead, among them two children. In Guazapa, a total of 624 rockets were launched, 30 houses were destroyed, and crops were burned. In the face of this destruction, death, hunger, and misery, as Christians we plead for an end to the war.*[5]

One of Laura's co-workers said, "Laura always challenged us to persevere, and we remember her words: 'I prefer to die with my people. Christ died in such a way, and I must also.' "

These terrible events were the crucible of hope and new life in El Salvador. In 1984 the very people who had been displaced by the bombings and invasions organized and formed the Christian Committee of Displaced People in El Salvador (CRIPDES). Two years later, in 1986, the repopulation movement was born, and began to effectively challenge the counterinsurgency strategy of the Salvadoran army to depopulate the areas of conflict controlled by the FMLN by repopulating them with displaced people.

In March 1986 hundreds of families were captured by the army in Chalatenango and turned over to the International Red Cross, and then placed in a refugee camp in Calle Real. Three months later these same families organized their return to the town of

San José las Flores in Chalatenango. A Mass was celebrated in the cathedral of San Salvador; then hundreds of people, both Salvadorans and internationals, accompanied them in a caravan of buses back to their homes in Chalatenango.

A month later there was a second repopulation — of the El Barillo cooperative located in Aguacayo, a village near the Guazapa volcano. This time the government took action and deported two dozen U.S. church people who had accompanied the refugees in their return. But the movement had already caught fire. Within a year the floodgates were forced open as thousands of refugees, and the hundreds of international people who accompanied them, forged a path in the wilderness back to the homes the refugees had abandoned because of the military repression.

On October 10, 1987, four thousand refugees from the camps in Mesa Grande, Honduras, repatriated to their homes in Chalatenango, Cuscatlán, and Cabañas. With the help of churches, popular organizations in El Salvador, and international solidarity, political space was opened. Over the next two years a tide of repatriations swept past military roadblocks and challenged official lies to bring the reality of the war to the light of day.

I went to the border of Honduras with hundreds of others to welcome the refugees. There we boarded buses and accompanied them to their homes in Chalatenango. The dam had been broken, and those who had been victims of the war now became actors in history as they began to rebuild their communities and to sow the seeds of a new El Salvador.

[13]

Land of Martyrs,
Land of Hope

October 1987 . . . Las Vueltas, Chalatenango

They came back just as they had left—on foot. All along the path from the village of El Zapotal to the town of Las Vueltas some carried chickens, others carried children; their packs and bundles seemed to form part of their bodies. This was the culmination of nine months of planning in the refugee camp of Mesa Grande in Honduras for their return to El Salvador. For many of these refugees it was the culmination of more than seven years in exile, a time of tears, and today a time of joy, just as the psalmist describes:

> *They went away, went away weeping,*
> *carrying the seed;*
> *They come back, come back singing,*
> *carrying their sheaves.*
> *(Psalm 126:6)*

"It was like a biblical event," Father Brendon Ford, an Irish Franciscan priest, declared in the Mass the following day in front of the church—a genuine giving of thanks for this day after so many years of living in exile. More than one thousand people were present in the plaza. It was a new page in the history of the Salvadoran people, written in the lined faces of these campesinos. Truly a new creation!

But not everything was joyful. This path of their return has been a path of thorns in years past, a real Way of the Cross filled with suffering and martyrdom. When we arrived near the town of Ojos de Agua, we stopped to rest and to wait for the other trucks in the caravan to catch up: "Look, there's the Sumpul River!" "And the hill that rises above the river?" "Las Aradas." These are names that evoke bitter memories of the massacre that occurred there May 14, 1980, when more than six hundred people were killed by the Salvadoran army as they tried to cross the river to safety in Honduras.

José, a man who had survived the massacre, narrated to me what happened that day. "You can't imagine how sad that day was! They threw babies up in the air and stabbed them with their bayonets." Once again the words of the psalmist came to mind and expressed for me the sadness that was too painful for many survivors like José to share:

> By the waters of Babylon, we sat down and wept
>   as we remembered Zion . . .
> How could we sing one of Yahweh's songs
>   in a strange land? (Psalm 137:1–4)

The People Have Come Back to Life!

It was especially moving for me to walk over the same paths where three years before we had accompanied the people in their flight from the army. I saw the faces of the people I had known — more tired, perhaps, but with an invincible hope. It has always been a great privilege for me to accompany the Salvadoran people. The last time I passed through Las Vueltas was the day after Christmas 1984. At that time the army carried out major invasions in the hills and valleys of Chalatenango. Now the people have come back to life!

As the church bells rang, many people drew near to the altar outside the church, facing the plaza. More than one thousand people, one thousand faces, one thousand hearts resonated with the same thought and hope. Moisés, a catechist I had met four years before in Chalatenango, addressed the people. It was his task to welcome the repatriated refugees. Like a "holy remnant," Moisés and 280 other people from Las Vueltas had remained in these hills through all the years of persecution and war. They never fled to Honduras nor knew the life of a refugee camp. Today, for the first time, these two peoples — repatriated refugees and faithful remnant — were reunited.

"Despite all our suffering," Moisés began, "we must go on. We are poor, and we have made an option for the poor. Like the people of Israel who were slaves in Egypt, we have passed through the wilderness to reach this promised land." Now and then the church bells rang, reflecting the joy written on the faces of the people. Father Brendon also spoke, comparing this moment in history to the exodus: "Let us go forward with a new spirit and a new heart. Let us look to the future with eyes of faith. In this way we can build the new society for which we all yearn, with justice, with peace, and with freedom."

We Want Justice and Bread for Everyone

One theme that was repeated by several of the speakers was that of victory. The return of the refugees was a victory that they themselves had won, a victory for the Salvadoran people. Neither the United Nations nor the Salvadoran government, regardless of their claims, was responsible for this return. Only when it was inevitable, and 4,500 refugees were prepared to set out on foot if necessary, did the UNHCR and the Salvadoran government accept a collective return of the refugees to their places of origin. It was a real victory of the people.

The next day, after the people had worked all day to fix the road and prepare tortillas, a Mass was celebrated to give thanks to God for the opportunity to work the land again. The church bells rang and the people gathered outside the church, looking out onto the plaza. Several FMLN combatants joined us. They asked if they could say a few words of welcome to the people who had returned.

For the next half hour we celebrated what for many was a family reunion, bringing together these people with the FMLN combatants, and parents with their daughters and sons. The significance of this encounter is profound, evoking painful memories of those who have died, anxiety about the future, but also hope for an embrace, a shared tortilla, a word of encouragement, an end to the war, and peace.

The Mass followed, and a communal reflection on the Gospel of Nicodemus and his question to Jesus: *"How can a person be born again?" (John 3:4).* "We want peace and justice for everyone," Moisés responded. "That's what it means to be born again. To struggle so that everyone may have justice and bread."

As the sun set over the hills surrounding the town of Las Vueltas, Brendon began the offertory prayer: "We give you thanks, Lord, for this bread and wine, fruit of the earth and the work of human hands." And so we concluded the liturgy, the work of a people who have come back to work the land and to reap its fruits so that they and their children might live in peace.

Come, Holy Spirit, and Fill Our Hearts

Sunday morning was one of those beautiful Chalatenango days, with a bright sun and a fresh breeze. As usual, we bathed in the crystal clear waters of the river that passes through the town. I went to eat breakfast in the shell of a house with no roof and damaged walls. It looked like the buildings in San Salvador that had been damaged by the earthquake the previous year.

This house had once been the National Guard headquarters. In October 1982 it was attacked and overrun by the FMLN. Now it had been converted into a collective kitchen for the newly returned refugees. I noticed two pictures on the wall, one of the Virgin Mary and the other of the Holy Spirit with this traditional prayer scrawled beneath the pictures: "Come, Holy Spirit, fill our hearts and light in them the flame of your love." An old woman named Emilia had put them there.

Emilia is one hundred years old, or so people say. She returned to Las Vueltas with her son, a granddaughter, and a great-grandson named Juan Ramón who was born two weeks ago. "When we left for the Sumpul River five years ago," her son told me, "I carried Emilia on my back." I asked Emilia, "How does it feel to be back?" "It's not easy," she complained, puffing on her cigarette. "I get headaches, I'm hungry, I sleep on the ground." Her answer was a sober reminder that as long as the war continues in El Salvador, the poor suffer.

Still, Emilia gives me hope. Behind her complaints I detected a smile and a fortitude that reminded me of Moisés' words: "Despite all our suffering, we must go on." This morning, as I looked over the valleys and hills that surround the town of Las Vueltas, I recalled Isaiah's prophecy of a promised land:

> No more will the sound of weeping
>   or the sound of cries be heard in her . . .
> For they will build houses and live in them,
>   plant fields and eat their fruit . . .
> They will be a people blessed by Yahweh
>   and their children with them. (65:19–23)

[14]

Arising from the Ashes

November 1987 . . . Copapayo, Cuscatlán

We arrived in the village of Copapayo on Sunday, November 1—All Saints' Day. On the way we passed through the town of Suchitoto, situated in the shadow of the Guazapa volcano, the heart of the conflictive area here these past seven years. It's a half hour walk from the church in Suchitoto to the shore of Lake Suchitlán; from there we traveled in boats until we came to the village of Copapayo.

The afternoon sun shone brightly over the waters of the lake; a breeze lifted our spirits as we talked and viewed the hills in the distance. Three weeks ago seven hundred refugees returned from the refugee camp in Mesa Grande, Honduras, to begin a new life here in Copapayo.

The previous Friday the people had celebrated Mass here to commemorate their loved ones who were killed November 4, 1983—at least 118 people died in the massacre. A delegation from the repopulation site in El Barillo was also there to welcome the people back to El Salvador. They read a passage from Exodus about crossing the Red Sea; and in the tradition of these Christian base communities, they interpreted their return in the light of the exodus event.

The people of Israel, after passing through the Red Sea, faced many difficulties in the wilderness. They complained to Moses: *"Why did you bring us out into the wilderness to die?"* (Exodus 17:3).

"What does this reading say to us?" Father Daniel Sánchez,

99

the celebrant, asked. "Even though we have left Honduras and returned to El Salvador," one man ventured, "we have not yet reached the promised land. We have to face difficulties in the wilderness as well. We still have a long way to go to reach the liberation for which we yearn."

"And what do these martyrs mean to you? These brothers and sisters, these mothers and fathers, these children and grandchildren who died here in Copapayo four years ago?" Father Daniel asked.

"They shed their blood for our liberation," a woman called out.

"They are a light," another woman said, "and we must try to follow their example."

There was not one word of vengeance or discouragement, only light and commitment. In the midst of the silence they lifted up the names of their loved ones who had been so cruelly assassinated in the massacre, expressing in this way what has always been the foundation of our faith since the time of the early Christians: "The blood of the martyrs is the seed of new Christians."

The Dark Night of Repression

What happened November 4, 1983, in Copapayo is not well known. I knew because I had heard Silvia's story in Chalatenango a few months after the massacre. If it were not for the survivors — real witnesses in the biblical sense of the word — that sad history would have been buried in the house where the last of the women and children were cruelly machine-gunned to death by the Atlacatl Battalion.

But a nine-year-old boy escaped from the house where the others were killed. Buried beneath the cadavers, covered with the blood of twenty-five women and children, he had miraculously survived. Hours later he fled across Lake Suchitlán to Chalatenango and finally to the refugee camp in Mesa Grande to testify to what happened. Two other children escaped as well. One week after the massacre the Salvadoran army returned to the village of Copapayo to scatter the bones and erase the memory of this massacre forever.

This morning I spoke with Vicente, another survivor of the massacre in Copapayo. He lost his wife and four children, ages one, three, five, and seven. While we spoke, Vicente took a stick and drew a picture of what had happened. Every now and then I asked a question to clarify some detail, but I felt a great silence in my heart – and a cry – as I listened:

> At 8 A.M. on the morning of November 4, the soldiers came down from the hills firing their machine guns and throwing grenades, causing great panic among the people. Many people dived into the lake and drowned; others fled in a boat, which was sunk by mortars and grenades. Those who ran were killed; women were raped and assassinated. A seven-year-old boy was ordered by soldiers to retrieve the boat that had been sunk. "I can't swim," he replied. So the soldiers took him by his arms and legs and threw him into the lake where he drowned. Some thirty people died at the edge of the lake.
>
> The rest of the people were captured and taken a short distance away where they received a lecture from an army official. "We are going to spare your lives, and give you medical attention and land to cultivate. Do you know who we are?" "No," the people answered, "We don't know." "We're the Atlacatl Battalion. And do you know who I am?" the official asked. "No, we don't know," the people responded. "I'm Colonel Domingo Monterrosa."

Vicente heard this conversation from where he hid in the water near the shore of Lake Suchitlán. When the soldiers first started shooting, Vicente plunged into the water and hid among the water lilies. His wife and children were gunned down at the shore. Colonel Monterrosa, the same man who commanded the Atlacatl Battalion when it massacred hundreds of people in El Mozote, Morazán, in December 1981, commanded his soldiers to return to the lake and fire into the water in case anyone was still left alive. Miraculously, Vicente survived the shooting.

> At 2 P.M. the soldiers took their captives to another village, La Escopeta. On the way they took the men aside and killed

them. Those who remained alive — about twenty-five women and children — were taken to another village, San Nicolás, and kept in an abandoned house overnight. In the morning they were machine-gunned to death in the house. The soldiers caved in the roof and left the bodies buried under the debris. Only the nine-year-old boy and two other children survived to tell the story.

Twelve young people who were captured near Copapayo were raped, cruelly tortured, and killed. Their bodies were left by the roadside, one by one, on the path leading from Copapayo to La Escopeta. One hundred eighteen people died in the massacre, including fifty-two children.

I didn't have any words for Vicente. I just shook his hand and said, *"Gracias."* But silence filled my heart — as did the cry of the people.

Our Only Crime Is To Be Poor

The morning of November 4 was especially beautiful. The natural beauty of the land seems to reflect the same qualities that characterize these campesinos — strength, simplicity, hospitality, and joy. Today we were going to the site of the massacre that occurred four years before, a little distance from the actual site where people are now living. We still had flowers from the All Souls' Day commemoration to place on the graves of the victims.

I accompanied Catalina, a woman who lost a son and a daughter in the massacre. I had met her daughter Silvia in Chalatenango three and one half years ago. Silvia was the first person to tell me about the massacre. This was the first time in four years that Catalina had been to Copapayo; and for me it was the first time.

We left the section of Copapayo where the people now live and traveled in boats to the valley across the bay where the massacre occurred in 1983. It seemed to me that people felt both joy and sadness. As we walked through the ruins of the old village, people gathered relics from their past — bottles, benches, grinding stones — things that would be useful to them in their new life.

When we passed by two of the houses that had been destroyed, someone called out: "That's where Chon used to live; and this is where Chencito lived." "Are they still alive?" I asked. "No, everyone, young and old, died in the massacre."

As we continued along the path leading to the cemetery, we walked in silence. "It's sad," Catalina remarked. But there were also moments of joy, seeing ripe papayas or a branch of bright red and white flowers known as *colación*. When we came to the cemetery the men began to cut the tall grass that hid the graves from view. Catalina went to each grave and placed flowers by each cross. One more small gesture of this suffering and heroic people who remember their dead — and their martyrs.

When we returned to the site where the people now live, many recalled their past, each one a witness, each one a survivor. I later spoke with Rosario, an elderly midwife in the community, and she summarized in a few words her unshakable faith: "It used to be a crime just to have a Bible, so we buried them. All this happened just as it was written in the Holy Scripture. Our only crime was to be poor and to cry out for justice. But God protected us with a divine cloak in the midst of the bullets."

A Rusty Chalice and Five Tortillas

Today, November 7, was a special day for the people. The priest and pastoral team from the Mesa Grande refugee camp had come from Honduras to celebrate with them. It would be a moment to recognize the fulfillment of their dream to return to El Salvador and an incentive for the refugees who still remained in Honduras to prepare to come back.

This Mass would also be special because it would be celebrated with the old chalice that had been buried by the people in Copapayo four years before. Together with the church bells, which had also been buried, it would be a symbol of hope, a sign that the people had returned to life.

"We celebrate this Mass in commemoration of the years you have suffered, of your yearning to return to El Salvador, and the fact that you are now here," the celebrant began. "This chalice, which was buried four years ago in Copapayo, holds the wine that is the symbol of your suffering and the blood of Christ." "This bread," he continued, lifting up the tortillas, "is our daily bread and the body of Christ. God's love has no bounds. God will consecrate this wine and this tortilla, and calls us to consecrate each day of our lives to bring new life to our people."

This Mass was special for me because it was so ordinary, mixing the daily bread of the people, a tortilla, with their suffering and their hope to begin a new life in this land; and offering up the cup of salvation, this rusty old chalice, together with the blood of the martyrs and the struggle of the people for justice.

The Salvadoran army continues to sow terror among the people in the countryside. But the poor have not lost their faith or their courage. The blood of their martyrs has really become the seed of a new people, and their hope is invincible. In small gestures and in their daily lives, there are clear signs that the people of Copapayo continue to bear witness to a more just and dignified peace for El Salvador.

[15]

How Beautiful on the Mountains

December 1987 . . . Santa Marta, Cabañas

I had never been to the village of Santa Marta before. But I had heard of this village near the town of Villa Victoria in Cabañas seven years ago. That was when five thousand campesinos fled this area to cross the Lempa River and take refuge in Honduras. I was on the other side of the river when that happened on March 18, 1981. Since then I had always wanted to visit Santa Marta.

We arrived November 24 in the town of Villa Victoria. I was surprised to see so many armed civil defense men walking in the plaza in front of the church. At the edge of the plaza the Salvadoran army had set up a post. Since the massive exodus of five thousand campesinos in 1981, this part of Cabañas has been controlled by the army. It has been a model of the army's pacification program since 1982. Now everyone is waiting to see what will happen with the return of one thousand refugees to Santa Marta.

It is four kilometers from the town of Villa Victoria to the village of Santa Marta, about two and one half miles. We traveled in a truck with campesinos from neighboring villages until we reached a path that led to Santa Marta. At that point we got off the truck and walked the last three kilometers. With the change in transport from riding to walking, we had entered more deeply into the world of these campesinos. Santa Marta is only five hours from San Salvador, but it is an entirely different world, full of natural beauty, solitude, and the rhythm of rural life.

This is where the exodus of five thousand campesinos began.

But it was not an exodus that led them directly to a promised land; instead, they came to a "wilderness," to a time of exile as refugees in Mesa Grande, Honduras. Today, however, they have come back to continue the march toward a land that really flows with milk and honey, with justice and freedom.

As we approached the village, I saw a woman and a dozen children mingling on the porch of a house. Marta ran out to greet us and give us a big hug. Once inside the house she told us how terrified she was. On September 1, just three months before, A-37 fighter-bombers dropped bombs over the area. "I was with my child on my way to the clinic in Victoria when the planes passed overhead."

One bomb fell on a house, killing a man and injuring seven adults and children. The next day the army came to apologize. But the damage was already done, and people were terrified; some even went to live in the town of Victoria. News of the bombing reached Mesa Grande, but it was too late to discourage the refugees in their plans to return. After seven years away from their homes, they were determined to come back, "even if we have to go on foot!"

The Death of Children before Their Time

When we reached the first shelters that the people had built, I saw many familiar faces. In one of these shelters I recognized Margarita, standing with her mother in the midst of seven children. *"Hola! Buenos días!"* I called out, and we greeted each other. I asked Margarita the name of the child who played at her side. "Víctor Emanuel. He's five years old." That's when I remembered her first child who had died six years before — he had the same name.

I will never forget the eyes of that small child who was dying of malnutrition. As the women sang and prayed the child gasped for breath and stared at us, as if he were trying to ask us something. Since then, the memory of his final agony has remained with me. The death of children before their time is a daily occurrence in the poorest of homes — something that scandalizes us and challenges our faith. For Christ is crucified in each child who dies of hunger.

But now the mother was happy because her family had returned home. Not exactly to their own house – the Salvadoran army had destroyed everything in Santa Marta in 1981 – but to the village where they were born, and this was reason to rejoice.

We passed the afternoon visiting families until evening, happy to be reunited. "It's just like we used to say," a woman reminded me: "See you in El Salvador!" This was the gift we all received today, this promise of returning to El Salvador that had been fulfilled.

Christ Suffers His Passion outside the City

The following day I went with Rodrigo, a teacher with whom I had worked six years before in the Mesa Grande refugee camp in Honduras. "What has been the fruit of your work all these years?" I asked him. "We made a survey last year in Mesa Grande," he told me, "and 85 percent of the adult population had learned to read and write." "And when you began, how many were literate?" "Only 15 percent. A good harvest!"

We walked to the place where the church in Santa Marta used to stand. Along the way we passed dozens of men clearing the land and building the first houses. They were very well organized. We came to the ruins of several houses. "Carlos lived here," Rodrigo told me, "and Pedro lived there." All I saw was the foundation of the house; the walls and the roof had been totally destroyed. When we came to the church only the entrance and the bell tower were left standing, nothing more. Everything else had been destroyed by the Salvadoran army in 1981.

Rodrigo told me the story of this church. During the 1970s Father Vicente Sibrián had promoted the efforts of campesinos here to organize themselves into farm worker unions, like FEC-CAS (the Federation of Christian Farmers in El Salvador) and the UTC (the Farm Workers Union). The majority of the land in this area was owned by one family. Little by little the conflict became more intense, until finally the first catechists and organized campesinos were killed by members of the paramilitary group ORDEN.

Even Father Vicente was threatened and he, too, fled with the people to take refuge in the mountains. All the people tell this story; it is part of their own history. This was in 1980. In March 1981 the Salvadoran army invaded, and five thousand campesinos crossed the Lempa River to take refuge in Honduras.

Crossing the Lempa River

That afternoon I talked to Luis. He told me that the men working in the saw mill nearby had found shrapnel from the bombs and bullets in the trees they were cutting into boards. I asked Luis to tell me the story of the exodus of the people to Honduras in 1981. He became animated and spoke as though it had happened only yesterday. The crossing of the Lempa River has left a deep impression on the people of Santa Marta, like a baptism by fire:

> *The bombing began on March 15, 1981. Later that day soldiers took up positions in the hills surrounding our village. That's when we decided to leave, but we couldn't cross the Lempa River; the Honduran army was waiting for us on the other side. We didn't know what to do. A handful of FMLN* compañeros *fought back an invading force of 1,500 soldiers. The night of March 17, five thousand of us met in the church in the village of Peñas Blancas and decided to cross the Lempa River at dawn to take refuge in Honduras.*

That's how it happened. I was on the other side of the river, visiting the refugees who lived in the villages there when I received the news from a Honduran catechist that thousands of Salvadorans had crossed the river. He had been notified the night before by one of the refugees who crossed to let people in Honduras know of their plans. That night the Honduran army, which had been guarding the border for two days, moved farther downstream.

Before dawn, on March 18, the refugees crossed. In the midst of falling mortars and machine-gun fire from a helicopter, five thousand people, the majority of them women and children, crossed the Lempa River. "It was a real baptism by fire," Lino, one of the catechists, had told me then. "It was like crossing the Red Sea; God divided the Honduran and Salvadoran armies like the waters of the Red Sea so that we could cross!"

Rejoice! This Land Is Yours!

In every visit to the repatriation sites we have always had an opportunity to participate in a liturgy of the Word or a Mass. It is a moment that allows people to give thanks for the gift of life and to hear words of solidarity and encouragement in return. Many people from foreign countries have found in this contact with the Salvadoran people and their struggle for liberation— especially in their encounter with the faith and the hope of the people—a source of strength for their own faith and hope.

The readings that appear at the end of the liturgical year announce a day of judgment that will prepare the coming of God's Kingdom in history. Even the natural surroundings change abruptly, and a strong north wind announces the coming of the dry season:

> Let those in Judah flee to the mountains. If you are on the housetop, do not come down to take anything with you. If you are in the field, do not turn back to fetch your cloak. How hard it will be for pregnant women and mothers nursing their babies! Pray that it may not be in winter or on a sabbath when you flee! (Matthew 24:16–20)

Norberto, one of the catechists I met after the Lempa River crossing seven years ago, spoke first. His words provided a sober reminder of the cruelty of the war:

> All these things happened to us, just as the reading said. We had to flee our houses to sleep in the mountains. We didn't even have time to take our belongings with us. A

*young girl who was pregnant stayed behind and was cap-
tured by the Salvadoran army. The soldiers ripped open
her womb, tore out the fetus, and threw it to the dogs.*

But not everything said was sad. We also heard encouraging
words from Father Jim Barnett, who also had come to visit Santa
Marta:

*Rejoice! You have come back home. This is good news,
and not only for you. I have told my friends in the United
States and my fellow priests in Latin America as well. This
land is yours! These houses are yours! This Word we have
heard and reflected on is yours! That's why I give thanks
to you, for your example. Thank you for being here, and
keep moving forward!*

How Beautiful on the Mountains

As our visit drew near to a close, I remembered the first Christmas I had celebrated with the people of Santa Marta in the refugee camp in La Virtud six years before. Then we looked with
hope toward the hills in the distance that led back to El Salvador.
Today, however, the people have returned to the land where
they were born. They are no longer refugees, but Salvadorans
and campesinos who have won the right to live in their own land,
work it, and make it produce for the good of the community.

Today the beautiful passage from Isaiah read each Christmas
morning will have more meaning and bring more joy to the community of Santa Marta. Today the Word of God has become one
with the people and "pitched its tent" in Santa Marta, where it
shines like a light "for all the ends of the earth to see":

*How beautiful on the mountains
   are the feet of one who brings good news,
who heralds peace and happiness,
   proclaims salvation and announces to Zion:
"Your God is King!" (Isaiah 52:7)*

THE HOUR
OF THE POOR

1987–1989: The Military Conflict as an Obstacle to Peace

Although progress was made in what the international community termed "the humanization of the conflict," there was a resurgence of violence, with a definite increase in attacks on the labor movement, human rights groups and social organizations. The FMLN carried out a campaign of abductions, summary executions and murders against civilians affiliated with or sympathetic to the government and the armed forces. The dialogue among the parties came to a standstill and it became clear that human rights violations . . . were the main obstacles to the peace process.

   —From Madness to Hope,
    Report of the Commission on the Truth
    for El Salvador, 37

THE CHURCH OF THE POOR
IN MORAZÁN
1987–1989

In September 1987, I met with friends from the Christian Base Communities of El Salvador (CEBES) who were working in northern Morazán, another area controlled by the FMLN in the northeastern corner of El Salvador. They had been working there since January 1981, three months after the Salvadoran army launched a major military attack against northern Morazán. Thousands of refugees fled to Honduras and eventually built six camps near the town of Colomoncagua as their numbers swelled to eight thousand. Thousands more, however, remained in Morazán, perhaps as many as 25,000.

The pastoral team in Morazán, like the civilian population, had been denounced by the local bishop—who supported the military and virtually abandoned the people of his diocese in northern Morazán. Consequently, they were forced to work under extremely adverse conditions as they accompanied the people of northern Morazán in their efforts to gain protection from persecution by the army.

The presence of the pastoral team in Morazán was crucial to the formation of community leaders and the development of community organizations.[1] The Christian base communities, and the Congregation of Mothers in particular, played a prophetic role in breaking the military blockade of Morazán and denouncing military attacks on the communities.

By 1985 the people of northern Morazán had begun to organize community councils and mobilize the people in the villages to demand an end to the military attacks on their communities, just as the repatriated refugees in Chalatenango had done. One of the first groups in Morazán to resettle were people from La Joya, a village which was destroyed at the same time as the massacre in El Mozote which took place on December 11–12, 1981.[2] In 1985 the people of La Joya repopulated the abandoned town of Jocoaitique. People from other villages, like Calavera and Estancia near the town of Cacaopera, also went back to their homes.

The stories from Morazán that the pastoral team shared with me were much like the stories I had heard in Chalatenango, filled with the same suffering and the same hope.[3] One story in particular symbolized for me the struggle of the Salvadoran people for life. María, a member of a small religious community, worked with the pastoral team in Morazán during the most difficult years of the war:

> Once, in 1984, I accompanied people as they fled from the army during a military invasion. We had to divide into two large groups to avoid detection. Sometimes we didn't have anything to eat, or we hadn't slept all night, but we still had to walk. We came to the abandoned village of El Mozote, where the massacre had taken place. On this occasion a woman in our group gave birth to a child.
>
> At the moment the child was born, the army was close by. We were down below in a ravine, and they were above us where we could see them. But a miraculous thing happened. As soon as the child was born, the people decided: "We must celebrate! Even though the soldiers are looking for us to kill us, this child is a sign that God offers us life."[4]

In March 1988 I accepted an invitation to work with the Christian communities of northern Morazán. I crossed the Torola River into northern Morazán at the beginning of Holy Week and would remain in Morazán until the following year. The work of the pastoral team in northern Morazán was to train pastoral workers and form local pastoral teams in each of the communities. They didn't speak about "the pastoral work of accompaniment" so much as about a commitment to build "a church of the poor." It was another step forward, not only to accompany the people in their struggle for liberation, but to discover the specific contribution of Christians and of a church of the poor to that struggle.

The pastoral team tried to encourage a critical consciousness in the people—not simply a political awareness but a discovery of Christian values that could contribute to the struggle for liberation. They promoted the formation of Christian base communities and actions of solidarity, and challenged people to discover what it means to be a Christian in the concrete situation in which they were living. These efforts also encouraged people to be critical of mistakes as they occurred within the liberation struggle and to work for a political and negotiated solution to the conflict that would guarantee a just peace.

The pastoral team also tried to strengthen a sense of hope in the people so that they would not lose their faith or their commitment to justice in the face of the suffering they endured. It was essential to encourage their hope for the liberation of the Salvadoran people and to begin to build in their own communities the new society for which they hoped.

Like the parable in the Gospel, the fruits of this labor enriched the pastoral workers a hundredfold as well. In María's words:

> I have more faith now because of having lived with these campesino brothers and sisters and learned from their courage and their profound faith in God. I thought that I was going to evangelize them. Now, with much humility, I realize that it is the campesinos who have evangelized us.[5]

If it had not been for the profound faith of the Salvadoran people based on the witness of the martyrs and the generosity of so many who have been killed in the struggle for justice, the struggle for liberation would not have achieved what it has. What follows is one chapter in the story of the Christian base communities of northern Morazán and the faith and courage of the people there.

[16]

Death and Resurrection in Morazán

Holy Week, 1988 . . . Perquín, Morazán

Today I arrived in Morazán. We crossed the Torola River at 8:30 A.M. I had dreamed of this day for a long time, and as we crossed the river I felt as though something new awaited us. I thought of another river, the Sumpul, which also evokes memories of suffering, and like the Torola River marks the boundary of areas controlled by the FMLN. Holy Week had already begun, and I was looking forward to celebrating Easter with the Christian communities in northern Morazán. I was surprised to hear that 25,000 people still lived in such a conflictive area after nine years of war.

The land here is poor and dry; still, the people plant corn, beans, and sorghum. Before the war, hemp was produced here, but in the past few years the Salvadoran army has burned the fields. With last year's drought the people are even more impoverished. They live off what they produce each day. When we came to the first village, Las Tijeretas, the leaders of the community met with us to give us their testimony about the bombing that occurred here on March 19. One woman was killed in the bombing, and her brother was captured by the Salvadoran army. People in the villages surrounding the town of Torola are still terrified.

That afternoon I visited Daniel and his wife Zoila and their two daughters. They received me with the same generosity and joy as many campesino families I had known, despite their poverty. Daniel told me, "Yesterday soldiers were transported by helicopter to the town of Perquín," about a three-hour walk from here. "How often does the army pass through Torola?" I asked him. "Every fifteen days." Despite the war, Daniel and his family live in the same house they have always lived in. Their love for the land has given them strength to endure the hardships.

Tonight is Wednesday of Holy Week. In many parishes people would be going to confession. Here in Morazán the people live Christ's passion in their daily suffering and not only in the liturgy and readings for Holy Week. I thought especially of the theme of reconciliation as a question for the church: "What have we done to our brothers and sisters?" How long have the people of Morazán had to endure the cruelties of the war without the support of the institutional church? Why have the Christian communities and the priests and catechists who accompany them been rejected by the local bishop, simply because they carry out their pastoral work in areas controlled by the FMLN?

Holy Thursday: "The Passover of Our People Is Near!"

I spent the night in Torola, a town that was destroyed by the Salvadoran army in January 1985. Only about sixty people live here now, and another eight hundred people live in neighboring villages. We left before dawn for Perquín in order to avoid any risk of bombing. These mountains are beautiful despite the destruction and scorched earth caused by the rockets and bombs that have exploded here. The land itself seems to reflect the passion and suffering of the people who work it.

When we arrived in the town of Perquín three hours later, I went to meet the pastoral team. What a joy to see old friends again and to meet the people of this town! Some 2,500 people live in Perquín. We ate breakfast in the house of one of the catechists, while others prepared the celebration for Holy Thursday. Only two days before, the Salvadoran army had landed troops here in helicopters; they left the same day. People were determined to celebrate Holy Week, despite their anxiety about a possible troop landing.

When we reached the town plaza, a huge mural painted on the side of the church greeted us, picturing Archbishop Romero and the words from his last homily: "In the name of God, in the name of this suffering people whose cries reach up to heaven more tumultuously each day, I ask you, I beg you, I order you: Stop the repression!" Despite the landing of troops here on Tuesday, the mural was left intact.

Inside the church, people had decorated the aisles with cedar boughs; the statues of the *Virgin Dolorosa* and Jesus of Nazareth were also colorfully adorned. Despite the war, or perhaps because of it, people celebrate their faith with great devotion, with a mixture of popular religiosity and revolutionary commitment.

Father Rogelio Ponseele, a Flemish priest, celebrated the Mass. He first came to Morazán in December 1980, after the parish house where he lived in San Salvador was bombed by death squads. The principal theme of his homily today was service to the people:

> *Jesus washes the feet of his disciples. It's a surprising gesture, because this task was exclusively reserved for the household servants. In this simple and humble gesture, Jesus summarizes his life. He has not come to dominate or to command, but to serve others, to be the last one in our midst even to the extreme of generously offering his life for others, breaking his body and shedding his blood for our salvation.*
>
> *The God whom Jesus reveals is a God who is near, a God who is profoundly in solidarity with us, a God who is supremely concerned about our people, a God who gives us sufficient strength to resist the terror of the airplanes and the threat of the bombs. In these difficult moments in which we live, moments of anguish and terror, we need to feel close to God, and we need to feel God close to us.*

Father Rogelio concluded this part of the homily with these words from Archbishop Romero: "We must always feel that God is near, so we can live through these difficult moments with our heads held high."

What is surprising here is the joy of these people who have

suffered so much; their smiles and their hope in the midst of the war are truly amazing. On this solemn night of Passover, which recalls the exodus of the people of Israel enslaved in Egypt, and the Last Supper of Jesus, Rogelio also spoke of the Passover of the Salvadoran people:

> *Today we are living through a decisive moment. Our belts are fastened, our sandals are strapped to our feet, our walking sticks are in hand, and we eat in haste because it's time to leave, it's time to take a decisive step from slavery toward liberation. The moment of our Passover is near!*

Today, when many people feel the burden of nine years of war and ask, "How much longer?" these words may be shocking. But from the perspective of the poorest of the poor — of those who suffer most because of the war — and from the perspective of the exodus and the gospel, Father Rogelio's words inspire hope:

> *Now that our people celebrate their Passover, let us not remain by the wayside but walk with our people. Let us continue to serve one another, following Jesus' example, generously serving our family, our community, and our beloved and suffering people on their journey toward victory.*

At this point Rogelio knelt down and washed the feet of four men, four women, and four young people from the community.

We returned home by the light of a full moon. More than two hundred fifty people had participated in the celebration. I was filled with joy and gratitude for this night when I could draw near to this suffering people, so full of hope. I recalled these words of Archbishop Romero:

> *Many times I have been asked here in El Salvador: "What can we do? Is there no solution for the situation in El Salvador?" And full of hope and faith, not just a divine faith but a human faith, believing also in the people, I say: "Yes, there is a way out!"*

Good Friday: A Crucified People Speaks of Hope

Today is Good Friday. I learned something about the history of the town of Perquín and the Christian base communities here. The influence of the fundamentalist churches is greater in Perquín than in other towns. "When we first celebrated Mass here in 1982," Father Miguel Ventura told us, "people closed the doors of the church on us. Today these same people are catechists."

Later that morning we had a procession of the stations of the cross through the streets of Perquín. As is the custom in many parishes, each station of the cross reflected the reality of El Salvador today. As we climbed a hill overlooking the town and church below, we knelt down before the twelfth station, where Jesus dies on the cross:

They crucified Jesus then. Today Jesus is crucified in the suffering of our people. More than seventy thousand people have died in this massive crucifixion. Like Jesus, we must be faithful to God and be willing to give up our lives for the liberation of our people.

That afternoon we returned to the church for the adoration of the cross. Father Rogelio led the reflection:

We must unite the life of Jesus to his death; his death on the cross was a consequence of his life. Jesus was killed on the cross because of his preferential option for the poor. The death of Jesus on the cross has been prolonged throughout history. Jesus dies today in countless people who are humiliated, repressed, and massacred.

Today, as Salvadorans, we can say that Jesus bears the cross and is assassinated in our crucified people. For Christians, the cross is the way not the goal; it is not the end. The cross is the way we must go forward. But we know that the death of Jesus is not fatal; it is a victorious death, because beyond the cross is the resurrection. The cross is the way to abundant life.

These words, spoken in Morazán by one who has accompanied the people throughout these years of the war, are credible to people here. They speak to their suffering and to their hope. During the prayer of the faithful, three women prayed. One said, "I pray in these humble words that we may walk the same path Jesus walked, bearing the cross. We should always obey when our Lord calls us to be humble before our people." I thought of the words of the prophet Micah: *"What does the Lord ask of us but to practice justice, to love mercy, and to walk humbly with God" (6:8).*

Another woman followed: "I pray to the Lord for the victims of the war so that God will always console their families and give them strength; and for our brothers and sisters who are refugees in other countries so that God will give them strength." Finally, a third woman spoke: "I pray for all the Christian base communities in northern Morazán—in Perquín, Torola, Joateca, Jocoaitique, and in the mountain villages—asking the Lord to help us grow in love."

Following these prayers we blessed the cross and proceeded through the streets with the holy sepulcher. Once again the streets of Perquín were filled with people. Even the traditional songs took on new meaning: "For your precious blood" (and the blood of the 70,000 dead in El Salvador) . . . "For your affliction in the garden" (and the affliction of these communities in northern Morazán, abandoned by the institutional church) . . . "For your long agony" (and the agony of nine years of war) . . . "For the cruel lashes . . ."

I recalled a testimony Rogelio had read in the afternoon celebration:

> *On February 28 two young men, Félix González, nineteen years old, and Mario González, sixteen years old, were violently taken from their houses at night by the Salvadoran army and tortured. At 1 P.M. the next afternoon their fingers, ears, and noses were cut off, and finally their throats were slit. Sebastián Gutiérrez, twenty-five years old, is still disappeared. This occurred in the village of Tepemechín, near El Tablón and the town of Sociedad in Morazán.*

During the procession we climbed the hill once again, over-looking the town of Perquín. A bright moon shone over the mountains. When we returned to the church the mural of Arch-bishop Romero greeted us: "In the name of God . . . in the name of this suffering people . . . stop the repression!"

Later that evening, in the convent, we ate a supper prepared by the townspeople: mangoes, bananas, coffee, and bread. On this night when Jesus was crucified, we witness once again the generosity of this crucified people who have not lost their faith, their hope, their love, nor their capacity to celebrate.

Easter: Passing from Death to Life

This morning I went to visit Míriam, one of the catechists from Perquín and the president of the Congregation of Mothers. Rosa, another catechist from the town of Jocoaitique, was also there. She told us the story of the massacre in El Mozote that occurred in December 1981. Hundreds of campesinos were assassinated by the Atlacatl Battalion that day:

> We were living near El Mozote, in the village of La Joya, when the massacre took place. We hid with the children in the underbrush and barely escaped with our lives. For the next five years we lived with other families from La Joya in caves, constantly on the run from the army. Many times we were bombed. In September 1985, with the help of the International Red Cross, we decided to join others in repop-ulating the town of Jocoaitique which had been abandoned until then. Almost four hundred people live there now.

That afternoon we left for the town of Jocoaitique to celebrate the resurrection Mass. A mother from La Joya and her child accompanied us. As we walked she told us of the hardships she endured during the five years she hid in the mountains after the massacre in El Mozote. I was amazed at the hope that she com-municated after such an ordeal. Father Miguel commented later: "Only those who are willing to take up the cross can truly announce the resurrection."

We arrived in the town of Jocoaitique in the evening and went to visit Rosa and her husband Pedro. Chepito, a fourteen-year-old *compa* (FMLN combatant) and Rosa's son, was there. When the El Mozote massacre occurred in 1981, Chepito was seven years old. For years he lived with his family in the mountains, hiding from the army. Now he carries an M-16 rifle which was sent by the United States to the Salvadoran army and later recovered by the FMLN in combat. We joined Rosa and Pedro for supper, while others helped prepare the Easter celebration.

Father Miguel Ventura received people warmly as the celebration began:

I know that your community has journeyed in the wilderness for a long time, trying to serve God and to do God's will. Tonight we are going to celebrate this resurrection Mass to give us strength to continue our journey.

What impressed me most was the enthusiasm with which the young people sang the songs: "Death, where is death? Where is my death? Where is your victory?" Those who sang in the choir could not have been more than ten years old when their relatives in El Mozote and La Joya were killed in the massacre in December 1981. Tonight they sang with conviction and, it seemed to me, with the joy of those who have passed from death to life: "He is risen! He is risen! He is risen! Alleluia!"

What does the resurrection of Christ mean to people in a country at war? What does it mean that Christ overcame death, and why has Christ not overcome death in El Salvador? Why are cadavers of innocent people still thrown in the streets? Could it be that the force of the resurrected Christ is not present in El Salvador?

Once again, the question that Job asks, *"Why do the innocent and just suffer?"*, cries out in the poor of El Salvador who have suffered seventy thousand deaths during nine years of war.

What is happening in our country? Why have so many of your relatives preferred to risk their lives rather than to give up this struggle? How do we explain the fact that our country continues to produce countless dead? Could it be that Christ, who overcame death, is not present in El Salvador?

No, dear brothers and sisters, here in El Salvador the force of the resurrected Christ is present in all the men, women, and young people who are willing to give up their lives so that others may have life. This is the true force of Christ's resurrection, and for this reason we have hope.

After communion people sang again with enthusiasm:

> When the poor believe in the poor,
> we can sing of freedom!
> When the poor believe in the poor,
> we will live together as brothers and sisters.

Before returning to the town of Perquín later that night, we visited Chepito's grandfather to bring him communion. Five years hiding in the mountains had weakened his resistance considerably. Still, the force of love in this community is very great. Holy Week was over. The war continues to cause victims among the poor in El Salvador. But the strongest impression with which I am left this Holy Week is that the hope of this crucified people is even stronger than the death caused by the war. Here the poor announce the Good News of the resurrection and a day of freedom with justice in El Salvador.

[17]

Dreams and Visions

May 1988 . . . Estancia and Calavera, Morazán

Today was a day like any other in northern Morazán. The morning sun shone brightly as the campesinos walked to their fields to plant corn, the land reflecting their joy over the first spring rains. Only the wall of the church in the town of Perquín showed signs of sadness. Before, the figure of Archbishop Romero and the words of his last homily—"In the name of God, in the name of this suffering people . . . stop the repression!"—looked out over the plaza.

Today, however, the face and the words were stained with black paint, a sign of the recent military operation. Still, we were happy because we were setting out to visit Estancia and Calavera, two villages near the town of Cacaopera, south of the Torola River, nearly a ten-hour walk from the town of Perquín.

On the way we passed through solitary places like Arambala, a town totally destroyed and abandoned. Over the ruins of one of the houses I read these words: "El Salvador is our country." What irony! The only country left to the people is in ruins because of the war. We continued our journey until we came to the ruins of the village of El Mozote, where we stayed the night.

El Mozote! The very name evokes indignation and silence: indignation over the massacre by the Atlacatl Battalion of hundreds of campesinos, most of them women and children, on December 11–12, 1981; and silence before the immensity of such evil. The only sign of life was the bright green vegetation which

125

flourished in the ruins of the houses, as a light rain fell on the village.

I stood in silence for a moment over the ruins of the chapel. Above me, a hill known as *Cerro de la Cruz*, "the Hill of the Cross," looked over the abandoned village. On this hill dozens of young women and young girls were "crucified" as they were raped, first by the officers, then by the soldiers, and finally killed. Here in the chapel the men were killed. The older women and the children were killed in a house. Only the ruins of the houses and the sky above remain as witnesses.

Once again the question of Job returned to me: *"Why do the innocent and the just suffer?"* "Why is God silent?" But what is scandalous is not the "silence" of God but *our* silence before these atrocities. The cry of the victims of the El Mozote massacre and of the seventy thousand victims of the war continues to demand prophetic words from the church: "In the name of God, in the name of this suffering people . . . stop the repression!"

Signs of Life in the Midst of War

We arrived in the village of Calavera in the late afternoon and slept near the banks of the Torola River. The next day we crossed the river and visited the home of Alejandro, just before an afternoon rain shower. We were received with warmth and joy. As we settled in until the rain passed, I heard the story of these communities for the first time. Like the people who escaped the massacre in El Mozote and La Joya, the people of Estancia and Calavera had to wander for years in the hills, fleeing from the army.

Alejandro invited me to sit in a hammock and listen while he told me their story. These two communities — Calavera and Estancia — began their "exodus" on October 10, 1980, with the first major army invasion in Morazán. More than 100 families from Calavera and 150 families from Estancia fled from their homes, which were later burned, and took refuge in the hills where they began their life "in the wilderness."

They spent four years there, fleeing from the army and exposed to the elements. Finally, in 1985, a few brave families dared to return to Calavera and live in their houses. Since then, they have remained in the village, despite threats of capture, torture, and assassination. Two months ago Hilario Pérez, a thirty-eight-year-old catechist and health promoter, was captured by the army and disappeared.

Today, their suffering "in the wilderness" has borne fruit in the vitality of these two communities, in their community councils, in their schools and clinics, in small projects like a chicken cooperative and a sewing workshop. Their faith and their joy bear witness to their determination to live, despite the death and destruction that they have suffered during nine years of war.

Later that afternoon we went to another house to celebrate a liturgy of the Word with the community. More than a hundred people came and crowded into the room, while the catechists and musical group prepared the readings and the songs. Little by little more people arrived, their feet covered with mud from the rain and their bright smiles lighting up the dark room. Dozens of children crowded around a table that served as the altar as we prepared to celebrate the liturgy with the community. Father Miguel greeted the people:

> It's always a joy for us to visit you. I congratulate you, because in the midst of so many difficulties, and after so many years of war, you have demonstrated that your faith in the God of life is stronger than death. Today we celebrate the Visitation, the visit of Mary to Elizabeth, an encounter between two poor women, just like this gathering between two poor communities today. Who believed in that time that this poor woman would be the mother of our Savior? Who believed that from this poor and humble people salvation would come?

Luisa spoke next. She is a young catechist who spent four years hiding with her family in the hills before joining the FMLN. Now she has returned to give birth to a son. She read the first reading from the prophet Zephaniah:

> Shout for joy, O daughter of Zion!
> Rejoice, O people of Israel! . . .

> Yahweh, your God, is in your midst,
>   like a hero who brings salvation;
> Yahweh will jump for joy when you appear
>   to renew this love with you. (3:14–17)

I looked at the faces of the people gathered, and tried to imagine how they had passed four years "in the wilderness," living beneath the rains in ravines and caves, out of fear of the Salvadoran army. Who would believe that from this poor and humble people in El Salvador such hope would come, not only for their own country but for all the peoples of the world? God will not abandon the people of El Salvador, but bring about the liberation for which they yearn. Life, not death, will have the last word—a faithful remnant will remain:

> For I will leave a poor and humble people in
>   your midst,
> whose only refuge is the Lord. (3:12)

During the Eucharist a list of fifty-two names was read, all people in the community who have died during these years of war. The people of Estancia and Calavera have a tradition of recalling their martyrs in each liturgy of the Word.

After the liturgy the fiesta began, with humble offerings of food and music. Tonight there is joy in the village of Calavera, the joy of the poor who have heard a word of hope and committed themselves to share this good news with other poor communities, confident that *"God is in their midst"* in their efforts to bring peace and justice to El Salvador.

Of Dreams and Visions

During the next few days we met with the local pastoral teams in the villages of Estancia and Calavera. I spoke with Saúl and Isaías, who accompanied these two communities during the four years they were hiding in the hills. Saúl spoke first:

> The military offensive of October 10, 1980, lasted twenty-two days. That's when the people had to leave their homes

and fields in Estancia and take refuge in neighboring villages. The soldiers burned twenty-five houses. But we never lost our faith in a living God. We celebrated the liturgy of the Word in the ravines and caves; we went for days without eating. During those first years of the war, we suffered terribly; but God loves us and will be with us till the last moments of our lives.

Isaías followed with his story:

In 1985 we began to promote Christian base communities by means of small reflection groups. In 1986 the Congregation of Mothers was formed, not only to increase the participation of women in the liturgies but also to strengthen their resolve to denounce the repression and the military blockade of their communities. I remember the text of Matthew 25, the last judgment, where it says we must feed the hungry and visit the sick and those in prison. This text has encouraged many of our communities to continue working for justice and a negotiated solution to the war.

I asked Isaías what inspired him to keep his faith through all these years of suffering "in the wilderness," and he told me the following story:

In September 1980 my father was captured and turned over to the National Guard in Perquín. He was later assassinated in front of the town cemetery. His death did not discourage me so much as motivate me to work even harder. I remember that my father told me, one month before he was captured, that if the day came when he would suffer on account of my commitment to justice I should try to be careful but keep working, so that I would always be able to serve our people.

My father couldn't read or write, but he was a dedicated Christian and this helped me to carry on. The words of my father have served me well, encouraging me to live my life for the sake of others.

As we talked Saturnino arrived. He was from the village of Estancia, and had been captured and tortured twice this year — once in March and once in May. In the midst of greetings and embraces, I asked him if he would also share with me what gave him strength to resist during times of trial:

> *Despite everything they have done to me, I am ready to give my life for our people. I was brought up with the Bible and recall where it says:* "Blessed are you who are persecuted for my sake, for yours is the Kingdom of God," *and also,* "Those who lose their life for my sake will find it." *These words gave me strength.*

What impressed me most about Saturnino's testimony was the source of his faith:

> *I draw strength from the example of my children, who gave their lives for our people. Yes, there are moments of suffering when you can no longer resist, but the courage and the blood of my children give me strength, and I want to follow their example.*

After hearing these last two testimonies, I remained silent. I didn't know what to say. I simply shook hands with each of them and said, *"Gracias."* Later, as I thought about what Isaías and Saturnino had said, I recalled that it was the death of a father and the death of a son which motivated each one of them to keep his faith alive and to struggle for life — giving up their lives, if necessary, out of love for their people. At that moment I remembered the words of the prophet Joel that we had been reading these days in preparation for Pentecost:

> *I will send my Spirit over every living being.*
> *Your sons and daughters will speak on my*
> *   behalf,*
> *   the old will dream dreams*
> *   and the young will see visions.*
> *In those days, even the servant men and women*
> *   will receive my Spirit. (3:1)*

Salt of the Earth, Light of the World

The next evening we celebrated one last liturgy in the village of Calavera before our departure for Perquín. The Gospel reading illuminated the journey of the people who suffer the war each day: *"You are the salt of the earth . . . You are the light of the world"* (Matthew 5:13–15). Father Miguel offered these words of encouragement:

> Our country has been soaked in blood these past nine years of war. All of you have paid a terrible price. Despite your sufferings, you have given a testimony of your faith in a God of life. Today we celebrate our faith in this God of life who acts through the poor in history. You are the salt of the earth! You are the light of the world! No one has suffered more than you the effects of the war; and no one has the same experience of faith as you in the God of life. The Gospel today illuminates our history. We must be salt and light for our people to illuminate the way ahead.

People recalled their years "in the wilderness," when they had to flee to the hills to escape the repression. The act of remembering together strengthens the people and deepens their hope. After several people had shared their memories, Father Miguel asked:

> Whom did you meet in the wilderness, if not the God of life? The God who calls us to love one another as brothers and sisters. This God of the wilderness who hears the cry of your suffering and promises you liberation.

The words preceding the Eucharist invited the people to live together as brothers and sisters, and to work for an end to the war. Five children were baptized, another sign of life, and they were received into the community with a song symbolic of the Salvadoran people's journey:

> We are the seed of a new world,
> a witness of love,

of peace in the face of war,
of light among the shadows,
a pilgrim church on earth.

A New Pentecost in El Salvador

The following morning we left for Perquín, arriving in the village of El Mozote in the afternoon. We walked over the solitary path which cuts through the center of the village, surrounded by the tall grass covering the ruins of the houses. Here life flourished before it was extinguished forever in the massacre of December 1981.

As we walked in silence, I recalled the testimony of life we had witnessed in the villages of Estancia and Calavera, two communities among dozens that have passed through the Calvary of these nine years of war. Unlike El Mozote, their story did not end in crucifixion. They encountered the God of Moses in the wilderness, who heard their cry and promised them liberation. They encountered the God of Job, who spoke to them out of the whirlwind of the bombs and bullets. They met the God of Jesus, who offered them life in abundance.

As we walked in silence, these words of Job came to my mind: *"I know that my Redeemer lives, and will speak the last word over the earth" (19:25).* These communities in northern Morazán, by their generosity and their faith, bear witness to the God of life who is stronger than the "gods" and idols of war, death, and oppression. They confirm once more the faith of the early Christian communities: "The blood of the martyrs is the seed of new Christians."

The words of Archbishop Romero, although stained by the Salvadoran army on the wall of the church of Perquín, are very much alive in the Christian base communities of northern Morazán: "Over these ruins the glory of God—which is the poor who live—will shine!" The vitality of the poor is one more confirmation that the day of Pentecost draws near in El Salvador, when the vision of justice and peace will flourish and the dream of freedom will become a reality:

Then I will send my Spirit over every living
      being.
Your sons and daughters will speak on my
      behalf,
  the old will dream dreams
  and the young will see visions. (Joel 3:1)

[18]

One Day in the War

September 1988 . . . A Letter to Friends

I never expected to write this letter. In fact, I had just sent each of you stories of hope from these communities in northern Morazán. We have been blessed this year by the opportunity to work with the people here on a daily basis. It's only very recently that the presence of the Salvadoran army has made our pastoral accompaniment impossible. On one occasion we were actually under direct fire when Salvadoran troops were air-lifted into our area and we found ourselves in the midst of a battle.

These circumstances were exceptional, but they provided us with an experience of war in all its brutality. We were also given a privileged glimpse of one day in the war and the suffering it causes. This raises the question of our responsibility as North Americans for U.S. policy in Central America.

We had returned to the villages of Estancia and Calavera in August to continue our pastoral work of accompaniment, and were preparing to go back to the town of Perquín. It was a bright September day and we had gone with Isaías to visit Marta, the widow of Hilario who had been killed by the Salvadoran army. Hilario had been a catechist and a health promoter before he was killed by the army last March.

There had been rumors of an impending attack by the FMLN on a military barracks nearby, and the threat of reprisals by the army. In the past, that would have been sufficient reason for people to flee to the hills to escape the repression. Now they had won a certain degree of "recognition" of their civilian status by the army; but the leaders of the community — including teachers, health promoters, and catechists — continued to be targeted, captured, tortured, and assassinated. That's what had happened to Hilario.

For that reason we had spent our nights with Pedro and María across the river, as a precautionary measure. So we retired early for the night, wondering what was going to happen. Several times during the night I woke up and looked at my watch before falling asleep again. At 1 A.M. we heard the first explosions.

"What's that?" I asked Isaías. "It sounds like it's coming from the other side of the Torola River." By now everybody had gotten up to see what was happening. "The FMLN must have attacked the army barracks in El Aguacate," Isaías added, "in the town of Corinto." We watched the flares dropped by the planes light up the sky and the hills below. It sounded like New Year's Eve. The explosions continued for half an hour; shots and bursts of machine-gun fire, however, lasted until dawn.

A little before dawn Isaías woke us. "Let's go," he said. "There may be reprisals in the morning. The army may bomb or strafe the banks of the river, and we are too close for safety." So we left Pedro and Maria's house and took refuge farther into the hills. At 6 A.M. the first helicopters came and began to strafe the banks of the Torola River and the surrounding area. From 6 A.M. until 9 A.M. the hills resounded with the sound of rockets and machine-gun fire. The Salvadoran army had begun its counterattack, and an FMLN patrol had been assigned to escort us out of the area of the fighting.

It all happened so quickly. Suddenly two helicopters hovered directly over the trees that sheltered us. I lay on the ground behind a rock, and each time the helicopter passed I pressed myself against the hard surface. The words of the psalmist flashed through my mind: *"The Lord is my rock and my salvation."* Then someone called out, "Let's go!" In the midst of the strafing by the helicopters we retreated under the cover of the trees, at moments sprinting and at moments stretched out flat on the ground.

We continued our retreat until we reached a safe place high up in the mountains above the Torola River where we rested for the remainder of the day. Late that afternoon we heard the sound of helicopters again, approaching our area, and took cover in a small gorge through which a small creek flowed. But since we were not familiar with the area, instead of going upstream to a place that offered some protection, we went downstream to the very spot where the helicopters had begun to strafe the gorge with bursts of machine-gun fire. The only thing we could do was duck down and crouch against the embankment as the bullets whirred through the trees above us, so close that the leaves fell on top of us. I wept.

"Let's go!" someone shouted, and we fled farther upstream, at moments wading through the water and at moments submerged in it, until we reached a small crevice in the rocks behind which we could duck. A waterfall drowned out the sound of the helicopter fire overhead. As evening began to enfold us in darkness, the helicopters departed. Once again we had found refuge, a safe haven where we could rest for the night.

I looked out over the Torola River valley below and was moved by the beauty of the surrounding mountains. We had not eaten all day, our clothes were soaking wet, but I fell asleep with a sense of gratitude for simply being alive. And so the first day passed. I thought to myself, "the worst is over."

Pray for Us Now and at the Hour of Our Death

We got up early the next morning and continued our journey until we reached Lemon Creek. I stooped down to drink from the refreshing waters and sat down beside a tree to rest. I remember that Corina and Mariyita sat nearby: Corina was a radio operator for the FMLN, and Mariyita made uniforms for them. Neither could have been much older than sixteen. Corina was very shy, or *"humilde,"* as the people here say.

Mariyita was more serious, although I once saw her smile. They had just joined the FMLN a few months before.

We had not been there long when we heard the sound of helicopters and the AC-47 gunship firing in the distance. A moment passed, and the firing came closer until suddenly the helicopters were directly overhead.

"Let's go!" someone cried out. "They're going to land

troops!" We fled down a deep gorge under cover of the trees which grew on either side of Lemon Creek. The planes and helicopters made passes overhead, firing bullets and rockets in our direction and dropping bombs. "We've been spotted!"

What followed is difficult to describe. We fled downstream, expecting the troops to land upstream. Whenever the helicopters passed directly overhead we lay flat on the ground beside the stream, desperately looking for protection behind the rocks; as soon as the helicopter had passed we advanced, running for our lives.

Once I looked across the stream to a *compa* who signaled to me with his hands, "Take cover!" I looked behind me at three people who had taken refuge behind a rock and called out: "Is there any room?" "No!" they called back. At that moment the A-37 fighter-bomber passed overhead and dropped a bomb a short distance ahead of us. We could not advance any farther. I felt resigned to my fate, *"conforme"* as the people here say. At moments I felt anger and at moments amazement. Despite such a concentration of fire-power from helicopters and planes we were still alive!

Suddenly I found myself alone, crouched behind a large rock to protect myself from the strafing of the helicopter, waiting for the right moment to cross to the other side of the creek. I looked behind me and saw no one. I didn't know what to do: whether to risk crossing the open creek and being strafed by the helicopter, or to retreat to see what had happened to the others.

Then I saw a familiar face, a catechist I had known from the Christian base communities before she had joined the FMLN. "Carmen!" I called out. The helicopter made another pass overhead, strafing the water below. "Let's go!" she cried, and we raced across the shallow water to the other side of the creek. We continued to make our way downstream under cover of the trees.

Suddenly we came out into the light of day. We had reached the very spot where the bomb had fallen only minutes before. The ground was in complete disarray, the tree limbs and branches were twisted and broken, the earth was covered with dust and leaves, and a strong odor like burning leaves permeated the air. The bomb crater was not very deep, but the destruction extended over a large area. Some bombs, we had been told, are attached to iron rods in such a way that they explode above ground and cause widespread destruction. We hurried to seek cover further downstream.

At last we reached a small ravine which led over dry rocks to a hill directly above us. I looked up and watched a helicopter circling overhead. For an instant I was paralyzed, certain that the helicopter could see every move I made. I could not bring myself to take another step forward and instead crouched on the dry rocks below. I felt like a wounded animal, waiting for the hunters to close in for the kill.

"Let's go!" Carmen called out. She waited to make sure I was coming. Soon we caught up with the others and stopped to rest. Soon we caught up with two *compas* who were debating whether the area we were about to enter was mined or not. But we couldn't go back; we had no choice but to press forward. We climbed out of the gorge to a plain above and hid ourselves in the thick vegetation for the rest of the day.

What more can I say? We listened to the rockets and the machine-gun fire until dusk. The army landed troops downstream, in the direction we were first headed, and not upstream as we had thought. Corina and Mariyita, we learned later, had continued downstream where they were ambushed by the soldiers. There had been an exchange of fire for several minutes while the planes concentrated their fire-power even more over the area where the fighting had taken place. About 1 P.M. the troops were finally air-lifted out of the area by nine helicopters.

When the last three helicopters passed directly overhead, I could see the faces of the soldiers. Most of them were young, with clean-shaven heads and camouflage uniforms. "If they fire in our direction," Carmen told me, "don't move." Suddenly shots passed over us in all directions. I simply closed my eyes and prayed in silence. "They're gone!" she called out jubilantly.

The last time I saw Corina she was sitting beside a tree with Mariyita holding an M-16 rifle that had been recovered in combat from the army. I remember reading a name etched on the frame of the gun: "Manuel Contreras." Could it be that he died in the attack on the military barracks? I also remember seeing these words on the frame of the gun: "Property of the U.S. government."

Later Carmen told me they had found Corina and Mariyita lying dead in the creek. Corina had been shot once in the head; Mariyita had been shot three times in the chest. Mariyita's body had been mined by the army with a booby-trap. Any attempt to move her body would trigger the mine to explode and cause others to die—a cruel trick to inflict more casualties.

I don't know what happened to Corina's M-16. What I do know is that it came from the United States, was paid for with U.S. tax dollars and passed from the hands of somebody like Manuel to the hands of Corina. One was forcibly recruited by the Salvadoran army; the other, the daughter of an FMLN *compañero,* volunteered to be a radio operator for the FMLN. Enemies in time of war, they were the son and daughter of the same people. Now both of them are dead.

The Poor Await a Prophetic Word

So the war goes on, costing seventy thousand lives, while U.S. "aid" to El Salvador has surpassed $4 billion in nine years. Just as the "Vietnamization" of the war in Southeast Asia placed a heavier toll on the Vietnamese to bear the cost of the war, so U.S. backing for the war in El Salvador has placed a heavier burden on the people of El Salvador: "The gringos provide the dollars, but the Salvadorans provide the dead."

What conclusion can we give to all this? "We must end the war before the war ends us," one of the Salvadoran bishops said not too long ago. If the fighting were to end tomorrow, the war would be far from over. The war is not only bullets and bombs; it has roots and causes. The poor in El Salvador, those who suffer the burden of this war each day, those who lack work and land, those who don't have enough food to eat or a place to live, those who organize to demand their rights—especially the right to live— those who suffer the repression: they are the ones "who provide the dead."

Even if the bullets and bombs were to be silenced, if there is no work, land, bread, shelter, and freedom for the poor who are the majority of the people in El Salvador, the silent war against the poor will go on as it has for generations to come.

The poor wait to hear a prophetic word from us—from the church and from people in solidarity alike. They wait to hear a voice that truly denounces injustice and defends the right of the poor to determine their own destiny. They wait to hear a voice resound: "In the name of God, in the name of this suffering people . . . stop the repression!"

They want to hear a voice cry out: "No! Not one dollar more for the war!" spoken with the same conviction as the early Christians who cried out to Caesar: "No! Not one grain of incense on the altar of the idols!" But it must be a "No!" spoken with conviction, with a willingness to radically change the way the First World condemns the poor of the First and Third Worlds to an early death by hunger or by war. A "No!" that expresses a willingness to risk our lives in defense of the poor and their struggle for liberation, justice, and peace.

The war continues in El Salvador: seven FMLN combatants were killed in the attack on the Salvadoran military barracks in El Aguacate, while unconfirmed reports from the army hospital in the town of San Francisco Gotera say that fifteen soldiers died in the attack, another twenty are in critical condition, and eight are said to be in a state of shock.

On September 22 and 23, as a response to the FMLN attack on the military barracks, the Salvadoran army indiscriminately bombed an area that includes the villages of Calavera and Estancia. They fired more than one hundred rockets, dropped five bombs, and strafed the entire area from 10 A.M. until 6 P.M. José Santos Pérez, a young catechist, was killed in this bombing as he returned from a literacy course offered by the parish in the town of Cacaopera. Four days later the Salvadoran army pulled two hundred fifty young men off buses and forcibly recruited them into the army to recoup the losses they had suffered as a result of the attack on their barracks.

Despite all that has happened, the people have hope! This hope is what enables us to go on in our pastoral work of accompaniment in the midst of so many difficulties and personal limitations. Because we are witnesses to the presence of a liberating God who hears the cry of the poor in El Salvador, who knows their suffering and accompanies them in their struggle for liberation, we share in their hope, too. We are witnesses to a God of life whose "glory" is, in the words of the martyred Archbishop Romero, "that the poor live."

This presence of a liberating God in the midst of war and in the midst of a revolutionary struggle; this presence of a God of life in the midst of death reveals not only a new face of God but a new face of the poor in El Salvador, a people who have become aware of their right to determine their own destiny, and their responsibility to liberate their people.

It is the poor in El Salvador who take the initiative to organize and to begin to live a new way of life in community. The poor are the ones who with so much sacrifice and generosity are able to offer their lives for others. The poor are the ones who look toward the future with an invincible hope. For all these reasons surely this is a critical time in Central America, a time of *kairos*, a moment of grace in which the old order is passing away and the new order is breaking into the present. It is the hour of the poor.

[19]

Where Is the Fiesta Going To Be?

November 1988 . . . Torola, Morazán

It is November now, All Saints' Day. Perhaps there is no place more appropriate than El Salvador to celebrate this day when we commemorate the saints and martyrs of the church. El Salvador has its share of saints and martyrs, beginning with Archbishop Romero and extending to the seventy thousand people who have been killed during the past nine years of the war.

Today we had the privilege to share this day with the people of Torola, a town in northern Morazán. Torola was the cradle of the Christian base communities in Morazán, and the revolution has roots here as well. The first Christian base communities were formed in Torola in 1973–1975, about the time the revolution first took root in Morazán. From this seed a new experience was born, of a church of the poor that accompanies the liberation struggle of the people.

Each time we walk the three hours from the town of Perquín to Torola, I meditate on the natural beauty of these hills, the destruction caused by the war, and the suffering of the people. Like the victim in the parable of the Good Samaritan who lies wounded by the roadside, the people of Torola have been wounded by poverty and repression.

As we walked, Evelyn, a young catechist who accompanied us, began to tell me about the beginnings of the Christian base communities in northern Morazán:

The church of the poor began in small reflection groups in Morazán. If we look back to the 1970s we can see how that seed has been growing. We met to reflect on the Word of God and to see what God was saying to us. In our communities nobody had access to education or health care; there was no way to even subsist.

The Bible told us that women and men are made in the image and likeness of God, but we saw that this image had been obscured by hunger and illiteracy and trampled by the military. The Bible told us that the situation of poverty in which we lived was not the will of God, but the fault of a few people who hoarded the wealth of the country and left the majority of us to starve.

As our communities developed, and our awareness grew, we experienced new life. We began to work together, to farm together, to undertake community projects together, to care for our sick together. We discovered that real change was possible and that we were capable of transforming our lives. We saw the fruits of our collective efforts. We began to take more seriously our Christian vocation and get involved in politics. That's how the base communities became involved in the struggle for liberation.

After the war began, we formed a pastoral team in Morazán. People needed to feel that they weren't alone, that the church was present to them at this painful time, helping to explain what was happening in our country and offering hope. It was the women, not the men, who took the lead. The men, because they had been persecuted, were afraid to get involved. But once the women got organized, their actions spoke to the men and inspired them, too.

We formed the Congregation of Christian Mothers and began to start schools, organize health clinics, and form baking and sewing cooperatives. We began to confront the military and demand our rights, forcing the army to allow food and medicines to be delivered to the communities in northern Morazán. As Christians, we have a responsibility to be involved in the struggles of our people. In this way we are helping to build the Kingdom of God.

When we reached the town, several people came out to greet us. I stood for a moment and watched the children playing in the plaza. What a contrast to the destruction of the war! All around us the houses were in ruin. These children, however, were signs of life in the midst of the destruction caused by the war.

As I looked around the plaza, I was struck by the silhouette of a malnourished child painted on many of the walls of the houses in town. Beneath the picture these words were inscribed: "For our barefoot children without bread, we vow to win—FMLN!" To understand the roots of the revolution in El Salvador it is enough to meditate on these children. Almost every one is barefoot and malnourished, their bellies extended from parasites.

But besides poverty, the children of Torola have also suffered the war. Just a few weeks ago, on October 17, the town was bombed. A helicopter fired a dozen rockets at a group of women and children as they gathered in the church to celebrate the feast day of San Lucas. One house was destroyed, and the church and the town hall were damaged. An A-37 fighter-bomber also dropped four five-hundred-pound bombs on neighboring villages.

We listened to these testimonies as we prepared to celebrate the All Saints' Day Mass. Abdomilia, a white-haired grandmother, told us how she barely survived the rocket attack. The kitchen where she had been working was completely destroyed by a rocket. Two women who had been baking bread there were gravely injured. A third woman, who suffered from epilepsy, was also injured.

When the Poor Believe in the Poor

The children also had their story to tell. They had taken refuge inside the church, beneath the statue of Santiago, the town's patron saint, barely escaping a rocket that struck the front of the church. Ironically, the rocket hit the very spot where these words had been scrawled on the wall of the church: "The people of Torola fled to the cities out of fear of the armed forces who fight courageously against poor and unarmed people."

What impressed me most, however, besides the poverty of the

children and the destruction caused by the bombing, was the courage and hope of the people. They are truly the poor of Yahweh. They are afraid, naturally; but what is most striking is their faith in a God of life who has liberated them from death. What stands out is their hope. The people wanted to celebrate their saints and remember their dead; and they have not fled to other more peaceful areas because they want to live in their home town of Torola and work the land.

Before the Mass began, the children asked, "Where is the fiesta going to be?" Neither poverty, nor the bombings, nor fear, nor the war, nor death have the last word, but rather their faith in a God of life, a God who celebrates life, a God of the poor, a liberating God who is victorious. The local music group began to play the songs of the saints and martyrs of El Salvador, beginning with Archbishop Romero, as the Mass concluded. Then squash and coffee were shared by everyone present. The children had their fiesta!

These events are little noticed in El Salvador because it is not easy to reach the conflictive areas. It is difficult to draw near to the poor who live on the margin of society and suffer poverty and repression. The poor have discovered something greater than poverty, war, or death in El Salvador. They have discovered their own dignity, and that when they believe in each other and participate in the struggle of their people for liberation, they have hope.

Today there is a crisis in El Salvador. It is a decisive hour, a day of judgment, when the wealthy and powerful sectors of El Salvador, and the government of the United States, will be judged by the Lord of history for bringing death and destruction upon the poor. It is also a time of grace, a moment of *kairos*, when the poor will be uplifted and justice shall be fulfilled.

As we approach the liturgical season of Advent, we discover signs of hope in the struggle for life in El Salvador. Only from the place of a crucified people is it possible to announce resurrection; only from the world of the poor is it possible to struggle for the liberation of the Salvadoran people. It is the poor of Yahweh who, like Mary in her Magnificat, announce the coming of Christ into the world of the poor as a poor and persecuted child:

> *My entire being celebrates*
>   *the greatness of the Lord . . .*
> *Who pulled the powerful down from their*
>   *thrones,*
>   *and put the humble in their place;*
> *filling the hungry with every good thing,*
>   *and sending the rich away empty.*
>   *(Luke 1:46–53)*

A decisive moment draws near as the poor prepare a path of justice and liberation in El Salvador. And we, like the children, ask, "Where will the fiesta be in El Salvador?"

Christ Is Born in Jocoaitique!

We left Torola early the next morning and returned to Perquín. From there we continued our journey until we reached the town of Jocoaitique. I had not visited Jocoaitique since Easter, eight months before. I had always been impressed by the people here, because I knew that they had escaped the massacre of hundreds of campesinos in the villages of El Mozote and La Joya in December 1981.

As we walked along the road beneath the afternoon sun, Pedro, one of the catechists from Jocoaitique, told us, "We must keep some distance from each other, in case the planes come to bomb." He also informed us that a commando unit of the Salvadoran army was operating in the region. The threat of an attack, however, did not seem to discourage Pedro's joyful spirit. His hope is as strong as ever, stronger even than his fear of death.

I thought of this hope in the context of the Advent season. Will a Savior be born in this martyred land of El Salvador? In the tradition of the *posadas*, José and María continue their pilgrimage in the Salvadoran people as they look for a place where their poor and persecuted children may be born. If peace ever comes to El Salvador, it will be these children who enjoy its fruits.

I thought of the people of Jocoaitique who have suffered this past month from the army repression. Twenty-five people were captured in November, including catechists, women from the

Congregation of Mothers, members of the Christian base communities, young people, and even a fifteen-month-old child. The accusation is always the same—"collaborating with the guerrillas."

We arrived in Jocoaitique in the late afternoon; the *posadas* were about to begin. We went directly to Pedro and Rosa's house. Like Pedro, Rosa is an active member of the Christian base communities; she is also the local president of the Congregation of Mothers.

Rosa had just been released from jail after eight days of interrogation by the army in the town of San Francisco Gotera. Her crime? "Collaborating with the guerrilla priests in Morazán."

"Is it a crime to go to mass?" Rosa asked her interrogators. "No, but these priests are guerrillas," her captors told her.

"I don't know about that," Rosa responded, "but I do know that they celebrate mass."

"Yes, but we know they encouraged you to denounce the army before the human rights commission," they replied.

"That's true, but you would have done the same if the bombs had fallen on your house."

"Never mind, we know that you're one of the leaders of the Oscar Romero Congregation of Mothers," they told her.

"All I can say is that I am a mother because I have ten children, and that Archbishop Romero was a prophet who was assassinated because he spoke the truth. That much I do know."

After her interrogation Rosa was taken to a cell to sleep on the cold floor without any blanket to cover her. Eight days later she was taken from the jail cell to the police headquarters and finally released. Rosa immediately went to San Salvador to denounce her capture and the capture of her husband, Pedro, to the human rights commission. Then she returned to Jocoaitique to encourage people to participate in the march for peace on November 21 in front of the cathedral in the city of San Miguel.

This story could have appeared in the Acts of the Apostles. What was said of the apostles Peter and John when they were released from jail could be said of Rosa: *"Once they were free they continued to preach the Word of God" (Acts 4:23)*. As she told us her story, Rosa served us a delicious supper of tamales made from the newly harvested corn. It was a sign of the joy we felt to be together again.

Tonight marks the beginning of Advent. The coming of Christ in history once again draws near and calls us to conversion. As we sat with Rosa and Pedro after supper, Santos, another community member who had been captured, recalled how the people of La Joya had lived for years in mountains, caves, and ravines, hiding from the Salvadoran army. Many children were born in these circumstances, in conditions similar to the ones in which Jesus was born.

Today we witnessed another sign of hope in the story of this martyred community of Jocoaitique. Once again the community is in danger, on account of these captures and threats by the army; and one of the catechists is still in jail. But their hope is greater than their fears. Instead of going to console the people of Jocoaitique, we were consoled by them.

Later that night, as we returned to the town of Perquín beneath a beautiful full moon in northern Morazán, I recalled a few lines of the song we had sung in Pedro and Rosa's home:

> *They come and go to Bethlehem*
> *along paths of joy,*
> *And Christ is born in all of those*
> *who offer their lives for others;*
> *They come and go to Bethlehem*
> *along paths of justice,*
> *And in Bethlehem are born*
> *those who learn to struggle.*

[20]

An Advent Meditation

December 1988 . . . *El Mozote, Morazán*

Once again the Advent season awakens our deepest longings and most fervent hopes, like a seed buried in the winter darkness, a light that shines in the distance, or the eagerly awaited return of a loved one. Here in Central America, where people have lived for generations in poverty and more than a decade in the midst of war, signs of hope never cease to amaze us with a surprising and subversive appearance that is truly gospel — and in the most unlikely places! Those who have only heard bad news and suffered even worse realities have suddenly been thrust upon the center stage of history and into the heart of the Advent mystery: Christ is born among the poor!

In countless manifestations this liberating presence of God in history has surprised us, just as Jesus' presence in Galilee surprised the people of his day:

> *Tell John what you have seen and heard; the blind see, the lame walk, the deaf hear, the dead are resurrected, and Good News is announced to the poor. (Luke 7:22)*

And in El Salvador the victims of the earthquake rebuild their houses, the refugees return to plant their fields, and the poor organize to defend their rights in a litany of popular organizations that recalls the bitter fruit of nine years of war: seventy thousand dead. The displaced, the unemployed, the marginalized, the political prisoners, the families of the disappeared, and the returning

149

refugees have joined together to struggle for a truly democratic and just society.

How distant at times these prophetic words from Isaiah seem from this Central American soil:

> They shall beat their swords into plowshares,
>   and their spears into pruning hooks;
> Nation shall not lift up sword against nation,
>   nor shall they train for war anymore.
> (Isaiah 2:4)

This week's Advent readings are a prophetic judgment on the state of affairs in our world at the close of a century that has witnessed more killing than any other. The litany of nations at war in the past decade alone is dramatic, and at the root of nearly every conflict is a life-and-death struggle of the poor for justice.

A few weeks ago I visited a village that has since become a symbol of the depths of cruelty of the war in El Salvador: El Mozote. In December 1981 this village ceased to exist after the Salvadoran army massacred hundreds of men, women, and children in their war of counterinsurgency against the poor. As I stood for a moment over the ruins of the chapel in El Mozote, the surrounding silence seemed to echo the age-old cry of indignation: *"Why do the poor and the just suffer?"* It is a question that more and more, like Job, we have made our own.

This week's Advent readings are a call to conversion. It is a time of crisis, a time of judgment when *"the entire universe will be moved and the Lord will come with power and glory."* A time of *kairos*, as Mary reminds us in the Magnificat, when the Lord will look with favor upon the poor of the earth and *"cast the powerful down from their thrones, while the rich are sent away empty-handed" (Luke 1:52).*

Before such a dramatic spectacle, Advent reminds us that Christ is born in the most humble of places and circumstances, in the heart of a poor family. *"Who is the King of Glory?"* the psalmist asks. A poor child, born in a stable or in a ravine, in search of refuge from the principalities and powers of the day: *"This is the King of Glory."* And the glory of God, Archbishop Romero reminds us, "is the poor who live!"

Torola, Morazán . . . Prepare the Way of the Poor

Not far from the village of El Mozote is another symbol of the destruction caused by the war: the town of Torola. This is where the first Christian base communities in Morazán were formed in the 1970s until the repression against the organized poor reached such unprecedented levels that the communities were forced into exile. Most of the inhabitants of these villages fled to the refugee camp in Colomoncagua, Honduras after their homes were burned and their relatives killed by the Salvadoran army in October 1980. Since then, several families have returned, and more than a thousand people still live in the surrounding villages.

I want to tell you about María, a barefoot, seven-year-old girl in tattered clothes with a contagious smile. María lives in Torola with her mother and six brothers and sisters. She brings us joy and lifts our spirits every time we visit this town, and the ruined and abandoned houses weigh heavily upon our thoughts. María has a shadow that follows her wherever she goes, painted on many of the walls in the town. It is the silhouette of a child painted in black, with an extended belly, a sign of malnutrition. Beneath the picture the following words are written: "For our barefoot children without bread, we vow to win! — FMLN." It is a reminder both of the roots of this conflict as well as one of the goals of the revolution: to end the hunger of these children.

According to UNICEF four hundred children die every week in El Salvador due to malnutrition — twenty thousand children each year. The mystery of this dramatic struggle for life and death in places like El Salvador is that, after nine years of war, the people have hope! In the past two years the people of Torola have organized themselves to meet the needs of their community, forming a cooperative to grow vegetables and to raise chickens. Beside the stark reality of hunger and malnutrition, the efforts of the community to meet the basic needs of the people is a light of hope.

What happens in Torola happens every day in thousands of communities throughout the world, where a life-and-death struggle of the poor, especially of the children, takes place. In *one day*, the nations of the world spend $3 billion on weapons of war

($1 trillion each year), while forty thousand children die of malnutrition (16 million children each year). The cry of the poor is a cry in the wilderness that shakes the very foundation of our faith as Christians and challenges us to respond. Before the mystery of the birth of Christ in our lives, the death of children before their time is a scandal.

This week's Advent readings remind us that we must prepare a way of righteousness in the wilderness of injustice before Christ can be born in the world today. We must make room for the Lord of history through our actions of solidarity with the poor. When justice rules in the world, *"every valley shall be lifted up, and the hills shall be brought low"* (Isaiah 40:4). Then *"the glory of the Lord shall be revealed"* in the poor who live, and a seven-year-old child named María will not die of malnutrition but live!

Calavera, Morazán . . . "I Will Do Something New"

Farther to the south, on the banks of the Torola River, lies the village of Calavera near the town of Cacaopera. A few months ago we celebrated the liturgy of the Word there. Gathered in an adobe house around the light of a kerosene lantern, I heard for the first time the story of this poor community, with its indigenous roots, the home of one of El Salvador's martyred priests, Octavio Ortiz.

This week's Advent readings focus on the joy that fills our hearts and is symbolized in the light of the rose-colored candle, a joy that is the heart of Advent:

> *Shout for joy, O daughter of Zion!*
> *Rejoice, O people of Israel! . . .*
> *Yahweh, your God, is in your midst.*
> *(Zephaniah 3:14–17)*

The joy of Advent is the presence of Christ in the world, a light that illumines the darkness of war and hunger and promises redemption with concrete signs of hope: the return of the refugees, the birth of a child in a ravine, and poor communities that organize so that their children may live.

In the face of so much war and injustice, what can we do? The challenge in the Gospel is as simple as it is direct: *"Whoever has two coats, give one to someone who has none. Whoever has food, feed the hungry" (Luke 3:11).* Justice is not only a divine mandate, it is a human possibility. The foreign debt of the Latin American nations equals the U.S. military budget for one year. In ten years these same nations pay in interest alone an amount equal to the principal of the debt. Why not cancel the debt altogether and convert military spending into resources for food, shelter, health care and education?

Every child born in Latin America is born with a $1,000 debt to the banks and nations of the developed world. Every year in Central America one hundred thousand children die of malnutrition. It is children like María and villages like Calavera who bear the burden of a debt they never contracted, from which they received no benefits, and which they can never pay.

Every hungry child in the world is a judgment on the rich nations. Already *"the axe is laid to the roots"* of injustice, whose bitter fruit is war and injustice throughout the world. It is a time of *kairos* in Central America, when the Lord looks with favor upon the poor:

> *Don't look back to times of the past;*
> *I am going to do something new.*
> *Don't you see it already happening in your*
> *midst? (Isaiah 43:18)*

El Carrizal, Morazán . . . "How Beautiful on the Mountains"

We celebrated the last week of Advent in the mountain village of El Carrizal, near the Honduran border. Marta lives there in a one-room wooden house. A tiny room serves as a kitchen, living room, dining room, and bedroom for her sister, brother, three children, and grandchild. Every time I pass her home I see her making the day's tortillas over a hot fire, while Norma, her ten-year-old daughter, sits in the doorway.

Norma is an exceptional child; she is disabled. Her head is the

size of an adult's, her fragile body smaller than her six-year-old
brother's, and her legs are severely crippled. Still, she manages
to walk to school each day, study her lessons diligently, and help
her mother with the household chores, gathering firewood and
carrying water.

These mountain communities are extremely impoverished.
There is a simplicity in the land and a strength in the people that
remind me of Appalachia. After a three-year drought the food
situation is critical. The military blockade of northern Morazán
prevents food in any quantity from entering or lumber from being
sold to earn a few extra *colones* to buy beans and corn. In June
1985 the entire village of El Carrizal was forcibly relocated by the
Salvadoran army as part of their effort to depopulate the region;
months later, however, the people returned.

Last June the people of El Carrizal celebrated the second anniversary of the Congregation of Mothers. Hundreds of people from
the surrounding mountain communities came to celebrate this
festivity, presenting testimonies and skits of the achievements of
the community during the past two years. One skit enacted the
story of how the mothers organized to prepare milk and bread
twice a week for the children in the community. Another skit
dramatized the capture of a member of the community council
by the army, and his subsequent release after the mothers pur-
sued the soldiers and demanded his release.

It was a day of celebration, an encounter between poor communities. Like Mary's visit to her cousin Elizabeth in the Gospel
for this fourth week of Advent, the solidarity of the poor generates
new life. This week's readings also remind us that the Lord works
in humble ways and with humble people:

> But you, Belen Efrata, although you are the smallest of all
> the peoples of Judah, you will provide me with the one
> who will govern Israel. (Micah 5:1)

The Lord of history has chosen the poor and humble of this
earth to judge the rich and proud; people like Marta, Luisa, and
María. And the King of Glory has chosen tiny nations like El
Salvador to judge the rich and powerful nations like our own.

Advent reminds us that the poor of the earth are the ones

favored by the Good News of Christmas. God has chosen sides with the poor and the humble of the earth, with the Marías and the Josés, and sojourns with the poor through history, preparing the way for the Kingdom. Then nation will not fight against nation, the hungry will be fed, and the oppressed will be free. Like the magi of old, we, too, are invited to accompany the poor on this journey.

[21]

Christmas in Morazán

December 1988 . . . Perquín, Morazán

It is December now in Morazán. I looked forward to celebrating this Christmas with the Christian base communities in northern Morazán. This year the people of Morazán received visits from several solidarity delegations from around the world, including Spain, Germany, the Netherlands, Switzerland, Belgium, Mexico, Brazil, and the United States. They had come to visit the conflictive zones and see for themselves this new life that is being born among the poor in El Salvador. Like the "magi" of old, they had come from distant lands to offer a word of solidarity and hope.

After many days and weeks of bombings and captures, the people of Perquín longed to celebrate Christmas Eve in peace. During the morning there was a festive spirit in the town, as people prepared piñatas, food, and banners for the evening celebration. But in the afternoon, all that changed.

About 4 P.M. a threatening plane appeared in the sky, an AC-47 gunship flew over Perquín. Slowly it circled the town, like a vulture hovering over its target. Then it began to machine-gun the edge of town, causing a deathly silence to come over the people. A moment later two helicopters and two A-37 fighter-bombers appeared and rained down rockets and bullets over the hills surrounding the town. This continued for an hour, and then the planes departed. People were shocked.

Little by little, people began to come out of their houses again. At dusk the *posadas* began, and statues of José and María were carried through the streets in procession and returned to the

church. It was night by the time we began the Christmas Eve
Mass; already hundreds of people had gathered to celebrate.

Herod Still Seeks the Child

The first reading was taken from the prophet Isaiah:

> *The people who walked in darkness*
> *have seen a great light;*
> *those who lived in the obscurity of death*
> *were illuminated. (Isaiah 9:1)*

The words of the prophet inspired hope in those present, the
same hope that the people of Israel must have felt centuries ago
as they endured the dark night of injustice and exile. One of the
catechists began to read from the Gospel: *"In those days the
Emperor dictated a law . . ."* As I listened to the reading, I could
just make out the dull roar of the AC-47 gunship circling overhead
in the darkness. Suddenly the sky outside lit up as the plane
dropped flares to illuminate the plaza below.

Immediately we stopped the reading of the Gospel, blew out
the kerosene lamp, and left the church in silence. The entire plaza
was so bright that we could clearly see the houses on each street
corner. We decided to leave the immediate area as quickly as
possible, so as not to get caught in the middle of a surprise landing
of troops. As we made our way through the coffee groves, we
took care not to be illuminated by the light of the flares. Meanwhile the AC-47 gunship and several helicopters continued to
machine-gun the hills surrounding Perquín.

The strafing continued for an hour, before the plane and helicopters departed. Soon we arrived at the house of one of the
catechists. Maribel was not there, but her grandmother, Chavelita,
was and welcomed us inside. Her home was typical of the homes
in Perquín: wooden walls made from boards cut at the saw mill
in town, a clay tile roof, and a dirt floor.

Soon Maribel arrived with her younger brothers and sisters,
and we heard what had happened in the plaza after the strafing
began. Several women had fainted, and children cried. These

children have never known what it is to live in peace. "I shiver every time the planes come," Maribel's little sister told us.

Chavelita, the grandmother, had a biblical interpretation of the event. "Herod is still looking for the child to kill him." For all its simplicity, this explanation revealed a profound truth. Herod still seeks to destroy the new life that is being born in these poor communities of northern Morazán. Still, we continue to witness something miraculous. Despite the tremendous diabolical power that the technology of war unleashes against the poor of El Salvador, it has not been able to destroy their hope!

"People of El Salvador: Your God Reigns!"

The following morning, Christmas Day, the plaza in the town of Perquín was filled with people and activities. The children played with the piñatas, and people enjoyed the Christmas festivities. In the afternoon we celebrated the Christmas Day Mass. Gloria, one of the catechists, read the day's reading from the prophet Isaiah:

> How beautiful on the mountains
> are the feet of one who brings good news.
> (Isaiah 52:7)

How beautiful that day will be when the people of Perquín can look up at the hills that were machine-gunned last night and hear the good news proclaimed to all: "Peace has come to El Salvador!" How beautiful that day will be when all the church bells will ring and voices will shout: "People of El Salvador, your God reigns!"

Father Miguel Ventura offered encouragement to the people after the disruption of the previous night's celebration:

God is with us, God has not abandoned us, and we must not lose faith in God or in our poor brothers and sisters. On this day, two thousand years ago, Jesus was born in the midst of great poverty much like that in which we live. Jesus was born in the midst of a poor people much like our *own. God chose to be born in the midst of conflict. Whenever the poor refuse to accept their misery and oppression, they are always persecuted. Jesus challenged this oppression, and that's why they killed him. We must learn to live our faith in the midst of a conflictive reality.*

As the Mass ended and we lingered to speak with friends, I felt grateful for the experience I shared this Christmas with the people of Morazán. I never expected that we would celebrate Christmas in quite this way, in the midst of poverty and persecution. Perhaps we had a privileged glimpse of the conflictive reality into which Jesus was born two thousand years ago. Now, like then, Herod still seeks the poor child to kill him and to kill her. Herod still seeks to eliminate whatever gives hope to the poor.

This is what Simeon prophesied to Mary centuries ago upon the occasion of Jesus' birth:

The multitudes of Israel are to encounter him, for their rise or their fall. He shall stand as a controversial sign, while a sword will pierce your own soul. (Luke 2:34–35)

Often, the church flees from poverty and avoids conflict at all cost. We condemn the poor and persecuted to remain poor and persecuted by our inaction or moderation. We refuse to put an end to this war and to all wars, and we do not really believe the poor will inherit the earth. We deny this Christ who is crucified each day in the poor, and we cannot truly announce the resurrection unless we are willing to share more fully in the sufferings of the crucified peoples of this world.

What We Have Seen Gives Us Life

Our friends from Europe, Latin America, and the United States have gone back to their countries now, after celebrating Christmas with these poor communities in northern Morazán. They promised to inform people in their countries about what they had seen and heard: U.S. policy continues to support a war against the poor in El Salvador, but the hope of the people for a just peace is firm. They came, like the magi of old, looking for the "star" that Archbishop Romero mentioned nine years ago in his Epiphany homily: "What we must save, above all, is the liberation process of our people."

On the last day before their departure, Father Miguel asked the visitors what impressed them most. This is what they replied: "A people in the midst of death who celebrates life . . ." "A people in the midst of war who loves peace . . ." "The children . . ." "The sense of solidarity among the poor . . ." "The strength of the community organizations and a people who is shaping its own destiny . . ." "The presence of community in the midst of war . . ." "A faith in God which is lived out in daily life . . ." "A poor, generous, and courageous people who bring life . . ."

[22]

The Last Word Is Life

March 1989 . . . Torola, Morazán

It's spring now in Morazán. Today we journeyed with two catechists, Serapio and Porfirio, to the town of Torola. We came to be in solidarity with the people there after a bombing raid last week killed five people in the nearby village of Junquillo. Three children and one woman were killed by the impact of the bomb that struck their house; a fourth child died on the way to the hospital. We hope to visit the families of the victims this afternoon.

As we drew near to the village, we could see the ruins of the house where the bomb exploded. Clay tiles from the roof were scattered in all directions, and pieces of children's clothing were strewn over the ground; only a shell of the house remained. We stopped at a neighbor's house and met Vicente, the father of the three children who were killed, and his three other children who survived. It's a miracle they are still alive! We also met Juan, the father of the fourth child who died, and Santillo, the brother of the woman who was killed. Of the fifteen people who were in the house, five were killed, five were injured, and five were unharmed.

Vicente described what happened. "The helicopters came at 7 A.M. and continued their strafing for two hours. Then an A-37 fighter-bomber dropped two bombs on the village. The second bomb destroyed my house." At one point Vicente broke down in tears and embraced his surviving children who sat by his side

161

as he talked: Dominga, six years old, Cando, four years old, and Marta, three years old.

That evening we returned to the town of Torola to lead a reflection with people from the Christian base communities. Church bells tolled over the silent, abandoned, and moonlit streets of the town, calling the dozen families who still lived in the town to the meeting. Abdomilia, a white-haired grandmother, was present. She had survived the rocket attack last October that damaged her house as well as the church where several children had been playing.

The reading selected for the evening reflection was meant to give people encouragement:

> We are tried in every way, but we are not discouraged; we are anxious, but not desperate; persecuted, but not abandoned; beaten down, but not defeated. Everywhere we bear the death of Jesus in our body so that his life may also be revealed in us. (II Corinthians 4:8–10)

We continued the reflection in light of the coming celebration of Holy Week and the passion, death, and resurrection of Christ in the poor of El Salvador today. Father Miguel Ventura, who was the parish priest here fifteen years before when the Christian base communities were first formed, led the reflection:

> The sufferings which you have experienced this past week are an indication of a profounder identification with Christ's suffering, as well as Christ's nearness to you in your suffering. These sufferings also reveal the force of the Spirit in our lives, and of Christ's resurrection.

We concluded the reflection with a song from the Salvadoran Mass, "When the poor believe in the poor," and the affirmation that it is only when the poor organize and unite that new life is generated. We witnessed this solidarity in Junquillo this morning in the actions of Vicente's neighbors after the bombing. They cared for the victims, buried the dead, and took Vicente and his surviving children into their homes. We also saw this solidarity in the determination of the community organizations to publicly denounce the bombing.

This experience of solidarity is so basic and so vital to the survival of these communities. The poor of Torola have not abandoned the conflictive areas, despite the bombings and the invasions, because they have overcome their fear and have united to build community organizations that provide for the needs of the people. This life-giving solidarity is one example of what it means for "the poor to believe in the poor."

Holy Thursday in a Mountain Village

All this week I have been thinking about Holy Week. Since the March elections we have not been able to visit the town of Torola because of the fighting between the FMLN and the Salvadoran army. The same is true of the villages of Estancia and Calavera, near the town of Cacaopera. It is difficult if not impossible to reach these communities at the present time. So I decided to accompany the pastoral team in the mountain communities near the Honduran border for these days leading up to Easter.

We left the town of Perquín early in the morning and passed through the little mountain village of Talchiga, visiting families of the victims who had been killed by the Salvadoran army a month before. This was the first time I had visited Talchiga. It was about three hours from our next destination, the village of El Carrizal. As we approached the village, it occurred to me that there could be no better place to celebrate Holy Thursday than with these families. I was struck by how isolated they were from other communities, and also by the suffering they had endured because of the recent army repression.

The people of Talchiga are desperately poor. We visited their humble houses, made of stick walls and thatched roofs, much like the houses in the village of Junquillo where the bombing occurred two weeks before. María Elena, the widow of Teodoro, welcomed us into her house and recounted in detail how the soldiers had killed her husband a month before while he was fishing. Later we walked to the spot where he is buried, near a stream. A single cross marks his grave.

Good Friday: Anniversary of Archbishop Romero

The following day we continued our journey to the village of El Carrizal and met with Father Pedro Declerq and the local pastoral team. The dawn hours are beautiful as the sun rises over the mountains of Morazán, and a fresh morning breeze greets the day. We met briefly in Santos' home before walking the remaining two hours to the village of Nahuaterique to celebrate Good Friday. Santos and her family used to live in the village of Jocote Amarillo until the time of the El Mozote massacre. Later the family moved to the mountains to escape the repression.

When we arrived in Nahuaterique later that morning, people were already preparing the stations of the cross for Good Friday. Today was the ninth anniversary of the martyrdom of Archbishop Romero, and the pastoral team was preparing the liturgy to commemorate his death. We listened to a recording of his homily on the Beatitudes, given one month before his assassination, over the loudspeaker in the church.

One passage in particular impressed me as Romero encouraged the pastoral leaders "to remain in your places, alongside the people during this time of persecution." I thought of these Christian base communities in Morazán and of the catechists, the priests, and the leaders of the communities who have accompanied their people during the past nine years of the war.

We walked outside the church to begin the stations of the cross. The reflections on the stations recalled the passion, death, and resurrection of Christ in the people of El Salvador. Each village reflected on one or two stations, and a single Way of the Cross for all the communities in northern Morazán was created. Testimonies of the victims of the assassinations in Talchiga appeared beside the testimonies of the bombing in Junquillo. Two things stood out for me: the awareness of the people of their oppression by the wealthy and powerful in El Salvador, and the hope they found in the struggle of their people for a just society.

After the final station we moved back into the church and continued to sing songs about Archbishop Romero: "Symbol of rebellion, that was your way to love . . ." A moment later we returned to the main plaza to witness a dramatic presentation of the passion of Christ presented by the young people of the village, who were dressed in masks. The drama was a contemporary enactment of Christ's passion in the people, complete with references to the death and destruction caused by the Salvadoran army.

We concluded the drama with this song about Archbishop Romero:

> *March 24:*
> *a day the Church will remember;*
> *Once again they have bathed in blood*
> *one who spoke the truth.*

As we left the village of Nahuaterique to return to El Carrizal for the night, a beautiful sun set over the mountains. We could see the city of San Miguel in the distance, to one side of the mountain peak of Cacahuatique; beyond that, another mountain range stretched from the city of Santiago de María to the town of Berlín in Usulután; beyond that, the twin volcanoes of San Vicente and Chinchontepec; and beyond that, more hills extending west to the capital city of San Salvador.

These mountain campesinos in northern Morazán are truly the "salt of the earth" of which the Gospel speaks. Fifteen years after the first seeds of revolution were planted in the sterility of these poor mountain communities, a promise of new life has taken root and borne fruit in the Christian base communities and community organizations of Morazán.

Easter Sunday: The Triumph of Life

Today is Easter Sunday! Today we celebrate the triumph of life over death, light over darkness, truth over lies, and liberation over five hundred years of bondage in the Americas. I left El Carrizal early yesterday morning to begin an eight-hour journey south to the villages of Estancia and Calavera. We had received word that the army had retreated, and I was going to meet two friends from the United States who had just arrived in Morazán. How suddenly plans change!

We passed through the village of Talchiga along the way and continued south for another hour to the next village, Masala, where we stopped to rest. These mountain paths are desolate, especially in the months just before the rainy season begins. We passed hours without seeing a single person, and all the houses we saw had been burned or destroyed by the army. One house we saw used to be a school for the children of Talchiga until five years ago; a bomb was dropped on the school and killed two children.

I thought of the abandoned villages I had passed through five years before in Chalatenango and the dry, barren, rocky soil. It was conditions such as these, in the midst of a sterile land and an abandoned people, that the prophet Isaiah said would be transformed:

> The wilderness and the arid land will rejoice;
> the desert will be glad and blossom . . .
> See, your God comes, demanding justice;
> Your God is the God who rewards,
> the God who comes to save you.
> (Isaiah 35:1– 4)

From the village of Masala we continued on until late afternoon when we reached the village of Calavera. We passed through the same hills where the helicopters and planes had attacked us six months before. As evening drew near, the sky turned a brilliant red and cast its colors over the hills surrounding the Torola River below. The air was filled with the haunting cry of the locusts—always a sign of Easter.

Apart from the locusts and the sound of our steps over the dry leaves and underbrush, an eerie silence enveloped us in its embrace. I thought of this same night, two thousand years ago, and the abandonment that the disciples must have felt the day after the crucifixion of Jesus.

As we descended the hills in darkness, we turned off our flashlights so as not to arouse the suspicion of a Salvadoran army patrol on the other side of the river. I could see the lights of the chapel and an occasional fire burning in a home in the village of Calavera, our final destination. What irony! We had come to celebrate the resurrection of Christ in a village that bears the name of the hill where he was crucified — Calvary.

But it is fitting that we celebrate the death and resurrection of Jesus here. Only a crucified people, like the people of Calavera who have lived for nine years beneath the bombs and in constant flight from the army, can truly announce the resurrection!

By now it was dark. We crossed a swinging bridge over the Torola River and entered the village of Calavera. Soon we reached the chapel, which was originally a chicken coop with a thatched roof surrounded by chicken wire. Hundreds of people had gathered inside. The room was illuminated by the paschal fire and by several smaller candles.

One of the catechists had just read the Gospel, and the reflection was about to begin. Father Peter Hinde and Sister Betty Campbell, my friends from the United States, were sharing the story of the miraculous crossing of five thousand Salvadoran campesinos over the Lempa River eight years before, the very place where my own journey among the Salvadoran people had begun. "God intervenes on the side of the poor and always in new and surprising ways," Peter concluded.

Father Miguel Ventura followed with the homily, recounting the struggle of the people for life after nearly a decade of war:

> Dear brothers and sisters, we have the opportunity to gather at this time as we remember nine years of a cruel conflict. Many of us have felt, perhaps, that the light of a negotiated solution to the Salvadoran conflict has been snuffed out. Nevertheless, your presence here tonight, and your nine years of active participation in the construction of this new society, is the clearest expression of the resurrected Christ. Tonight we will celebrate that life we have lived for nine years, a life and a light that gives hope to many on this Salvadoran pilgrimage.
>
> A few weeks ago, several of our brothers and sisters took part in the anniversary celebration that proclaimed that Archbishop Romero, like Jesus Christ, lives in our history! Tonight we are going to join in the celebration of the resurrected Christ and of Archbishop Romero resurrected in his people.

Brothers and sisters, I want to share with you tonight what the resurrection of Christ means to us. What does Christ say to a people at war who have suffered seventy thousand dead, more than a million refugees and displaced people, seven thousand disappeared, and thousands of political prisoners? What do the events of two thousand years ago have to say to us? That is why we have come together tonight, to illuminate the meaning of our journey.

The silence was penetrating. I recalled the first Easter vigil I had celebrated with the Salvadoran people eight years before in a marginal community of San Salvador. There, too, there were no lights; the electricity had gone out and only the paschal candle on the altar illuminated the celebration. Father Miguel continued:

In the time of Jesus there also was a question to clarify. Who has the last word in history? Will it be death or life? Who will have the last word? Will the Roman Empire have it? Will the oppressive powers that condemn the poor have it? Will death or life have it?

I believe that this night is most propitious for affirming that someone has the last word, and that we are not walking toward death but advancing day by day toward life. It is Christ whose enemies put guards around his tomb to deny his resurrection. It is Christ who rises victoriously and says in a loud voice: "The God of life has the last word!"

Brothers and sisters, you who have wandered these hills; you who have left loved ones along the way; you whose children have died and watered this soil with their blood; you whose family members have been imprisoned and tortured; I ask you: "Who has the last word in history?"

How often we have each asked this question in our heart of hearts, and many times without any answer. The campesinos have a saying: "The darker the night, the closer the dawn," but how long the night has been! Again the silence is penetrating.

You, brothers and sisters, are the living testimony that Christ is the last word, your profound faith is the last word.

*We are gathered as a people of God, as a church of pilgrims,
in the midst of this martyrdom, in the midst of these trials,
proclaiming that God has the last word! So tonight, dear
brothers and sisters, we must announce to the peoples of
this world that God dwells among our people, that God
does not permit our people to get down on its knees to
worship false gods. We accept and confront the trials and
challenges of the future, illuminated on our journey by this
great night of resurrection.*

*That is why we are here: to proclaim that death does not
have the final word, but Christ does! The God of life does!
Our people, organized in our struggle for justice and truth,
do! The mothers, the students, the young people, the farm
workers, all those who walk hand in hand with their brothers and sisters to build this new society have the final word!
This is the greatness of our people.*

A cool breeze blew through the chapel, and the paschal candle
flickered. Our hearts were afire, yearning to hear a word of hope.
The liturgy continued with an offertory of the achievements of
these communities: bread and milk from the mothers, pencils and
paper from the teachers, syringes and medicines from the health
promoters, a Bible from the catechists, bread and wine from the
people.

Prayers were lifted up for those who had died during these
past nine years of the war—this lasted fifteen minutes!—and several children were baptized. All these were signs of the vitality of
this people and the triumph of life over death.

We ended this long liturgy with a traditional Easter song:
"*Resucitó!* He is risen! Alleluia!" Then Father Miguel gave the
final blessing:

*Tonight we have said that history is not a dark night. We
are saying tonight that our history is light. It is this light that
the resurrected One has poured into our history. So we
continue our pilgrimage. Many people will believe tonight
thanks to your faith; thanks to this light that illuminates us
and shines in all directions.*

Now, dear brothers and sisters, go forward! This night

gives us an answer: the God of life, the God of the resur-
rection has the final word! In the most difficult moments
that you live, remember: the idols of power and money do
not have the final word. As Archbishop Romero said, the
God of life has the final word: "The glory of God is the
poor who live!"

The following morning I prepared for the journey to San Salvador. It was one year since I had crossed the Torola River to
accompany these communities in northern Morazán. Now as I
prepare to leave, I know one day I will return. I can still hear the
voices of the people singing the song that reflects their journey
of suffering and hope:

> *Heroic Morazán,*
> *they could not defeat you . . .*
> *and together we will struggle*
> *until our liberation!*

BLOOD OF THE MARTYRS

1989–1991: From the "Final Offensive" to the Signing of the Peace Agreements

The fighting that raged up to December 12 cost the lives of over two thousand people from both sides . . . The 1989 offensive was one of the most violent episodes of the war. The guerrilla forces took cover in densely populated areas during the skirmishes, and urban areas were the targets of indiscriminate aerial bombardment. The critical situation in the country bred such violations as the arrest, torture, murder and disappearance of hundreds of non-combatant civilians. It was against this backdrop that the Jesuit priests and two women were murdered. The parties realized that a decisive military victory was not within their grasp and resumed in greater earnest the negotiating process which led to the signing of the peace agreements . . . on January 16, 1992 . . . putting an end to twelve years of armed conflict in El Salvador.

> —From Madness to Hope,
> *Report of the Commission on the Truth for El Salvador, 39*

THE SEEDS OF NEW LIFE
1989–1991

When I left Morazán at the end of Holy Week 1989, I returned to San Salvador. Within six weeks, Alfredo Cristiani, from the ARENA party, would take office as the new president of El Salvador. Already the struggle for peace was beginning to intensify in the capital. The National Debate for Peace, a coalition of over eighty popular organizations and churches, drew thousands of people into the street to demonstrate for a negotiated solution to the war and a just peace.

Throughout the summer, negotiations between ARENA and the FMLN for peace continued. It soon became apparent, however, that ARENA was going to dismantle the few reforms that the Christian Democrats had achieved, breaking up the agricultural cooperatives, lifting price controls on basic goods, and privatizing banks and exports, imposing their own neo-liberal economic model on the poor. The popular organizations fought back, and repression against their leaders intensified. The FMLN responded by attacking military installations in San Salvador.

On October 31, the labor federation FENASTRAS was bombed in the middle of the day, killing ten people, including union leader Febe Elisabet Velásquez. The office of COMADRES, where the mothers of the disappeared worked, was also bombed.[1] Eleven days later, on the night of November 11, the FMLN launched its largest military and political offensive of the war, occupying a third of San Salvador[2] — including most of Soyapango, a poor neighborhood on the periphery of San Salvador where I was staying at the time.

For five days, fighting took place in the poor neighborhoods of San Salvador, but the army was unable to retake the neighborhoods from the FMLN. On the night of November 15, at a high-level meeting with President Cristiani, the army decided to begin bombing the poor sectors of the city, killing hundreds and injuring thousands of civilians.[3]

That same night a small group of military officers, including the military High Command, gave orders to kill the six Jesuits and not leave any witnesses. During the early morning hours of November 16, the Atlacatl Battalion—the same army battalion responsible for the massacre of thousands of civilians at El Mozote, Copapayo, Los Llanitos, and the Gualsinga River—occupied the Central American University (UCA) and assassinated six Jesuit priests and two Salvadoran women.[4]

In response to both the bombings and the killings, the FMLN occupied the wealthy neighborhoods of San Salvador, which the army did not bomb, and then withdrew from the city. In the following weeks, the army searched houses, clinics, and churches, captured hundreds of people, and deported more than thirty foreign missionaries and humanitarian workers.

On November 30, I was captured with four others by the Treasury Police in the "April 22" parish house in Credisa, a neighborhood in Soyapango on the eastern edge of San Salvador. We were held at gunpoint for two hours as the police searched the house and then taken into the streets and placed on the back of a pick-up truck to be taken to the police headquarters. There we were blindfolded, our hands were tied behind our backs, and we were forced to remain standing the entire night while we were interrogated. Four days later I was deported to the United States.

The FMLN offensive broke the impasse of the negotiations, making clear both the military power of the FMLN as well as the military impunity of the Salvadoran army. The killing of the Jesuits and the bombing of civilian neighborhoods brought severe denunciations from governments and peoples around the world.

In April 1990 the negotiations for peace between the FMLN and the Salvadoran government were resumed, laying the groundwork for the signing of the Peace Accords and the end of the war two years later.[5] The U.N. Secretary General and his special representative, Alvaro de Soto, played a crucial role in moving the negotiations forward, as did other nations, including the United States.

Three months after my deportation, I returned to El Salvador for the tenth anniversary of Archbishop Romero's assassination. It was the first large public demonstration since the November offensive and once again opened political space for the people to mobilize for peace. For the next nine months I went to work as part of a pastoral team (CEBES) with the Salvadoran refugees who had repatriated four months before from Colomoncagua, Honduras, to Ciudad Segundo Montes in northern Morazán.[6] They named their resettlement site Segundo Montes, in memory of the Jesuit priest who had visited them in Honduras one month before he was assassinated by the Atlacatl Battalion in November 1989.

On February 11, 1990 the village of Corral de Piedra[7] in Chalatenango was attacked by helicopters that fired rockets at a house where several people had taken refuge. Four children and one man were killed in the attack; another sixteen were injured, twelve of them children. At first the army denied any responsibility for what had taken place; subsequently they blamed the FMLN. But the evidence against them was indisputable. Sister Ann Manganaro, to whom this book is dedicated, cared for the wounded and denounced the attack in San Salvador. The community was later renamed Ignacio Ellacuría, in memory of the Jesuit martyr.[8]

In January 1991, I left El Salvador to return to the United States and help with the work of solidarity. Throughout 1991, negotiations between the Salvadoran government and the FMLN continued, bearing fruit with the signing of the Peace Accords on January 16, 1992, in Chapúltepec Park in Mexico City. This was to be the beginning of a new era in the struggle for a just peace in El Salvador.

What follows is the story of those first four months after the November 1989 offensive, which prepared the way for a renewal of negotiations and the beginning of peace in El Salvador. Much remains to be done. The causes that gave rise to the war, particularly the extreme poverty, the lack of strong democratic institutions, and military impunity remain to be resolved.

Before there can be genuine reconciliation in El Salvador, the church has insisted, there must first be truth and justice. The Truth Commission has made a major stride toward letting the truth be known; but the struggle for justice continues.

[23]

The November Offensive

January 6, 1990 . . . A Letter to Friends

On November 30, 1989 I was detained by the Salvadoran security forces and four days later forced to leave the country. At about 5 P.M. eight uniformed Treasury Police burst into the "April 22" parish house in Credisa where I was staying at the time. They pointed their M-16s at five of us and held us at gunpoint for two hours while they searched the house. We were later taken in the dark to the Treasury Police headquarters in a police truck and an unmarked car with polarized windows and three heavily armed men inside. At the headquarters we were blindfolded, handcuffed, and forced to remain standing the entire night.

At different times during the night we were interrogated, still blindfolded and handcuffed, but no accusations were made. Then, about midnight, we were taken outside and placed on the back of a pick-up truck for some unknown destination. "You had better start praying," one policeman joked, "because you're never coming back here again." As we rode through the streets of San Salvador, it all seemed like a dream. I had imagined this scene hundreds of times before, as I heard countless stories of disappearances and death squad missions. But I never imagined it would happen to me.

When we arrived at our destination, I could just make out beneath my blindfold what I knew to be the headquarters of the National Police, located one block from the main plaza in front of the cathedral of San Salvador. Once inside, we were again interrogated. "How long have you been fighting for the FMLN?"

the interrogator asked us. "We work for the church," I replied. "The church?" he replied with a sarcastic laugh. "We know that Archbishop Rivera Damas is a subversive."

A little later I was threatened by this same man: "How long have you had that beard? Do you know we have a machete in the corner to shave it off? Or maybe we should take you all up in a helicopter and dump you out." But nothing happened. An hour later we were taken back to the Treasury Police headquarters and forced to remain standing the rest of the night.

The following morning Father Carlos Díaz, a Spanish Dominican priest, and I were turned over to immigration authorities for deportation. The three Salvadoran co-workers picked up with us did not fare so well, however, spending the next fifteen days in detention where they were subjected to beatings and torture. Estela, twenty-eight years old, a single mother who coordinated the daycare center in the parish, and José, thirty-eight years old, a catechist and a father of six children, were both subjected to the *capucha*—a form of torture in which a hood filled with lime is placed over the head to suffocate the victim and force "a confession." Santiago, twenty-eight years old, the music director in the parish, was held for several weeks and then released. But Estela and José remained in prison.

I had first met José eight years before, when I went to the border to meet the refugees crossing the Lempa River into Honduras. As we were being led away by the Treasury Police, my thoughts flashed back to that scene by the Lempa River, and a young man with a gaping hole in his neck from a gunshot wound, lying on the ground. It was José. Later he worked as a catechist in the refugee camp in Mesa Grande, before returning to El Salvador. We had met several times in Chalatenango. Eventually he came to work with the pastoral team in the "April 22" parish. Now the war had brought us together still one more time.

In many ways it still seems like a dream. I had decided to stay in El Salvador and had just talked with friends to reaffirm my decision when I was captured. Now I am back in the United States. The prayers and concern of so many of you have made this transition easier. Currently I am working with the churches and the solidarity community to end U.S. military aid to El Salvador and to support a peaceful settlement to the war that involves all social sectors of the nation and the FMLN.

As we move into the 1990s, I still find hope in the words of Archbishop Romero's 1980 Epiphany homily:

> *I want to reaffirm, as a person of hope, despite all these doubts, that I believe a new stream of salvation will break through . . . What we must preserve, above all, is the liberation process of our people which has cost them so much blood . . . We dare not lose it.*

I think, too, of the death of the six Jesuits, their housekeeper Elba Ramos, and her daughter Celina who were brutally assassinated by the Atlacatl Battalion last November 16. How ironic! This Salvadoran mother and her fifteen-year-old daughter left their house to stay with the Jesuits because they thought it would be safer, only to meet their deaths that same night. They, too, are a reminder of the 75,000 Salvadoran martyrs who have been killed these past ten years—so many humble men and women, even children, some of whose names we know and most of whose we do not.

As we prepare to celebrate the tenth anniversary of Archbishop Romero's martyrdom this March 24, his words are more instructive now than ever:

> *I rejoice that the blood of the church is mixed with the blood of our people, because it is a sign that the church is really with the people.*

So, too, we may rejoice in the witness of these six Jesuit priests for their commitment to defend life, to tell the truth about El Salvador, to promote justice for the poor, and to give up their own lives so generously so that the poor in El Salvador might live. Their names, like Archbishop Oscar Romero's, are inscribed in the hearts of the Salvadoran people they loved so well: Ignacio Ellacuría, Ignacio Martín-Baró, Segundo Montes, Amando López, Juan Ramón Moreno, and Joaquín López López.

I went to their funeral at the UCA one week after the beginning of the FMLN offensive. It was the first time we had been able to leave our neighborhood since the fighting began. Hundreds of people had gathered in the auditorium in a great outpouring of love for the victims and outrage at the abominable crime that had been committed by the Salvadoran military. The funeral Mass was one more testimony to the ancient truth of the church: "The blood of the martyrs is the seed of new Christians!"

The Marginal Communities Struggle To Survive

I came to San Salvador in April 1989, after accompanying the Christian base communities (CEBES) in northern Morazán for the previous year. The transition from a conflictive area in the countryside to the city is never easy, but I was blessed with support from many friends and an invitation from Father Jim Barnett to work with the pastoral team in the "April 22" parish in Credisa, a neighborhood in Soyapango on the eastern edge of San Salvador.

The "April 22" community is one of the poorest I have seen in the city. During the war it has doubled in size, as thousands of displaced families from the countryside fled to the capital. The hill on which the "April 22" community is built used to be the city dump, and you can still dig down ten feet or more and find garbage. Yet the way people tell it, their journey here eighteen years ago was like an exodus, out of a precarious existence along the banks of the sewage-filled rivers of San Salvador to a firmer piece of land which at that time was the city dump. This became their "promised land!"

The people who live in the "April 22" community are as diverse as the country. They come from all fourteen departments and represent all views on the political spectrum. Many families have sons who were drafted into the army; others have sons who joined the FMLN during the November offensive. The only thing these families share is their poverty and their faith.

During a lull in the fighting last November I walked with Father Gerardo Potter, one of the parish priests, to the "April 22" clinic to get medicines and paused to look at the hundreds of shacks that dot the hillsides. Every one had a white flag! Unfortunately many were still hit by the government planes and helicopters that strafed and bombed the poor neighborhoods where the fighting took place.

The parish projects are a real witness to the creativity of the people and their initiative. After the earthquake, the parish team discovered that seven out of every eight households in the "April 22" community are headed by single mothers, and most have four to six children to feed. So daycare centers were opened. Later schools and clinics were started, and young people from the neighborhood were trained as teachers and health promoters. Carpentry and artisan workshops provided many people with skills to earn a living and the experience of working cooperatively.

These activities, however, are a source of empowerment that is considered subversive by the government in El Salvador. During the FMLN offensive last November the churches did what they have done throughout the war, providing sanctuary to refugees, distributing food to the hungry on an emergency basis, and treating the wounded in clinics — all of which were considered "subversive" activities.

According to the army's logic, if you took in refugees, "you might be harboring guerrillas," and on several occasions the army raided churches and captured and beat refugees, violating the law of sanctuary. If you distributed emergency food rations to hungry people in the parish, "you might be feeding guerrillas," and on several occasions the army prevented food from reaching the poor communities where fighting had taken place, violating humanitarian law.

If you treated the wounded, "you might be treating guerrillas," and on several occasions the army raided church clinics and confiscated the medicines, violating medical neutrality. In fact, most of the wounded treated were civilians, although church policy, from the archbishop down to the parish worker, was to respect medical neutrality and treat anyone — government soldier, FMLN guerrilla, or civilian.

Moments of Terror and Courage

The testimonies I heard and the scenes I observed in the poor neighborhoods during and following the November offensive were tremendous! On Saturday night, November 11, the FMLN launched its largest offensive of the war, occupying over a third of San Salvador — mostly poor neighborhoods — and holding them for up to five days. The next morning FMLN guerrillas put up a barricade near the railroad tracks in Credisa, one-half block from the "April 22" parish house where I was staying.

By noon government helicopters had begun to strafe and rocket the immediate vicinity. The people who lived in the shacks near the railroad tracks suffered the most. By the end of the day twenty civilians had been wounded, including several children, and were treated in the parish clinic. At least two people from the parish were killed. Street fighting continued until Tuesday night, right in front of the parish house. By Wednesday both the army and FMLN guerrillas had moved to another neighborhood.

In Mejicanos, a poor neighborhood on the northern edge of San Salvador where I had worked in 1987, the young people of the "San Francisco de Asís" parish and the Passionist priests performed a heroic work, carrying wounded civilians on stretchers from the outlying areas of the neighborhood to the church for treatment. They worked continually for five days, often beneath the bombing and the strafing. Three hundred civilians were treated at the church, 150 of whom had to be carried on stretchers. Another 50 wounded were carried to the nearest Red Cross station ten blocks away.

The army had denied the Red Cross access to the Mejicanos neighborhood for five days — a clear violation of the Geneva Conventions. Many of the wounded died for lack of medical attention. The young people in the parish told me they personally had buried twenty-one people, but that many more remained buried in the ruins of their houses.

On Saturday, November 18, after a week of fighting, four hundred people who had taken refuge in the Mejicanos church, including forty orphans, left on foot for the center of San Salvador. They could no longer endure the heavy mortaring to which the neighborhood had been subjected since Thursday. The mortars had been launched from the direction of the First Army Brigade, two miles away. I visited the people from Mejicanos on Sunday in the convent where they had taken refuge. They told everything that had happened.

Many other neighborhoods were affected. In Zacamil, where Fathers Rogelio Ponseele, Pedro Declerq, and several sisters worked to promote Christian base communities in the 1970s—and where the Maryknoll priests now work—the fighting was particularly intense. There, too, base community members courageously faced persecution by the army.

The community of Emanuel, a marginal neighborhood in Zacamil, was burned to the ground after army planes strafed it from the air and the shacks caught fire. When I went back to see the families I had worked with there, they were literally standing in the ashes. One woman showed me her dress which was full of bullet holes; it had been hanging on the line to dry when the strafing occurred. These families first fled from the war in the countryside years ago; then their homes collapsed in the earthquake and they built this community of Emanuel in 1986; now it had been destroyed and they were trying to rebuild again.

The story was the same in other neighborhoods and parishes of the capital. The amazing thing is that people were beginning to rebuild! Despite the repression, despite the absence of any political space, there were rays of hope in the organizing efforts of the people to rebuild their homes and carry on their struggle for life and a just peace.

"Let Us Be Filled with This Hope!"

So what does the future hold for El Salvador? The *kairos* document, which was signed by Christian base communities in Central America, illuminates very well the journey of the Salvadoran people for the coming decade. It says:

> *It is a critical time in Central America . . . Either we close the door on the possibility of hope for the poor for many years or as prophets we open ourselves to a new day for humanity and for the church . . . Either we are on the side of the poor or on the side of the Empire; with the God of life or the idols of death; with the God of Jesus Christ or the false gods of Christendom.*

Shortly after I arrived in the United States last month, I received a letter from a friend, Father Jerry Zawada, a Franciscan priest who is currently in federal prison for resisting nuclear weapons. In the isolation of his jail cell he found these words from one of Archbishop Romero's homilies and sent them to me:

> *Let us sing a song of hope and be filled with a cheerful spirit, knowing that this Christian life that came to us with Christ through the Virgin Mary and takes flesh in all believers is the presence of God who makes us a promise. No, brothers and sisters, El Salvador need not always live like this. "I will tear off the veil of shame that covers all peoples. I will wipe away the tears of all those mothers who no longer have tears for having wept so much over their children who are not found"* (Isaiah 25:7–8).
>
> *Here, too, in El Salvador, the Lord will take away the sorrow of all those homes that this Sunday suffer the mystery of dear ones abducted or murdered or tortured or tormented. This is not of God. God's banquet will come; wait for the Lord's hour. Let us have faith; all this will pass away like a national nightmare and we shall awake to the Lord's great feast. Let us be filled with this hope. (October 15, 1978)*

[24]

Monseñor Romero:
Risen in the People!

March 24, 1990 . . . San Salvador

Ten years is a long time. So much has happened in ten years. So much has changed in the lives of the Salvadoran people, and, tragically, so much has remained the same. If it were not for the blood of the martyrs, it would all seem so futile, so tragic: so many deaths, so many people disappeared, so much death and destruction.

Today I marched in the streets of San Salvador to commemorate the tenth anniversary of Archbishop Romero's death. As I marched, I found myself surrounded on all sides by a human shield of love and solidarity. The march became for me a walking meditation on the passion, death, and resurrection of the Salvadoran people. The faces of the people were alive with hope and seemed to say: "You see, we are still alive! They killed our loved ones, but they couldn't kill us all."

I saw Carmen, from the Committee of Mothers of the Disappeared, marching alongside me. She and hundreds of mothers like her were the first to take to the streets and denounce the government repression years ago, when nobody dared to speak. They took her children away from her, but they couldn't stop the love that gave birth to them, nursed them, reared them, struggled for them, and finally wept for them because she could not find their bodies to bury them.

A little later I saw Mirtala, an organizer for the Christian Committee for the Displaced of El Salvador (CRIPDES), standing on the back of a pick-up truck taking pictures of the march. The police captured Mirtala twice during the last six months and tortured her, but they couldn't take away her courage and her love for her people. Nor could they take away the courage of her mother, a brave woman who was captured because of her work with the Committee of the Mothers of the Disappeared.

I knew Mirtala's sister, Sonia, before she was killed last October. After the second Sumpul River massacre in June 1982, a group of refugees had fled to Honduras to escape from the army. "We buried a child last night," they told me, "beside the river. We haven't eaten for fifteen days and the child died." Two years later, when I met Sonia in Chalatenango, she told me the same story. The child who died by the river was Sonia's child.

I knew Mirtala's brother, Orlando, a fine man. He had been secretary general of the Federation of Farm Workers (FTC) and spoke fondly of the conversations he used to have with Archbishop Romero. Most of Orlando's brothers and sisters were killed by the army. Later he joined the FMLN and continued to struggle until his death during the November offensive.

How many more stories can I tell you? I saw María, a catechist from the Christian Base Communities of El Salvador (CEBES). She told me the story of returning to El Mozote in 1985 as she fled from the army. There she hid with dozens of families among the ruins of the houses and the memories of the dead. They killed hundreds of people in El Mozote, but they couldn't take away María's love for her people or her determination to announce that "life, not death, has the last word!"

By the time we reached the cathedral, people had already entered the sanctuary. Once inside, we found the tomb off to one side where Archbishop Romero is buried. In the center of the cathedral the altar was covered with paper flowers placed on huge palm leaves. Six bright red candles fluttered in the breeze between the two side doors. The cathedral was filled to capacity, and people overflowed into the streets.

A picture of Archbishop Romero was hung across the altar, next to these words from Revelation:

> *They have triumphed through the blood of the Lamb, and*
> *because of what they proclaimed, even to the point of sac-*

rificing their lives for Him. For all this, rejoice, heavens and all you who live in them! (12:11)

After the Mass was over, I went over to the tomb of Archbishop Romero, literally carried on a wave of people, and placed a bright yellow flower I had picked on the tomb. A small child looked around and smiled, and then moved the flower forward until it lay in front of a young woman. Suddenly I stood face to face with Silvia, a catechist from Copapayo whom I had not seen since 1984. She was a survivor of the massacre of 118 people there on November 4, 1983.

Silvia escaped across Lake Suchitlán to the town of San Antonio los Ranchos. There she was wounded by flying shrapnel from a bomb that exploded while she washed clothes in the river, the sharp metal slicing her cheek in two, disfiguring her forever. "I've never been to the tomb of Archbishop Romero before," she told me. "That's why I came today. My mother stayed home to take care of my eleven-month-old baby. When are you coming to see her?"

Today the people of El Salvador took back the streets for a few precious, beautiful moments. One day, even these streets that have seen so much blood, so much pain and suffering, so many tears and oppression, will see joy and peace. Proud and free, filled with hope, and surrounded by love, thousands of people filled the streets of San Salvador to commemorate the anniversary of their beloved pastor, crying:

"Archbishop Romero, you live in the hearts of the people!"

[25]

On the Road to Emmaus (I)

April 1990 . . . *Segundo Montes City, Morazán*

Returning to Morazán is like returning to an overflowing spring of water. At least that's how I experienced it this year. I had celebrated Holy Week here these past two years. This year, however, there are so many more people with the repatriation of 8,400 refugees from Colomoncagua, Honduras. They had come to build a new community, which they named "Segundo Montes," after the Jesuit martyr who was killed by the army last November 16. He had visited the refugees in Honduras only a month before his death.

The returning refugees say this about their new life:

> *We are no longer refugees nor do we want to be again. We want to reconstruct the experience we lived in the refugee camps without building another refugee camp in El Salvador. We want to contribute to peace, building schools, promoting health, creating new opportunities for work, and producing for basic needs so that everyone can live a better life.*

And of Segundo Montes, in whose name this new community was founded, they say:

> *One day a gray-haired and bearded man with an amiable smile arrived in the refugee camp, umbrella in hand, followed by a group of curious children who had never seen*

*anyone open an umbrella before. This man later told us
that before he came here he didn't see any future for the
poor in El Salvador. But during his visit with us he changed
his mind, he saw hope, he saw the sun shine brightly over
Colomoncagua, and the possibility of a future in El Salvador.*

You feel this hope and future today in Morazán, after ten years
of a war that has cost the lives of 75,000 Salvadorans, a war that
continues to take the lives of humble men and women through
indiscriminate bombings and cruel assassinations, repressing an
organized people who struggle for a just peace in El Salvador.
The following story is an account of what I saw and heard during
these days of Holy Week in Morazán.

The Triumphal Entry of the Refugees into Morazán

For days the locusts have been announcing Holy Week. Last
night a hard rain fell. Today the dawn was refreshing, and a light
breeze blew. The delegates of the Word, both men and women,
and the catechists here prepared the liturgy today, selecting an
open spot beneath some *amate* trees in the new settlement called
Los Hatos.

"That's how we celebrated at first in Honduras," one man
said, "beneath the trees."

"And that's how Jesus celebrated," a woman added, "wherever he happened to pass the night, conversing with the people."

As people arrived from the other settlements, we formed a
circle to bless the palms. Pedro, a lay delegate, explained the
significance of the day:

*Sisters and brothers, now that we have arrived in our land
of El Salvador, we are going to celebrate this Palm Sunday
in a new land. Today we not only celebrate the triumphal
entry of Jesus into Jerusalem, but the triumphal entry of
our people into Morazán after ten years of living in exile.
Today we are on a new march in this new land. Today we*

are not going to celebrate a Holy Week of sorrow but of hope.

As the catechists blessed the palms with water, "recalling the water of our baptismal commitment," we walked along the path in procession, returning to the spot where we were going to celebrate the Mass. For the past ten years the people have been on a journey, fleeing through the hills to reach Honduras, only to return over these same paths to repopulate their lands and begin a new life in El Salvador. Even though the war has not ended, the people have returned more determined than ever to end the war and the injustice that gave rise to it.

Today's readings recall Jesus' passion, the same passion that these people have experienced: *"He humbled himself and was obedient unto death, even a shameful death on a cross"* (Philippians 2:8). The Gospel reading of Jesus' passion ends with the soldiers sealing his tomb with a rock. Not a single word of hope or resurrection. It appears that death has triumphed.

But it is not that way. Father Dennis Leder, S.J., began the celebration with a word of hope:

> *Sisters and brothers, today as we recall the passion of Jesus, we recall as well the willingness of Jesus to live among the poor, to defend them, and to share their fate. Be assured that Jesus is in our midst. God is with the poor, with those who suffer, with the disappeared, with the tortured, and with those who are assassinated today.*

An older campesino made this message of hope even more concrete:

> *Today we recall this holy city, made holy by the blood of our brother Segundo Montes and the blood of all the martyrs who have died in our struggle. It's because of their sacrifice that we have reached this holy land which God promised us and gave us.*

During the communion I thought a lot about these words as I looked at the faces of the people: faces of old people who rejoice now that they have returned to die in the land where they were born, faces of many mothers and fathers like Exaltación and Alejandro who have lost five children — including their son Father Octavio Ortiz — in the war, faces of hundreds of children born in Honduras who have come to know this land for the first time.

It has been ten years of a difficult walk over these paths stained with blood. But the faces of the people expressed joy, not sadness. Their eyes radiated and shone with joy. They had returned to Morazán, the land of their birth, to work the land, build a new community, and contribute to peace in El Salvador.

As dusk fell we sang a song which tells the story of Emmaus, and how the disciples recognized Jesus "in the breaking of the bread." It is a song that illuminates the journey these repatriated refugees have taken: remembering their history, illuminating it with the Bible, and transforming it in community.

A Tragic History Illuminated by the Bible

The history of the past ten years in Morazán is marked by particular events. If you ask the repatriated refugees, "When did you first leave home?" most of them reply, "After the October invasion." The "October invasion" refers to a military operation of ten thousand soldiers here in northern Morazán on October 10, 1980 (before the general offensive of the FMLN, which took place January 10, 1981), when the Salvadoran army bombed and shelled the civilian population in their villages, burning their homes and their crops, and forcing thousands of humble campesinos and their families to flee to Honduras to save their lives. The refugees arrived in Colomoncagua in December 1980, where they stayed until their return to Morazán in November 1989.

Many such army invasions occurred here in northern Morazán these past ten years. But the darkest chapter of all was the massacre that occurred in El Mozote, December 11–12, 1981, when hundreds of men, women, and children were massacred by the Atlacatl Battalion. Only one woman, Rufina Amaya, survived to tell the story. It was not until November 1989 — eight years later — that the refugees — and Rufina — left Honduras to come back to their homes in Morazán.

That's how the repatriated refugees remember their history, and they also illuminate it with the light of the Bible. I went to a liturgy of the Word in the settlement of Los Quebrachos. It was a lovely Sunday morning. We met beneath the trees around a table, surrounded by the beauty of the mountains of Morazán. In the distance we looked out at the hills surrounding El Mozote.

The reading for the day was from the prophet Ezekiel, about the valley of the dry bones. It is an appropriate symbol, since the land of Morazán is not only watered with the blood of the martyrs; it is also scattered with their bones as in the case of El Mozote:

My people, I am going to open your tombs; I am going to take you from them and return you to the land of Israel. I will put in you the spirit of life and you will be revived; and I will install you in your own land. (37:12–14)

If it were not for the blood of the martyrs, of all those who have given their lives for the liberation of their people, it would be difficult to give a reason for our hope. Because it would seem that death had triumphed, that death has the last word, and not life and resurrection. I do not know a single repatriated family that has not lost two, three, even five or more children or dozens of relatives during these ten years of war. The deaths of these martyrs inspire a commitment in those who still live to follow their example, even to the point of giving up their lives for the cause of justice and out of love for their people.

Next we read the Gospel for the day, the resurrection of Lazarus. One of the mothers, who had lost three sons, told us, "When I saw my youngest son for the last time he told me: 'Mama, if one day I die, don't think that they killed me, but rather that God has called me to give my life.' " These words reflect the same wisdom as Jesus when he says: *"Nobody can take my life from me, I offer it freely" (John 10:18).* This is the faith of a people who offer signs of a new life and resurrection in their return to Morazán and their determination to work the land and to build a new life together.

Building a New Life Together

Not only do the repatriated refugees remember their history and illuminate it with the Bible; they also transform their history in community. It's impressive to see this new life they are creating, inspired by new values: mutual aid, the common good, cooperation, popular democracy, and solidarity. They build their houses and plant their fields collectively. They have formed community kitchens and daycare centers to enable a fuller participation of women in all activities of the community.

When they left for Honduras in 1980 they were 85 percent illiterate; now 85 percent can read and write, the fruit of their efforts to train their own teachers to serve the community. In the health sector they trained health promoters who diagnose and treat illnesses, assist at births, and educate the community about preventative health care. More than one thousand people have learned a new skill in one of the workshops where they make clothes, shoes, hammocks, clay pots, tin utensils, and crafts. All this will serve as an economic base for the community to produce to satisfy their basic necessities.

Through popular assemblies they put into practice a genuine participatory democracy. And they offer solidarity to other marginal communities in Morazán, sharing what they themselves have learned and sending community teachers to teach in other communities which have never had the opportunity to learn. "Our community development," they say "will be our contribution to peace in El Salvador."

These are all signs of life in the midst of a war that has caused 75,000 deaths in ten years.

The poor in Morazán, despite the suffering and persecution they endure, continue to give testimony of their faith in the resurrection. Their eyes have been opened through their efforts to build a new life together, like the eyes of the two disciples in the story of Emmaus at the breaking of the bread.

Even now the people continue on the road to a new Pentecost where *"the old will dream dreams and the young will see visions,"* like Juana, an eighty-year-old great-grandmother who has returned to see her native land after ten years in exile, or

Isabel, a young catechist with whom I read the psalm of the returning exiles:

> *They went away, went away weeping,*
>   *carrying the seed;*
> *They come back, come back singing,*
>   *carrying their sheaves. (126:6)*

[26]

On the Road to Emmaus (II)

April 1990 . . . Segundo Montes City, Morazán

Holy Week is upon us. Already there are signs of its presence like the first rain showers that refresh the earth or the song of the locusts in the evening. Today I passed by a little *ranchito* and was greeted with a slice of freshly baked bread and a cold drink. People are preparing for their first Holy Week in Morazán in ten years. "This is not going to be a Holy Week filled with sorrow," they say, "but with hope."

Early in the week we met with the pastoral team in Segundo Montes City to prepare for Holy Week. The people are quite eager to be of service to the community. Some of them have worked more than twenty years as delegates of the Word. They are the ones who have had to discern the signs of the time during these past two decades since the Latin American Bishops Conference in Medellín and its call for a preferential option for the poor. These have been decades filled with social convulsions, violence, persecution, and liberation struggles that have awakened the consciences and hopes of the popular majority in El Salvador, Central America, and the Latin American continent.

These delegates of the Word and these catechists have lived these difficult years of repression by "remaining in their places," as Archbishop Romero called on them to do, in a region that has been abandoned by the institutional church for the past ten years. They are, in the words of the Gospel, *"salt of the earth," "light to the world,"* and *"leaven in the dough."*

Later that evening we prepared the table that would serve as

194

an altar, recalling the words of the first martyred priest in El Salvador, Rutilio Grande: "Let us go to the banquet, to the table of creation, where everyone has a place and no one lacks what he or she needs." We met beneath the trees as the lay delegates read the readings for the penitential rite.

This penitential service challenged me, particularly since the people have suffered so much injustice. They have been the victims of such cruelty and abomination. What sin do the poor of El Salvador have, especially when you compare their personal sins to the "structural sins" of war, poverty, and oppression for which U.S. policy is in no small measure responsible? Without a doubt, the Salvadoran poor identify more with a crucified Christ than with those who crucified him.

The penitential rite, however, is an important moment for the people as they remember their lack of generosity or solidarity, and the times they have been discouraged.

Next, one of the lay delegates read from the First Letter of Paul to the Corinthians:

> Sisters and brothers, you must not forget our ancestors who walked behind the cloud and crossed the Red Sea together. In this way they remained united with Moses when they were baptized in the cloud and the sea. (10:1–2)

The people gathered here tonight recalled their journey these past ten years, passing through a "Red Sea" of so much suffering, fleeing for years "in the wilderness" and exiled to the refugee camps in Honduras, walking always toward a "promised land." It has been a real baptism of fire and blood! Ramón, one of the delegates, recalled their journey:

> Each time the army invaded they burned our houses, destroyed our crops, and killed our people. We were baptized in this suffering, but we never lost sight of our hope to return one day to our beloved country.

Truly these are profound experiences that the oppressed peoples of Central America have lived. It may not be that "history repeats itself," as is sometimes said, but it does advance. The story of the people of Israel illuminates the journey of this oppressed people today as they struggle for their definitive liberation. In this sense, not only does the Bible illuminate the history of the oppressed peoples of Central America, but the history of the oppressed today deepens our understanding of the ongoing pilgrimage of the people of God in history, as related to us by Scripture.

Holy Thursday: The Passion of the Repatriated Refugees

Today we celebrated the beginning of the passion of Jesus: the washing of the disciples' feet and the Last Supper. Once again we met beneath the trees, this time in the settlement of San Luis, around a table adorned with flowers. More than one hundred people gathered around the table that served as an altar, faces of a people who have lived the passion and the resurrection in their own flesh during these past ten years of war. This reality was the point of departure for one of the delegates' opening words for the celebration:

> Just as the people of Israel recalled their liberation from slavery in Egypt, in the paschal supper we, too, recall our own history, how we lived under oppression, how we organized to struggle against injustice, how we had to flee to the hills to take refuge in Honduras, and how we prepared ourselves there, learning many things so that when we returned one day we could help rebuild our country.

After this introduction the story of the exodus and the Last Supper were read. Father Dennis Leder began the reflection:

> Sisters and brothers, today we recall the Passover that the people of Israel celebrated in Egypt, a Passover which is the sacrament of liberation from slavery, the same Passover which Jesus celebrated as the Eucharist centuries later. Today we are beneath these trees in Morazán, two thousand years later, celebrating that same Passover.

One by one the people began to share their own reflections. Some recalled the past ten years in exile as a lesson for the future: "Just like the people at the Passover supper with their shoes on and their walking sticks in hand, we should be prepared to face the challenges of the future." Others recalled the years in exile as a new way to live as Christians: "We are poor, and we should live together in community with a spirit of solidarity as a church of the poor."

People also expressed gratitude for having returned to El Salvador:

I want to give thanks for being here in our country today, after ten years in exile. It is a blessing from God to be able to pass from slavery to this Promised Land, as it will be a blessing one day to be with our loved ones who so generously gave their lives for our liberation.

That's what Alejandro said, the father of Father Octavio Ortiz, the Salvadoran priest killed eleven years before. In all, five of Alejandro's children have been killed during these ten years of war.

It is impressive to see how this ancient history of the exodus continues to be a reality today in the liberation struggles in Central America, and how the oppressed peoples here identify themselves as a people of God. They also offer signs of service and solidarity. They want to build a new life in community here in Morazán where the gestures of the Eucharist and the washing of the feet become incarnated in their daily lives and in the very structures of the society that they are creating.

This Holy Thursday was an occasion for joy and a sign of hope for all who shared in the celebration. Tonight we ate supper in the humble *ranchito* of one of the lay delegates in this community, enjoying the hospitality and generosity of these campesino families of Morazán. The next day we proceeded to the settlement of Los Hatos, and later of Los Quebrachos, to celebrate the Way of the Cross on Good Friday.

Good Friday: A Martyred People Announces Resurrection

This year marks the third Holy Week I have celebrated in Morazán. The first was in the town of Perquín two years ago; last year I accompanied people from the villages of Estancia and Calavera, on the Torola River, near the town of Cacaopera; and this year in Segundo Montes City, near the town of Meanguera. Each year has been different, with a little more freedom for the people of Morazán.

But this freedom has not been without a price; it has been won at the cost of much blood and suffering. Those who have sown this freedom with their lives are no longer here; today others enjoy the fruits of their generosity. This has always been the faith of the church since its beginning in the catacombs when the Eucharist was celebrated over the relics of the martyrs, a church that was born from and continues to be nourished by the blood of the martyrs.

Today we celebrated Good Friday in the settlement of Los Hatos, accompanying the people in their Way of the Cross this morning. It is a traditional procession, but the content that the repatriated refugees give it is full of life and suffering. The stations of the cross speak of the passion the people of Morazán have lived during ten years of war and struggle for liberation.

We listened attentively to the catechists call out each station: *"The women weep over Jerusalem."* A second catechist responds: "How many mothers here have not wept over their children who have been killed!" *"Jesus falls for the third time"*: "Many are the witnesses who have fallen and envelop us now like a cloud!" *"Jesus is stripped of his garments"*: "Like so many who have been stripped of their lands, their lives, their dignity!" *"Jesus is nailed to the cross"*: "Like our people who are crucified!" *"Jesus dies on the cross"*: "Like so many who have died in this war!"

These *via cruces*, which are repeated in villages and streets throughout El Salvador, are very traditional, but they express the heart of the poor, full of suffering and pain, but also of people's hope. The very act of walking over these rocky paths recalls all the flights of the people through the hills and ravines to escape the army, many times at night. That's why this popular religiosity expresses so well the passion, death, and resurrection of the Salvadoran people.

In the afternoon we celebrated the Adoration of the Cross in the settlement of Los Quebrachos, looking at the beautiful mountains which surrounded us on all sides. The Suffering Servant passage from Isaiah was read, and then the Gospel story of the trial and passion of Jesus as he is called before the secular and ecclesiastical authorities of his day. One of the catechists offered this reflection:

> It's a sad history which reflects our own history. Today there are also priests and bishops who refuse to denounce injustice. Today there are still soldiers who carry out orders to kill their own people. Today Jesus still suffers in our people.

This celebration moved me, perhaps because we celebrated it in such a memorable place, looking at the hills that surround the martyred village of El Mozote in the distance. In front of the altar the people had placed a cross, a sign of the suffering of hundreds of campesinos massacred at El Mozote; a sign, too, of the generosity of the martyrs and of Jesus.

We reflected on the meaning of the cross. Father Dennis began the reflection:

> Today this cross is a symbol not only of the death of Jesus but also of his offering of love for us. Today we recall not only Jesus but all of our martyrs, including Archbishop Romero, Father Octavio Ortiz, Father Segundo Montes, and all of our family members who have shared the cross of Jesus, generously giving up their lives for our liberation.

A lay delegate also spoke:

> Before, we thought that the army had eliminated our faith in El Salvador. Later priests, sisters, and catechists were killed. Then thousands of poor women, even pregnant women, and children were killed. But they could not finish

*off all of us. We discovered that all these martyrs live today
in our people and continue to inspire us, giving us strength
in our struggle for liberation.*

We carried the cross in a short procession and then formed
two lines, singing these traditional songs: "Come, sinner, to the
foot of the cross and adore the blood of my good Jesus." Those
who view this ritual from the outside may think that it is passive
or perhaps alienating, blessing the suffering of the people. But in
reality it expresses much more. Lived from within, with faith, it
is exactly the opposite of resignation and offers a response to the
question that the massacre at El Mozote awakens in us: *"Why do
the just and the innocent suffer?"*

Today it seems clearer to me than ever that the Way of the
Cross is a commitment the people make to follow the example
of the martyrs who offered their lives in the struggle for justice
and the liberation of their people.

And if there were any doubts, the song which the people sang
about the martyrdom of Father Octavio Ortiz, who was killed in
El Despertar, dispelled them:

> *Let us go forward with all of our strength,*
> *and erase every sign of sadness;*
> *five brothers are calling us*
> *to continue the struggle.*
> *We must go forward*
> *and never lose our ideals;*
> *that's what the martyrs of El Despertar*
> *cry out to us to do.*

Easter Vigil: The Resurrection of a People in Exile

Perhaps it was inevitable. It would have been unreal if the war
did not make its presence felt during Holy Week in Morazán. As
Saturday dawned, we heard the sound of machine guns and
rockets fired by the helicopters that flew near the settlements of
the repatriated refugees. More than one hundred soldiers penetrated the area during the night hours, and early on Saturday the

sounds of war were heard. I thought of the reading for Holy Week where the soldiers guard the tomb of Jesus, *"so that he won't be raised from the dead."* The same is true today: the wealthy and powerful do not want to see the resurrection of the poor in El Salvador.

But the people want to celebrate their Easter. They have returned to live in Morazán after ten years of exile, and they want to experience the power of the resurrection in their lives! We passed the morning meeting with the lay delegates and catechists, sharing experiences of other catechists who were visiting from as far away as the town of San Francisco Gotera in Morazán, and San Salvador. It's a propitious time, on this day of Holy Saturday, to share and deepen this hope for new life. And always, when poor communities get together, they generate new life.

In the afternoon we shared our reflection with other communities in northern Morazán that are accompanied by Fathers Rogelio Ponseele and Esteban Velásquez, the same communities I had worked with the previous year. These are moments of great joy and great hope. In spite of the abandonment of the region by the bishop, the people of northern Morazán continue to share their faith and bear witness to the gospel as they struggle for their liberation. Rogelio and Esteban are hopeful that one day they will be able to carry out their pastoral work of accompaniment without persecution and with the full backing of the institutional church.

When we returned to the settlement of Los Quebrachos for the night, the people were gathering for the Easter vigil. We met beneath the trees by the light of a kerosene lantern. A bonfire was lit and the blessing of the fire took place. Then the Easter candle was lit. Beneath the stars of an immense sky over Morazán, illuminated by the lantern and the candles, we celebrated the most profound and ancient mysteries of our faith and our humanity: the passion, death, and resurrection of Jesus in our lives and in history.

We read the story of creation, followed by the Exodus reading about the liberation of Israel from slavery in Egypt; finally, the story of the resurrection was read. One of the catechists began the reflection:

*Tonight we celebrate three steps, three passages in the life
of our people: from darkness to light, from slavery to freedom, from death to life. They are passages which our people have undertaken during these ten years of war and
struggle for liberation. Tonight, too, we celebrate the baptism of these children as a sign of new life in our midst, as
we recall the passage of Jesus from death to resurrection.*

I thought again of the question that was posed one year ago
tonight as we celebrated the Easter vigil under the shadow of the
war in the village of Calavera. Could it be that after ten years of
war, 75,000 deaths, and 1.5 million people displaced from their
homes, in the midst of a profound social and economic crisis,
that the resurrection has no power here?

On the contrary, the presence of these 8,400 repatriated refugees, their return to their homes in Morazán after ten years in
exile, and all the acquired learning and skills they bring back with
them to build a new life together and a new model of society in
El Salvador, based on justice, cooperative labor, and solidarity—
all this is testimony of the resurrection of Christ in the poor of El
Salvador. With this conviction we ended the Easter vigil and
walked to our homes to rest for the night, waiting for a new day
to dawn.

Christ's Resurrection, El Salvador's Liberation!

The following day, Easter Sunday, we went to the town of
Meanguera to celebrate the Easter Mass. More than three hundred people participated, and fifty children were baptized. It was
the first time in ten years that the church bells rang in this town,
which was abandoned in 1980 when the refugees fled to Honduras.

The celebration of Holy Week ended with these words of hope:

*This is a most propitious day to celebrate these ancient rites
of our church, because today we are living the resurrection
of Christ in the resurrection of our people. We have passed
over paths of suffering, death, and martyrdom, but these*

paths have led us to this resurrection. We have returned to our homes in Morazán after ten years in exile in order to begin a new life together. Death has not won out, but life has the last word!

Today the people are beginning to rebuild their lives in Morazán. One symbol of this new life is the repopulation of Arambala, a town that was abandoned eight years ago after the massacre in El Mozote. Today it has come back to life with the return of several families to their homes there. Like the ancient prophecy of Ezekiel, the dry bones begin to revive again in a resurrected people who search for life and for liberation. And so the banners this day proclaim the good news throughout Morazán: "Christ's Resurrection, El Salvador's liberation!"

EL GRITO
DE LIBERACION DE ESTE PUEBLO
ES UN CLAMOR QUE SUBE HASTA DIO
Y QUE YA NADA NI NADIE
LO PUEDE DETENER.

EPILOGUE

Every Tear Shall Be Wiped Away

February 1, 1992 . . . San Salvador

Who could believe it? They came from all parts of El Salvador, streaming down the highways—with no soldiers in sight—waving their red handkerchiefs as bright as their smiles, many with tears in their eyes. I saw friends from years past, their faces and their stories reaching back to 1980 and the beginning of the war that had now come to an end. The war is over! Who could believe it?

Like a river they came, streaming through the streets of San Salvador, thousands of rivulets that began in the mountains a decade ago as far away as the border with Honduras in La Cañada and Las Aradas in Chalatenango and La Guacamaya in Morazán. Now twelve years later the people flow into the streets of the *Plaza Cívica*, renamed the Plaza of the Martyrs, to celebrate their victory, the end of the war: *"They went away, went away weeping, carrying the seed; They come back singing, carrying their sheaves" (Psalm 126:6).*

We walked through the streets, beginning at the monument of *El Salvador del Mundo*, where so many marches have begun, and where now the government celebration was beginning (but only a handful of people stayed), and we marched toward the Plaza of the Martyrs as the sound of Beethoven's "Ode to Joy" filled the air:

Come, sing, dream as you sing,
live and dream of a new day,
in which all people will become
brothers and sisters.

My eyes filled with tears. Twelve years, twelve long years, and now the war is over! As we marched I saw many familiar faces. Catalina was there from the village of Corral de Piedra, renamed Ignacio Ellacuría after the February 5, 1990 bombing, which killed four children and one adult. Across the way I saw Chepe, from the village of Copapayo, site of the November 4, 1983 massacre, which killed 118 people. And a little farther along I saw Pedro from the village of La Joya in Morazán. Pedro escaped the El Mozote massacre that killed hundreds of people on December 11–12, 1981. He filed the criminal complaint in the Salvadoran courts, formally accusing the Salvadoran military of the El Mozote massacre.

So much sadness, so much suffering, so much blood shed in these twelve years: 75,000 dead, and each victim had a name, a hope, a loved one, a dream. Today, however, we marched jubilantly to the sound of the "Ode to Joy," and triumphantly to "The People United Will Never Be Defeated." The faces and the smiles, the tears and the joy, the red banners and the cries, our steps and the blue sky overhead all mingled with the music as we entered the Plaza of the Martyrs, carried forward by the stream of people flowing to the center of San Salvador where for twelve long years they dreamed to come.

How Beautiful on the Mountains

The war in El Salvador lasted twelve long years, although its roots go back generations, perhaps centuries, to the beginning of the conquest. Five hundred years of domination and exploitation, five hundred years also of incredible faith and resistance. The armed struggle began twenty-two years ago, then broke out into open war January 10, 1981, but the military dictatorship goes back at least to 1932 and the massacre of 30,000 people, including Farabundo Martí for whom the FMLN (Farabundo Martí

National Liberation Front) is named. Today, February 1, 1992, the first day of peace in El Salvador, marks the sixtieth anniversary of Farabundo Martí's execution before a firing squad.

Since the FMLN military offensive in San Salvador in November 1989, and the army's assassination of the six Jesuit priests and the two women, the situation of the war in El Salvador changed. Even the United States realized that there was no military solution to the conflict, and a process of negotiation began that ended with the signing of the Peace Accords in New York December 31, 1991, and in Mexico January 16, 1992. For weeks during the month of December I followed closely the advances and the obstacles, the declarations and the rumors, but never did I dream that peace was so close at hand.

The Advent readings in December took on special poignancy as we all hoped for peace:

> Shout for joy, O daughter of Zion!
>   Rejoice, O people of Israel!
> Yahweh has lifted the sentence of your
>   condemnation
> and has driven your enemies away.
>   (Zephaniah 3:14-15)

And the Christmas reading that I had last heard the year before standing in the ruins of the church in Mozote:

> How beautiful on the mountains
>   are the feet of one who brings good news,
> who heralds peace and happiness,
>   who proclaims salvation
>   and announces to Zion:
>   "Your God is king!" (Isaiah 52:7)

Now, however, these feet have multiplied by the thousands, these tired and weary feet of so many humble campesinos who have walked these mountains by night fleeing from the military in years past have been converted into the jubilant feet of these same campesinos who come to celebrate their victory of peace!

On Epiphany this year I remembered in a special way Archbishop Romero's homily twelve years before, given just two months before his death. I carried these words with me all these years as a reminder of that star of hope to which he alludes:

> *I want to reaffirm my conviction as a person of hope that a new ray of salvation will come . . . What we must preserve above all is the liberation struggle of our people . . . The star which guides our people must be this: How can we guarantee that this struggle of the people for social justice does not stop or wither away but go forward?*

Who could believe it? It was like a dream, and we rubbed our eyes and embraced each other to assure ourselves that it was real. It is only the beginning. Much work remains to be done; there are still many dangers and risks. But today, at least, we celebrate the peace as a triumph of the people.

You Have Risen in Our People!

Ever since we arrived in San Salvador January 30, two days before the cease-fire went into effect, I was struck by the absence of soldiers in the streets—and the presence of the FMLN everywhere, from sympathizers with their red handkerchiefs, to the unarmed combatants, to the General Command. You would have to have been in El Salvador during these past twelve years to appreciate the difference!

Early Saturday morning we went to the installation of COPAZ, the Commission for Peace, which is made up of representatives from the government and the FMLN, as well as the entire spectrum of political parties in El Salvador. Each representative had their turn to speak, but the loudest applause was for the FMLN representative on the commission, Joaquín Villalobos. It was incredible just to see the array of political forces and declared enemies sharing the same platform.

But what touched me in a special way was the humanity of Villalobos' discourse:

> *Nobody can doubt that the FMLN has defended the interests of the poor during these years of struggle . . . We are*

*proud of our role in the transformation of the country, but
we are also aware that we committed errors and this is the
moment to say to the nation with humility that we recognize
this . . . In order for there to be economic development and
stability, there must be profound changes in the ownership
of land . . . But whoever believes they have the absolute
truth or the perfect economic model is mistaken; only consensus will offer a true solution.*

The names of many martyrs were recalled as well — Archbishop Romero, the six Jesuit priests, Guillermo Ungo — and they
received long applauses as well. Only the mention of Major Roberto D'Aubuissón, founder of the death squads and the ARENA
party, evoked sharp disapproval from the people gathered.

Once in the Plaza of the Martyrs we heard more speeches by
each of the five leaders of the General Command of the FMLN.
Shafik Handal reminded the people that the Peace Accords are
"the responsibility of everyone, not just the FMLN and the government," and he called on all present to solemnly affirm their
commitment to defend them:

*They told us over and over again that the FMLN had no
popular support. But look at you! Your presence here today
is a confirmation of the fact that the FMLN has its roots in
the people. There is not a single Salvadoran family here
today which has not lost a son or a daughter, a spouse or
a parent, or somebody to the military repression during
these past twelve years of the war.*

The speeches went on into the night, but it was the faces of
the people and their joy, the reencounter between hundreds of
unarmed FMLN combatants filing past the crowd and shaking the
hands of the people one by one, the remembrance of loved ones
not present, that touched my heart. Overlooking the crowd
below, a banner of Archbishop Romero hung on the front of the
cathedral with these words painted on it: "Archbishop Romero,
you have risen in our people!"

Now Lord, You May Dismiss Your Servant in Peace

The next day, Sunday, we went to Mass in Calle Real, a small village nine kilometers north of San Salvador. This is the parish of Monsignor Urioste, the Vicar of Pastoral Work in the Archdiocese, and briefly the successor to Archbishop Romero until Bishop Rivera Damas was named to take his place. Just days before, in a celebration here in Calle Real, Monsignor Urioste compared the Peace Accords to a blueprint of a house waiting to be built, where all of us are master-builders. This is the sense of the Medellín documents as well: "Peace is a permanent task, the fruit of justice and of love," and each of us is called to become "artisans of peace."

Today's Gospel recalled the story of Simeon:

> *Now Lord you may dismiss your servant in*
> *   peace,*
> *because my eyes have seen your salvation*
> *which you display in the sight of all peoples.*

How many elderly people must identify with his joy! A story was told about Pedro, a campesino who last heard from his son when he received a letter from him explaining his decision to join the FMLN in the mountains: "Father," his son wrote him, "if I live to see the day of peace, let's meet in the plaza in San Salvador to rejoice."

On Saturday Pedro went to the plaza to celebrate with everybody else the inauguration of peace, but his joy was tinged with the sadness that marks the feelings of so many these days. His son was not there; he had been killed in the fighting years before. I looked up at the cross that hung beside the altar—a huge wooden cross adorned with flowers that seemed to speak of this joy and sadness.

The next day we celebrated a liturgy in Resurrection Lutheran Church with Bishop Medardo Gómez. Once again I was struck by the readings chosen for this day—the Road to Emmaus—which is traditionally read the Monday after Easter. Yet there is a festivity in the air much like Easter. Even the words on Archbishop Romero's banner in the Plaza of the Martyrs were written in the past rather than the future tense: "You *have* risen in our people!"

Bishop Gómez compared the Peace Accords to the birth of a child:

> On December 31 the child was born. On January 16 the umbilical cord was cut. On February 1 the child was baptized. And on October 31, when the first stage of the peace process is completed, the FMLN is demobilized, and the military is restructured, the child will be confirmed.

Later that morning we went to the UCA chapel where the five FMLN commanders were welcomed by the rector of the university, Father Francisco Estrada, S.J. "We will continue to accompany you," he told the FMLN, "and offer you our critical perspective." Shafik Handal recalled the years of fruitful dialogue and debate between the FMLN and Father Ignacio Ellacuría, the former rector of the UCA and one of the Jesuit martyrs.

But it was Joaquín Villalobos who surprised people with his candid admission: "We have come here today not only to render homage to the Jesuit martyrs, but to say to Ellacuría that he was right," referring perhaps to Ellacuría's commitment to a negotiated settlement to the war.

Father Jon Sobrino, S.J., spoke movingly of El Salvador as "holy ground," and spoke of the cross as the place where "great suffering and great love" converge. Following his words the five FMLN commanders placed a wreath of flowers on the tombs of the six Jesuit martyrs and proceeded to the rose garden where the six had been killed by the Atlacatl Battalion on November 16, 1989. There Obdulio, the husband and father of the two women who were killed with the six Jesuits, clipped a rose for each of the FMLN commanders.

A New Heaven and a New Earth

In the following days we made two trips to the countryside to return to these "holy places" where so much suffering and so much love have converged, places where I had spent most of my time in El Salvador during the past decade: Chalatenango and Morazán. These are places that recall the prophecy of Isaiah invoked by Jon Sobrino in the chapel of the UCA on Monday:

> *I will create a new heaven and a new earth,*
> *and the former things will not be remembered*
> *   nor come to mind again.*
> *For I will create Jerusalem to be a joy*
> *   and its people to be a delight.*
>   *(Isaiah 65:17–18)*

I thought of Archbishop Romero's words as well: "Over these ruins the glory of God will shine!"

We traveled over the highway to Chalatenango without encountering a single military roadblock! It may not seem significant to someone visiting El Salvador for the first time, but these roadblocks in the past have isolated thousands of poor families in regions that effectively became condemned by the military as "free-fire zones" and targets of indiscriminate bombings.

Today, however, we passed without any problem through the town of Chalatenango on our way to the repatriated communities of Guarjila, Ignacio Ellacuría, and San José las Flores, before crossing the Sumpul River to Nueva Trinidad and finally to Arcatao, our destination.

What joy to see Esperanza after so many years! I recalled those early years in 1983–1984 walking these same paths with her and so many others as thousands fled the invasions of the Salvadoran army, walking by night and hiding in the hills by day. Esperanza received us warmly and prepared a hot meal of beans and tortillas for us. We sat and reminisced as she recalled the sufferings of past years.

As we talked, Dalila, her eight-year-old niece, showed us a picture of her father who was killed along with her mother when Dalila was two. What does peace mean to so many children like Dalila who are orphans of this war?

Esperanza recalled the day and month she left her home— June 13, 1980—to hide in the hills. She recalled the May 1982 army invasion, which killed hundreds of campesinos near the

Sumpul River (the second Sumpul River massacre). She recalled the November 1985 bombing that injured her two-month-old son, and the March 1986 army invasion, when she hid with her child in the house of an evangelical family, filling the kitchen with smoke to obscure her presence from the soldiers.

After she related these stories, Esperanza showed us a picture of Mario, her eighteen-year-old son who had fought in the FMLN and was killed in December 1990. She spoke with a tinge of sadness, but also joy and expectation at the coming birth of another child due any day now.

These days are filled with anxiety about the future, especially with the question of land tenure. Every campesino living in the conflictive areas controlled by the FMLN is guaranteed land by the Peace Accords, but how this will be worked out when the original owners return remains to be seen. "We are ready to give back the houses to the prior owners," Esperanza told us, "but we expect them to help us to resolve the problem of land and housing for all of our families displaced by the war."

The United Nations is separating the FMLN and the Salvadoran army and concentrating them in a limited number of locations. Both sides seem relieved that the war is over, but there is concern about security once the FMLN is demobilized in October. Already the death squads have begun to reappear, and many of the problems that gave rise to the war, like land, remain to be resolved. The problem of reconciliation between those who have suffered so many deaths and those responsible for so many massacres must be also worked out. "There will be no reconciliation without truth and justice," Archbishop Rivera Damas has said.

On our way back to San Salvador the next day we stopped in El Paisnal at the site where Father Rutilio Grande, S.J., and two others were killed March 12, 1977. He was the first of a long line of priests, nuns, and catechists who have been killed these past fifteen years because of their option for the poor and their commitment to justice. *"Padre Rutilio, your cross is not only of wood but of light,"* the popular song goes.

And All Tears Will Be Wiped Away

Two days later we traveled to Morazán to visit the communities north of the Torola River which, until the return of the refugees from Honduras in November 1989, had remained isolated from the rest of the country by the military blockade at the river. With the return of eight thousand refugees, however, and the construction of Segundo Montes City, the military blockade was broken and the entire region opened up.

These mountains are so beautiful, filled as they are with so much joy and sadness. During the past few days the FMLN commanders have been meeting with the FMLN combatants in the camps designated by the United Nations to celebrate the cease-fire. Just two days ago Joaquín Villalobos had been in Morazán and, as he had stated at the UCA, he said that Segundo Montes had been right in his conviction that the solution to El Salvador's conflict was the disappearance of both armies — that of the FMLN and that of the government. Segundo Montes was one of the Jesuits murdered November 16, 1989, the same week the refugees returned from Honduras and gave his name to their new community.

We stayed the night in Perquín and spoke with Esteban Velásquez and Rogelio Ponseele, two priests who have accompanied the Christian communities in these areas of conflict and FMLN control in Morazán. Both are here by reason of conscience, despite the lack of support from the local bishop who is a military chaplain. Esteban shared with us news about the struggle over land and a meeting soon to take place between the returning mayors (mostly from the ARENA party) and the communal organizations of the people that replaced the mayors these past ten years of war. They will be meeting soon to resolve the problem of land. Without land for these campesinos who have suffered the most in the twelve years of war there will be no peace and no reconciliation.

Esteban also shared with us the difficult questions that lie ahead as to whether or not to accept the economic funding of the United States channeled through the Agency for International Development (AID). During the war AID money has been used to support counterinsurgency programs of the Salvadoran army. Many people asked us, "Would you accept money from the person who armed the man who killed your brother?" Yet alternative economic models will require outside capital. The question is from whom and on what terms.

The next morning we traveled with Esteban and Rogelio to Segundo Montes City. Along the way Rogelio recounted his words in the Plaza of the Martyrs February 1. It was his first time there in twelve years since he left San Salvador to go to the mountains of Morazán in December 1980.

I told the crowd that I came to Morazán to bring faith and hope to the people, and they in turn taught me the meaning of faith and hope. I came to evangelize and in turn I was evangelized by the people.

Later Rogelio read from a poem entitled "The Political Party":

Unless you've come to give your heart and life,
    don't bother to join . . .
because here a wound is the most coveted
        flower.
This place is fit only for sacrifice.
Here you must be the last to eat, the last to have,
    the last to sleep, and the first to die.

I thought of many friends, now dead, and the generosity of their lives: Darío, Ana Elsy, Mireya, Dora. In the midst of so much sacrifice and suffering, they always managed to smile.

Rogelio also recalled how he ended his words in the Plaza with a reading from the book of Revelation:

I saw a new heaven and a new earth . . . Here is the dwelling of God among the people. God will pitch a tent among them and they will be God's people. God will be with them and wipe every tear from their eyes. There will be no more death or mourning, crying out or pain, for the world that was has passed away. (Revelation 21:1-4)

The words reminded me of that most popular of songs in El Salvador, also sung on February 1 in the Plaza of the Martyrs, *"El Sombrero Azul,"* and the verse: *"May joy come to wash away the suffering."* Joy has come at last to El Salvador, the streams of people in the streets that day have washed the years of suffering—if not "away," at least with the healing waters of justice and peace and the hope for reconciliation and new life.

Marina was with us, filled with a contagious spirit of joy. She is one of dozens of catechists who have accompanied her people during all these years of war. I remember Marina's story, how she fled at age fifteen from her home in Torola in October 1980 and hid in the hills from the army. She and her sister-in-law each gave birth to children in the hills, only her sister-in-law died in childbirth and Marina nursed both children until they reached Honduras in December 1980. A year later Marina's child died in the refugee camp in Colomoncagua.

So many people have died, and so many children. The suffering of the children, especially, is hard to bear. "May joy come to wash away the suffering" of these children and bring new life to El Salvador!

El Salvador: Standing on Holy Ground

Now as we close our journey to El Salvador and prepare to leave, my thoughts go out toward the future. What will become of El Salvador? Who will remember? What are the tasks ahead? "This is the most significant moment in our history since our independence from Spain," said Facundo Guardado, one of the FMLN commanders. "It is the first time a revolution has been negotiated," U.N. mediator Alvaro de Soto commented. But the way ahead is filled with risks and dangers.

With the collapse of state socialism in Eastern Europe and the Soviet Union, and the defeat of the Sandinistas in the 1990 elections in Nicaragua, there appears to be no viable alternative to the free-market capitalism of the "New World Order" that the United States is trying to impose on the rest of the world. The results, however, have been disastrous for the poor of the Third World, and unless there are profound economic and political changes in the relations between the North and the South, the poor will continue to be the victims.

But the dream of a democratic socialism—political democracy with social and economic justice—remains alive, and El Salvador will provide a testing ground that many third-world nations will be watching. "We claim the right to dream," Eduardo Galeano said after the collapse of the socialist bloc in the 1990s, and if the past twelve years are any key to the future, El Salvador will continue to be "holy ground," a place of great suffering but even more, a place of great love and great hope for the poor and the oppressed of the entire world.

Notes

Introduction: Truth Crushed to Earth

1. Phrase used by Dr. Martin Luther King. See also Psalm 85:10-11: *"Mercy and truth shall meet, righteousness and peace shall kiss. Truth shall spring out of the earth and righteousness shall look down from heaven."*

2. Report of the Commission on the Truth for El Salvador, entitled *From Madness to Hope: The Twelve-Year War in El Salvador*, available in English or Spanish upon request from the United Nations Office of Public Information.

3. "The Commission on the Truth registered more than 22,000 complaints of serious acts of violence that occurred in El Salvador between January 1980 and July 1991. Over 7,000 were received directly at the Commission's offices in various locations. The remainder were received through governmental and non-governmental institutions. . . . Those giving testimony attributed almost 85 percent of the cases to agents of the State, paramilitary groups allied to them, and the death squads. . . . The complaints registered accused the FMLN in approximately 5 percent of the cases. . . . Despite their large numbers, these complaints do not cover every act of violence." *From Madness to Hope*, 43.

4. Jose María Tojeira, S.J., the Provincial for the Central American Province of Jesuits, said: "The amnesty law passed by the government in recent days is an offense to justice. Few people in El Salvador doubt the need to look for legal mechanisms to grant pardon, after a civil war which has lasted for more than a decade; but the current amnesty law was passed in a capricious and indiscriminate, and apparently illegal, manner without any consensus. All of which makes one think that it is a mockery of justice. . . ." *Carta a las Iglesias* (UCA, San Salvador), #279, April 1-15, 1993.

5. Between 1980 and 1992 the United States sent over $6 billion to the government of El Salvador, most of which was spent on direct military aid, or economic support funds to bolster the war economy.

219

6. Of the twenty-seven military officers cited in the Jesuit massacre, nineteen were graduates of the School of the Americas in Ft. Benning, Georgia. Of the twelve military officers cited in the El Mozote massacre, ten were School of the Americas graduates. Of the five military officers cited in the murder of the four U.S. churchwomen, three were School of the Americas graduates. Of the three military officers (or ex-officers) cited in the assassination of Archbishop Romero, two were School of the Americas graduates. See *School of the Americas Watch*, P.O. Box 3330, Columbus, GA 31903.

7. Under international law, and the Conventions and Protocols of Geneva, serious crimes against civilians occurred in both nations. No provision was made by the Peace Accords to bring to justice those responsible for human rights violations in El Salvador. The Ad Hoc Commission named more than a hundred military officers and called on them to resign from active duty. Not since the Nuremberg Trials in Germany have military officials been tried for crimes against humanity. In February 1992, the United Nations Security Council set up a War Crimes Tribunal to investigate crimes against civilians in Bosnia, and has subsequently appointed judges to try the cases. But nothing similar has been done for El Salvador. See "Terror, Tribunals and the Truth," by Tina Rosenberg, *The Washington Post*, March 14, 1993.

8. "The chairman of a House subcommittee charged yesterday that the Reagan administration lied to Congress for years about the Salvadoran armed forces' complicity in murder, and he said that 'every word uttered by every Reagan administration official' about the observance of human rights in El Salvador should be reviewed for perjury. 'This Congress ten years ago established a process whereby President Reagan would certify that improvements were being made in human rights in order to continue military aid to El Salvador. It now is abundantly clear that Ronald Reagan made those certifications in defiance of the truth.' " *The Washington Post*, March 17, 1993.

9. "Declaring human rights central to United States policy, Secretary of State Warren Christopher appointed a panel today to investigate charges that State Department officials misled Congress about atrocities by the military in El Salvador throughout the 1980s." *The New York Times*, March 25, 1993.

10. "Report of the Secretary of State's Panel on El Salvador," United States Department of State, July 1993.

11. "Report of the Secretary of State's Panel on El Salvador," United States Department of State, July 1993, 1-3.

12. *"Then you will know the truth, and the truth will make you free"* (John 8:32).

13. *El Salvador: A Spring Whose Waters Never Run Dry* (EPICA, 1990), 7.

14. Ignacio Ellacuría, S.J., *"Violencia revolucionaria en el Tercer Mundo y en América Latina," Carta a las Iglesias* (UCA, San Salvador), 167.

15. *El Salvador: A Spring Whose Waters Never Run Dry* (EPICA, 1990), 73.

16. The Peace Accords were signed January 16, 1992 in Chapúltepec, Mexico by President Alfredo Cristiani and the General Command of the FMLN. On February 1, 1992 a cease-fire took effect, formally ending the twelve-year civil war.

17. This is the figure which is commonly accepted and used by the Archdiocese of San Salvador, the Jesuits, and the press generally. See "75,000 Deaths," the lead editorial in *The Washington Post*, March 18, 1993: "As part of the peace machinery that the United Nations constructed for El Salvador, a 'Commission on the Truth' was formed to deal with the unspeakable civilian slaughter — 75,000 deaths — in its civil war." See also "Truth, Lies and El Salvador," the lead editorial in *The New York Times*, March 16, 1993: "A United Nations Truth Commission now confirms what the Reagan Administration sought to cloud — that terrible crimes were perpetrated in freedom's name by the armed forces of El Salvador. . . . The report itself is a cathartic memorial to 75,000 victims of a twelve-year civil war."

18. *El Salvador: A Spring Whose Waters Never Run Dry* (EPICA, 1990), 7.

19. *The Washington Post*, January 27, 1982, and *The New York Times,* January 27, 1982.

20. On February 8, Assistant Secretary of State Thomas Enders told the Senate Foreign Relations Committee: "We sent two Embassy officers to investigate recent reports of a massacre in the Morazán village of El Mozote. They reported that while it is clear that an armed confrontation between guerrillas occupying El Mozote and attacking government forces occurred last December, no evidence could be found to confirm that government forces systematically massacred civilians in the operation zone." Assistant Secretary of State for Human Rights Elliott Abrams told the same Senate Committee: "This case is an interesting one in a sense, because we found, for example, that the numbers, first of all, were not credible because, as Secretary Enders notes, our information was that there were only 300 people in the canton. It appears to be an incident which is at least being significantly misused, at the very best, by the guerrillas." Ten years later, after the release of the Truth Commission report, Enders said: "I was wrong," but he continued to boldly defend

U.S. policy "as the only way to end human rights abuses while preventing a communist takeover. Under our influence violence against civilians peaked, fell and ended." *The Washington Post*, March 21, 1993.

21. "On August 22, 1982, in the place known as El Calabozo situated beside the Amatitán River in the north of the Department of San Vicente, troops of the Atlacatl Rapid Deployment Infantry Battalion (BIRI) killed over 200 men, women and children whom they were holding prisoner. The victims had converged on El Calabozo from various directions, fleeing a vast anti-guerrilla military operation which had begun three days earlier in the area of Los Cerros de San Pedro and which involved, in addition to the Atlacatl BIRI, other infantry, artillery and aerial support units." *From Madness to Hope*, 125-126.

22. "On December 10, 1981, in the village of El Mozote in the Department of Morazán, units of the Atlacatl Battalion detained, without resistance, all the men, women, and children who were in the place. The following day, December 11, after spending the night locked in their homes, they were deliberately and systematically executed in groups. First, the men were tortured and executed, then the women were executed, and lastly, the children in the place where they had been locked up. The number of victims identified was over 200. The figure is higher if other unidentified victims are taken into account. . . . In the course of *Operación Rescate* massacres of civilians also occurred in . . . La Joya . . . La Ranchería . . . Los Toriles . . . Jocote Amarillo and Cerro Pando. More than 500 identified victims perished at El Mozote and in other villages. Many other victims have not been identified." *From Madness to Hope*, 114-121.

23. Rufina Amaya's testimony appears in *El Salvador: A Spring Whose Waters Never Run Dry* (EPICA, 1990), 20-21.

24. Maryknoll radio interview, 1984, Maryknoll, N.Y.

25. January 6, 1980 homily.

26. February 18, 1980 homily.

27. February 15, 1980 interview with *Prensa Latina*.

28. February 15, 1980 interview with *Prensa Latina*.

29. Archbishop Oscar Romero, *Voice of the Voiceless* (Orbis Books, 1985), 179-82.

30. March 1980 interview.

31. *"We preach a crucified Messiah . . . For the Jews, what a great scandal, and for the Greeks, what nonsense!" (1 Corinthians 1:23).*

32. I am indebted to the Christian Base Communities of El Salvador (CEBES), and the experience of working with their pastoral team, for this reflection.

33. Jon Sobrino, S.J., *"Iglesia Popular, Iglesia de los Pobres y Con-*

flicto Eclesial," *Carta a las Iglesias* (UCA, San Salvador), #48: "The church of the poor was forcefully reclaimed during Vatican II . . . following the lead of Pope John XXIII, who considered this expression as an excellent ideal for all of the Church. The preferential option for the poor, so clear in Medellín and Puebla, demands important changes in our understanding of what constitutes the church and its mission." See also Jon Sobrino, *The True Church and the Poor* (Orbis Books, 1984).

34. The National Debate for Peace in El Salvador was created in September 1988, when a broad spectrum of social sectors responded to an invitation of Archbishop Rivera Damas of San Salvador to participate in a forum whose objective was to establish a consensus for a political and negotiated settlement to the war. Only social sectors representing the right refused to attend. The conclusions of the forum were later published in *Debate Nacional, 1988,* and are available from the Archdiocese of San Salvador. See also, "A History of the National Debate for Peace in El Salvador," unpublished article available from the Washington Office of the National Debate for Peace in El Salvador.

35. The Christian base communities in El Salvador are predominantly Catholic, but there is a strong participation of Lutherans, Baptists, Episcopalians, and some Evangelicals. The participation of Christians in the struggle for justice and peace has fostered a profound sense of ecumenism.

36. In 1972 and 1977, fraudulent elections were held in which the opposition, made up of the Christian Democratic party (PDC), the National Revolutionary Movement (MNR), and the National Democratic Union (UDN) won a popular majority. In 1984 and 1989, elections were held during a time when the war and military repression made it difficult, if not impossible, to hold free and fair elections.

37. Since the signing of the Peace Accords, the international community pledged $800 million in reconstruction aid, of which the U.S. pledged $250 million. The Peace Accords make clear that all sectors of Salvadoran society should be involved in the planning, administration, and evaluation of a national plan of reconstruction. The Salvadoran government has resisted collaborating with community organizations and non-governmental agencies which represent the poor, and few if any reconstruction funds have reached these organizations.

38. *Justice in the World,* #6.

39. Archbishop Oscar Romero, *Voice of the Voiceless* (Orbis Books, 1985), 185.

40. "Declaration of Independence from the War in Vietnam," address delivered at Riverside Church, New York City, April 4, 1967.

The Beginning of a Journey: 1981–1983

1. "On March 24, 1980, the Archbishop of San Salvador, Monsignor Oscar Arnulfo Romero y Galdámez, was assassinated while celebrating Mass in the chapel of the *Hospital de la Divina Providencia*. The Commission finds that former Major Roberto D'Aubuissón gave the order to assassinate the Archbishop, and gave precise instructions to members of his security force, acting as a 'death squad,' to organize and supervise the assassination." *From Madness to Hope*, 127-131.

2. "On May 14, 1980, units of military Detachment No. 1, the National Guard and the paramilitary *Organización Nacional Democrática (ORDEN)* deliberately killed at least three hundred non-combatants, including women and children, who were trying to flee to Honduras across the Sumpul River beside the hamlet of Las Aradas, Department of Chalatenango. The massacre was made possible by the cooperation of the Honduran armed forces, who prevented the Salvadoran villagers from landing on the other side. . . . On October 26, 1992, surviving witnesses of the Sumpul River massacre filed a judicial complaint with the Chalatenango Court of First Instance, which was declared admissible under the title 'on verifying the murder of six hundred people.' " *From Madness to Hope*, 121-124. See also the statement of the Diocese of Santa Rosa de Copán, Honduras, dated June 19, 1980, and published five days later in the Honduran newspaper *El Tiempo*. This statement was endorsed by the Archdiocese of San Salvador on June 29, 1980, and by the Honduran Conference of Bishops two days later on July 1.

3. "On November 27, 1980 . . . political leaders of the *Frente Democrático Revolucionario (FDR)*, representing an important sector of Salvadoran society, were abducted, tortured and, after a short period in captivity, executed in San Salvador. . . . The Commission on the Truth concludes that it was an operation carried out by one or more public security forces." *From Madness to Hope*, 58-62.

4. "On December 2, 1980, members of the National Guard of El Salvador arrested four church women after they left the international airport. Church women Ita Ford, Maura Clarke, Dorothy Kazel and Jean Donovan were taken to an isolated spot and subsequently executed by being shot at close range. . . . The Commission on the Truth finds that the arrest and execution of the church women was planned prior to their arrival at the airport. Deputy Sergeant Luis Antonio Colindres Alemán carried out orders of a superior to execute them. . . . The Minister of Defense at the time, General José Guillermo García, made no serious effort to conduct a thorough investigation of responsibility for the murders." *From Madness to Hope*, 62-66.

5. "The Archbishop Oscar Romero Christian Legal Aid Office reported the following numbers of civilian victims: 1980 (11,903), 1981 (16,266), 1982 (5,962)." *From Madness to Hope*, footnote #10, 202.

6. "On March 17, 1981, as they tried to cross the Lempa River to Honduras, a group of thousands of peasants was attacked from the air and from land. Between twenty and thirty people were reported killed and a further 189 reported missing as a result of the attack." *From Madness to Hope*, 29. See *The Washington Post*, May 10, 1981, and *The New York Times*, June 8, 1981. For a moving account of the Lempa River crossing, see Yvonne Dilling, *In Search of Refuge* (Herald Press, 1984).

7. "In November 1981, in Cabañas Department, a counterinsurgency operation surrounded and kept under attack for thirteen days a group of one thousand people who were trying to escape to Honduras. This time between fifty and one hundred people were reported killed." *From Madness to Hope*, 30.

8. *"Habla el Comité Diocesano Pro-Refugiados de la Diócesis de Santa Rosa de Copán del Occidente de Honduras,"* paid ad in the Honduran newspaper *El Tiempo*, March 24, 1982.

9. See Renato Camarda, *Forced to Move: Salvadoran Refugees in Honduras* (Solidarity Publications, 1985).

In the Wilderness of Chalatenango: 1983–1985

1. "In addition to the massacres described here, the Commission received direct testimony concerning numerous other mass executions that occurred during the years 1980, 1981, and 1982, in which members of the armed forces, in the course of anti-guerrilla operations, executed peasants — men, women and children who had offered no resistance — simply because they considered them to be guerrilla collaborators." *From Madness to Hope,* 114-126.

2. "On December 25, Monsignor Gregorio Rosa Chávez reported that 6,096 Salvadorans had died in 1983 as a result of political violence. . . . In the interior of the country, the number of displaced persons climbed to four hundred thousand; this, added to the approximately five hundred thousand Salvadorans which UNHCR estimated to be in the United States, and the two hundred thousand in Mexico and Central America, represented twenty percent of the country's total population." *From Madness to Hope,* 34.

3. For a moving account of life in the communities on the Guazapa volcano, see Dr. Charles Clements' book, *Witness to War: An American Doctor in El Salvador* (Bantam Books, 1984).

4. The *Dallas Morning News,* March 9, 10, 11, 12, and 13, 1983.

5. "Attacks against the non-governmental Human Rights Commission were systematic during the period. On October 3, 1980, María Magdalena Henríquez, press secretary of the Commission, was abducted by uniformed police. Her body was found later. On October 25, Ramón Valladares, the Commission's administrator, was murdered. On December 4, 1981, security forces abducted the Commission's director, Carlos Eduardo Vides, who then disappeared. In August 1982, the Treasury Police abducted América Perdomo, director of public relations, who also disappeared. On March 16, 1983, Marianela García Villas, the Commission's president, was killed when a military patrol ambushed a group of displaced persons." *From Madness to Hope,* footnote #11, 202.

6. For an excellent background and description of these communities, see Jenny Pearce's book, *Promised Land: Peasant Rebellion in Chalatenango, El Salvador* (Latin American Bureau, London, 1986). Distributed in the United States by Monthly Review Press.

7. "In November, troops from the Atlacatl Battalion invaded an area close to Lake Suchitlán under rebel control, and 118 people were reported killed as a result of the actions." *From Madness to Hope,* 33, and footnote #62, 208. See also *The New York Times,* November 18, 1983, and *The Washington Post,* November 19, 1983.

8. "Between July 17–22, sixty-eight civilians were executed by army troops during a military operation in Los Llanitos, Cabañas." *From Madness to Hope,* footnote #75, 209. See also *The New York Times,* September 9, 1984; *The Boston Globe,* September 9, and October 1, 1984; and *The Miami Herald,* September 9, 1984.

9. "Between August 28–30, a further military operation by the Atlacatl Battalion in Las Vueltas, Chalatenango resulted in the massacre of some fifty civilians on the banks of the Gualsinga River." *From Madness to Hope,* footnote #75, 209. See also *The New York Times,* September 15, 1984.

10. Just as Assistant Secretary of State Enders had sought to discredit accounts of the El Mozote massacres nearly three years earlier, his successor as head of the State Department's Bureau of Inter-American Affairs, Elliott Abrams, attempted to discredit accounts of the smaller-scale massacres at Los Llanitos and the Gualsinga River. Abrams discussed them on the ABC television program *Nightline* several months after they occurred. A representative of Americas Watch, Aryeh Neier, also appeared on the broadcast:

Ted Koppel: "Secretary Abrams, why was neither of those incidents reported [in the State Department's country report on El Salvador]?"

Secretary Abrams: "Because neither of them happened. Because it is a tactic of the guerrillas every time there is a battle and a significant number of people are killed to say that they're all victims of human rights abuses."

Aryeh Neier: "That's why *The New York Times* . . ."

Secretary Abrams: "Ted, there's one very important point here."

Aryeh Neier: " . . . and *The Boston Globe*, and *The Miami Herald*, and *The Christian Science Monitor*, and Reuters, and all the other reporters who went to the scene and looked at what took place, they were simply being propagandists for the guerrillas? Is that right?"

Secretary Abrams: "I'm telling you that there were no significant — there were no massacres in El Salvador in 1984." Americas Watch, *El Salvador's Decade of Terror* (Yale University Press, 1991).

A New Heaven and a New Earth: 1985–1987

1. See passage cited at the beginning of this chapter introduction, *From Madness to Hope*, 36.

2. For documentation from *Tutela Legal* in 1985, see "Guazapa: The Cry of a Crucified People" (CRISPAZ: Christians for Peace in El Salvador, 1985).

3. "One should not forget that it is the supposed distinction between the 'masses' and the civilian population that has been the pretext used by the United States Embassy in its attacks on the Archdiocese Legal Aid Office to justify the deaths of all the unarmed civilians who happened to be caught in combat areas. According to the Embassy, these civilians who suffer violence at the hands of the armed forces are 'something more than innocent bystanders' in the conflict, given that they offer logistical support to the guerrillas, or at least share the same ideological aspirations; for these reasons they constitute legitimate military targets." *"Los Masacres de Cabañas y Chalatenango,"* Estudios Centroamericanos, September 1984, (UCA, San Salvador). This reasoning by the Embassy is in opposition to Protocol II of the Geneva Conventions which protects civilians in a civil war, regardless of whether they give logistical support, information, or sympathy to one party in the conflict.

4. For a moving account of Laura's life, see Renny Golden's book, *The Hour of the Poor, The Hour of Women: Salvadoran Women Speak* (Crossroad, 1991).

5. Letters of Laura López, from *"Fe y Práctica,"* (Coordinadora

Nacional de la Iglesia Popular [CONIP], 1985). For an English translation, see "The Life and Testimony of Laura," unpublished manuscript compiled by Reverend Bill Dexheimer.

The Church of the Poor in Morazán: 1987–1989

1. *Equipo pastoral, Comunidades Cristianas de Oriente, "La opción preferencial por los pobres como respuesta a las exigencias del momento actual,"* December 4, 1984, published in *Estudios Centroamericanos* (UCA, San Salvador, 1985). The full reflection was published under the title, "El Salvador: To Give a Reason for Our Hope" (CRISPAZ: Christians for Peace in El Salvador, 1985).

2. *From Madness to Hope,* 114-121. See section on El Mozote cited in the introduction to the book.

3. For a moving account of the life of the Christian base communities in Morazán see *Death and Life in Morazán: A Priest's Testimony from a War-Zone in El Salvador,* Father Rogelio Ponseele talks to María López Vigil (Catholic Institute for International Relations, London, 1989), available in the United States from EPICA. See also Venancia's story in Renny Golden's book, *The Hour of the Poor, The Hour of Women: Salvadoran Women Speak* (Crossroad, 1991).

4. Interview with María, pastoral worker with CEBES, 1985. The full interview was published under the title, "The Last Word is Life: Testimonies of Christian Communities in a Time of War" (CRISPAZ: Christians for Peace in El Salvador, 1985).

5. Ibid.

The Seeds of New Life: 1989–1991

1. "In the early morning of October 31, 1989, persons unknown placed a bomb at the entrance to the offices of the *Comité de Madres y Familiares de Presos Políticos, Desaparecidos y Asesinados de El Salvador Monseñor Oscar Arnulfo Romero* (COMADRES) in San Salvador. Four people, including a child, were injured. At midday, a bomb was placed in the offices of the *Federación Nacional Sindical de Trabajadores Salvadoreños* (FENASTRAS) in San Salvador. Nine people were killed and over forty injured. As a result of the attack, the FMLN decided to suspend peace negotiations with the government. The Commission on the Truth finds that the bomb attacks on the offices of COMADRES and FENASTRAS on October 31, 1989 were part of a systematic pattern of attacks on the lives, physical integrity, and freedom of members of these organizations. The government of El Salvador failed in its duty to guar-

antee the human rights to which the members of these organizations are entitled as individuals and as members of their organizations." *From Madness to Hope*, 92-96.

2. "At 8 P.M. on Saturday, November 11, 1989, the FMLN launched the biggest offensive of the war just a few days after the bombing of FENASTRAS headquarters. The impact of the offensive on the capital and other cities led the government to decree a state of emergency. Beginning on November 13, a 6 P.M. to 6 A.M. curfew went into effect. The fighting that raged up to December 12 cost the lives of over two thousand from both sides and caused material damage amounting to approximately 6 billion *colones*." *From Madness to Hope*, 39.

3. "At 6:30 P.M. on November 15, there was a meeting of the General Staff with military heads and commanders to adopt new measures to deal with the offensive. Colonel Ponce authorized the elimination of ringleaders, trade unionists, and known leaders of the FMLN, and a decision was taken to step up bombing by the air force and to use artillery and armored vehicles to dislodge the FMLN from the areas it controlled. The Minister of Defense, General Rafael Humberto Larios López, asked whether anyone objected. No hand was raised. It was agreed that President Cristiani would be consulted about the measures." *From Madness to Hope*, 49-50.

4. *From Madness to Hope*, 45-54. See passage cited in the introduction to this book.

5. "The Geneva Agreement (April 1990), witnessed by the Secretary General, marked the beginning of an irreversible embracing process drawing up an agenda and timetable (Caracas Agenda, May 21, 1990); human rights (San José Agreement, July 26, 1990); reforms in the army and the judicial and electoral systems and the establishment of the Commission on the Truth (Mexico Agreements, April 27, 1991); and finally the Chapúltepec Agreement, the starting point for the cessation of hostilities, disarmament and the implementation of the agreed institutional reforms." *From Madness to Hope*, 39.

6. For a moving account of the repatriation from Colomoncagua, Honduras, to Segundo Montes City in Morazán, El Salvador, see Steve and Beth Cagan's book, *This Promised Land, El Salvador* (Rutgers University Press, 1991).

7. Also known as Guancorita, and alluded to in the Truth Commission report, *From Madness to Hope*, 12.

8. For a moving anthology of writings from the Jesuit martyrs, see the book by Jon Sobrino, *Companions of Jesus: The Jesuit Martyrs in El Salvador* (Orbis Books, 1990). See also, *Mártires de la UCA* (UCA Editores, San Salvador, 1992).